Praise for *The Wise King*

"Simon Doubleday's *The Wise King* delves into the legend and reality of Alfonso the Wise, medieval Spain's most storied king. Doubleday skillfully locates this patron of culture, poet, crusader, would-be Roman emperor, ruler over Christians, Muslims, and Jews, within the broader historical trends, cultural developments, and noble networks of a medieval Europe on the cusp of the Renaissance. This book vividly brings to light a historical character who remains largely unknown to the English-speaking world."

—Brian A. Catlos, professor of religious studies at the University of Colorado and author of *Infidel Kings and Unholy Warriors*

"Simon Doubleday's biography of the famous Spanish king Alfonso X is extremely original. Each chapter is written around a central aspect of Alfonso's character and interests—love, astronomy, hunting, fatherhood, friendship, healing, anger—allowing Doubleday to tell the interweaving stories of a life, and providing the reader with a means to meditate on its resonance for his or her own life."

—Jesús R. Velasco, chair of the Department of Latin American and Iberian Cultures at Columbia University

"Simon Doubleday's book is an engaging and scintillating account of how the modern gaze into the medieval mirror can foster wisdom and humanity in contemporary readers, princes and paupers alike."

—Stanislao Pugliese, professor of history at Hofstra University and author of the NBCC-nominated *Bitter Spring: A Life of Ignazio Silone*

The
WISE KING

A Christian Prince, Muslim Spain,
and the Birth *of the* Renaissance

Simon R. Doubleday

BASIC BOOKS
A Member of the Perseus Books Group
New York

Designed by Cynthia Young
Map by Brian Shotwell

Library of Congress Cataloging-in-Publication Data
Doubleday, Simon R., author.
The wise king : a Christian prince, Muslim Spain,
and the birth of the Renaissance / Simon R. Doubleday.
    pages cm
Includes bibliographical references and index.
ISBN 978-0-465-06699-5 (hardcover) — ISBN 978-0-465-07391-7 (e-book)
1. Alfonso X, King of Castile and Leon, 1221–1284.   2. Castile (Spain)—History—
Alfonso X, 1252–1284.   3. Castile (Spain)—Kings and rulers—Biography.   I. Title.
DP140.3.D68 2015
946'.02092—dc23
[B]
2015027714

10 9 8 7 6 5 4 3 2 1

For Benita, Beatriz, and Breogán

Contents

	Prologue	xvii
ONE	Players	1
TWO	Lovers	29
THREE	Stargazers	53
FOUR	Hunters	81
FIVE	Laughter	105
SIX	Friends	127
SEVEN	Father	151
EIGHT	Healers	175
NINE	Anger	203
	Epilogue	225
	Acknowledgments	239
	Notes	241
	Index	293

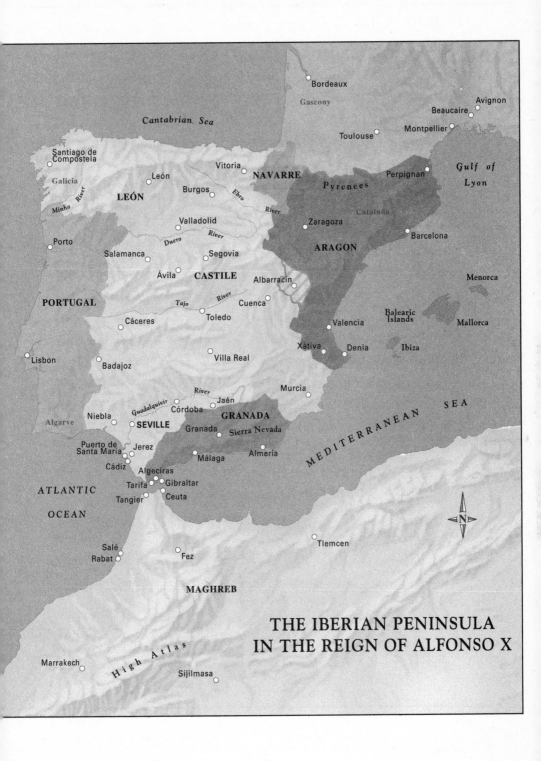

THE IBERIAN PENINSULA
IN THE REIGN OF ALFONSO X

A. Alfonso X of Castile and León

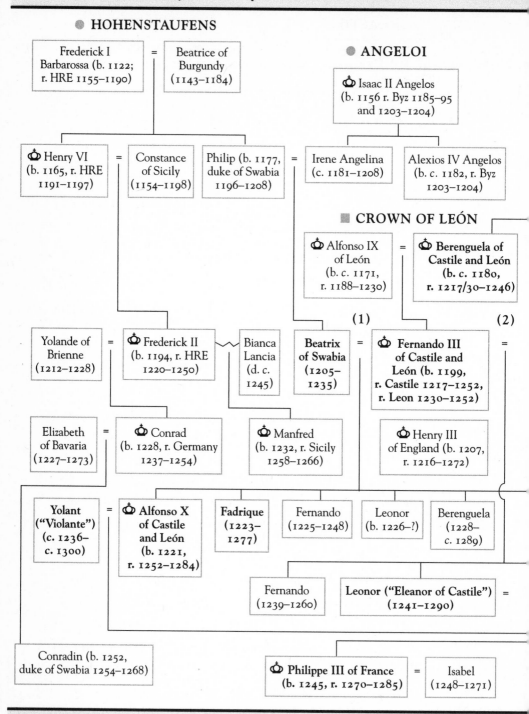

HOHENSTAUFENS

Frederick I Barbarossa (b. 1122; r. HRE 1155–1190) = Beatrice of Burgundy (1143–1184)

ANGELOI

Isaac II Angelos (b. 1156 r. Byz 1185–95 and 1203–1204)

Henry VI (b. 1165, r. HRE 1191–1197) = Constance of Sicily (1154–1198)

Philip (b. 1177, duke of Swabia 1196–1208) = Irene Angelina (c. 1181–1208)

Alexios IV Angelos (b. c. 1182, r. Byz 1203–1204)

CROWN OF LEÓN

Alfonso IX of León (b. c. 1171, r. 1188–1230) = **Berenguela of Castile and León (b. c. 1180, r. 1217/30–1246)**

(1)   (2)

Yolande of Brienne (1212–1228) = Frederick II (b. 1194, r. HRE 1220–1250) ⌇ Bianca Lancia (d. c. 1245)

Beatrix of Swabia (1205–1235) = **Fernando III of Castile and León (b. 1199, r. Castile 1217–1252, r. Leon 1230–1252)** =

Elizabeth of Bavaria (1227–1273) = Conrad (b. 1228, r. Germany 1237–1254)

Manfred (b. 1232, r. Sicily 1258–1266)

Henry III of England (b. 1207, r. 1216–1272)

Yolant ("Violante") (c. 1236–c. 1300) = **Alfonso X of Castile and León (b. 1221, r. 1252–1284)**

Fadrique (1223–1277)

Fernando (1225–1248)

Leonor (b. 1226–?)

Berenguela (1228–c. 1289)

Fernando (1239–1260)

Leonor ("Eleanor of Castile") (1241–1290) =

Conradin (b. 1252, duke of Swabia 1254–1268)

Philippe III of France (b. 1245, r. 1270–1285) = Isabel (1248–1271)

LEGEND

Bold indicates a primary role in text

Byz Byzantine Empire

c. Approximate Date

HRE Holy Roman Empire

● Key Dynasty Maternal Branch

■ Key Dynasty Paternal Branch

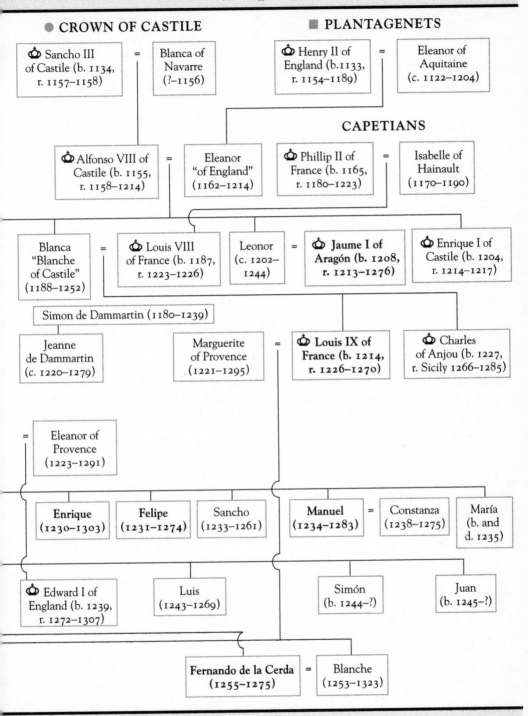

CROWN OF CASTILE

PLANTAGENETS

Sancho III of Castile (b. 1134, r. 1157–1158) = Blanca of Navarre (?–1156)

Henry II of England (b.1133, r. 1154–1189) = Eleanor of Aquitaine (c. 1122–1204)

CAPETIANS

Alfonso VIII of Castile (b. 1155, r. 1158–1214) = Eleanor "of England" (1162–1214)

Phillip II of France (b. 1165, r. 1180–1223) = Isabelle of Hainault (1170–1190)

Blanca "Blanche of Castile" (1188–1252) = Louis VIII of France (b. 1187, r. 1223–1226)

Leonor (c. 1202–1244) = Jaume I of Aragón (b. 1208, r. 1213–1276)

Enrique I of Castile (b. 1204, r. 1214–1217)

Simon de Dammartin (1180–1239)

Jeanne de Dammartin (c. 1220–1279)

Marguerite of Provence (1221–1295) = Louis IX of France (b. 1214, r. 1226–1270)

Charles of Anjou (b. 1227, r. Sicily 1266–1285)

= Eleanor of Provence (1223–1291)

Enrique (1230–1303)

Felipe (1231–1274)

Sancho (1233–1261)

Manuel (1234–1283) = Constanza (1238–1275)

María (b. and d. 1235)

Edward I of England (b. 1239, r. 1272–1307)

Luis (1243–1269)

Simón (b. 1244–?)

Juan (b. 1245–?)

Fernando de la Cerda (1255–1275) = Blanche (1253–1323)

 Ruler

= Marriage

⌄⌄ Non-Marital Relationship

B. Yolant of Aragon

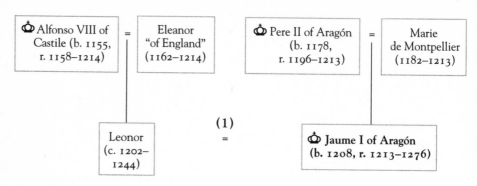

■ **CROWN OF ARAGON**

♔ Alfonso VIII of Castile (b. 1155, r. 1158–1214)	= Eleanor "of England" (1162–1214)	♔ Pere II of Aragón (b. 1178, r. 1196–1213)	= Marie de Montpellier (1182–1213)

Leonor (c. 1202–1244)

(1) =

♔ **Jaume I of Aragón** (b. 1208, r. 1213–1276)

| ♔ Alfonso X of Castile and León (b. 1221, r. 1252–1284) | = Yolant ("Violante") (c. 1236–c. 1300) | Constanza (1238–1275) | = Manuel (1234–1283) | ♔ Pere III of Aragón (b. 1240, r. 1276–1285) | ♔ Jaume II of Mallorca (b. 1243, r. 1276–1311) |

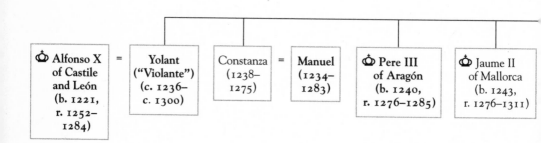

LEGEND

Bold indicates a primary role in text

c. Approximate Date

● Key Dynasty Maternal Branch

■ Key Dynasty Paternal Branch

♔ Ruler

= Marriage

CROWN OF HUNGARY AND CROATIA

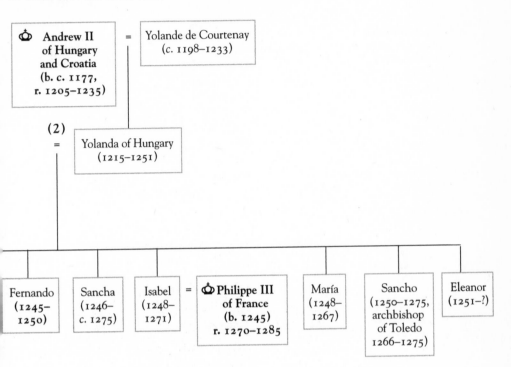

♛ Andrew II of Hungary and Croatia (b. c. 1177, r. 1205–1235) = Yolande de Courtenay (c. 1198–1233)

(2) = Yolanda of Hungary (1215–1251)

- Fernando (1245–1250)
- Sancha (1246–c. 1275)
- Isabel (1248–1271) = ♛ Philippe III of France (b. 1245) r. 1270–1285
- María (1248–1267)
- Sancho (1250–1275, archbishop of Toledo 1266–1275)
- Eleanor (1251–?)

C. Children and Selected Grandchildren of Alfonso X

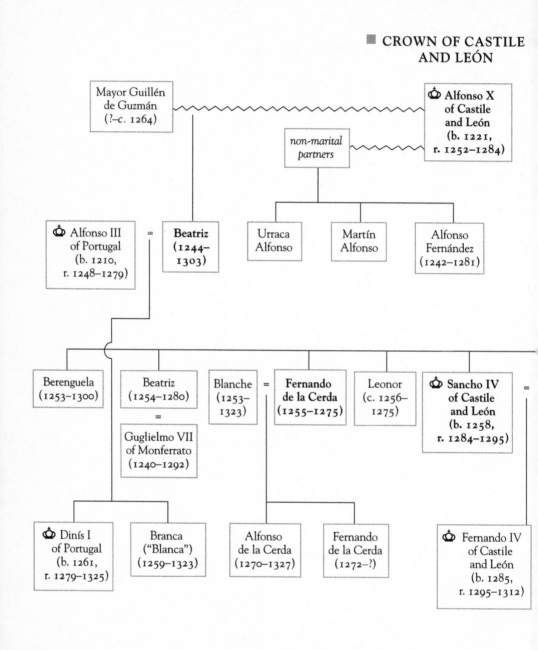

CROWN OF ARAGON

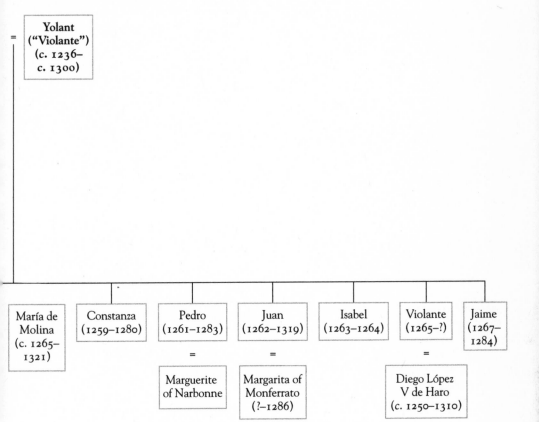

= Yolant ("Violante") (c. 1236–c. 1300)

María de Molina (c. 1265–1321)

Constanza (1259–1280)

Pedro (1261–1283)
= Marguerite of Narbonne

Juan (1262–1319)
= Margarita of Monferrato (?–1286)

Isabel (1263–1264)

Violante (1265–?)
= Diego López V de Haro (c. 1250–1310)

Jaime (1267–1284)

PROLOGUE

Sometime around the year 1237, a Spanish prince approaching the age of sixteen opened a book and began to read. The text was titled the *Book of the Twelve Wise Men*, and as the young man quickly realized, it was one of the "mirrors for princes," the sage manuals of advice that medieval rulers valued so highly. Through stories and colorful examples, these exemplary texts allowed readers to sharpen their sense of how to live well. In a work of this kind, you might glimpse the space that separated the person you were from the person you might still become.

The book could not have fallen into the hands of a more receptive reader. The prince—whose name was Alfonso and who, as the eldest sibling, was heir to the Spanish realms of Castile and León—was a sharp and curious young man, eager to advance his skills in the arts of ruling. His father, Fernando III, was a devastatingly effective military leader, the paragon of Christian warrior values, whose reign was a critical phase in the centuries-long campaign to colonize central and southern Spain, wresting the Iberian Peninsula from Islamic rule. The previous year, Fernando had occupied the beautiful city of Córdoba, which had once been the center of a powerful Spanish caliphate. Alfonso was in some ways cut from the same cloth: after his accession to the throne in 1252, he would pursue new conquests in the south and in North Africa. He aspired to become Holy Roman Emperor, a title that would allow him to take on the mantle of the supreme ninth-century ruler Charlemagne and fulfill a dream that had long been close to the hearts of the kings and queens of Castile. He hoped, in this way, to hold sway not only in a large part of Spain but also in a vast continental patchwork of territories stretching over much of Germany and Italy.

But Alfonso—a man with a voracious appetite for ideas and, paradoxically, a deep admirer of the culture that flourished in the same Muslim territories he was busily annexing by force of arms—was more innovative than his father. As Alfonso X, king of Castile and León, he would soon be celebrated as El Sabio, the Wise. A "Renaissance man" before the Renaissance—or, to be precise, before the Renaissance is traditionally believed to have begun—Alfonso was the most intellectually impassioned of all medieval rulers and the most creatively inspired. While other kings sought strength through cultural renewal, none equaled his commitment to literature, architecture, and the arts; single-handedly, he exorcises the myth that medieval Europe was mired in a dark age.

Linked by marriage, faith, culture, and commerce to all the kingdoms of Christendom, he stood out among his illustrious contemporaries, his realm a beacon of light and learning. His half sister, Leonor—Eleanor of Castile—helped to transmit much of this cultural energy to northern Europe when, in a successful attempt to defuse tensions with Henry III of England, Alfonso arranged for her marriage to Prince Edward, the future Edward I. The union ushered in a period of close collaboration between the two expansionist realms, and despite the misgivings of her island subjects, Leonor would be instrumental in reenergizing cultural life at the English court.

Alfonso himself married into the royal family of the other great Christian realm in medieval Spain, Aragon, through his betrothal to Yolant, daughter of Jaume I (r. 1213–1276), conqueror of Valencia and the sunbathed island of Mallorca. Yolant, who was sometimes known in Castile as "Violante", was for many years a valuable, skillful, and independently minded partner in rulership, as well as mother to most of his children, becoming one of a considerable number of politically powerful Iberian queens. She and Alfonso arranged for the betrothal of their eldest son, Fernando de la Cerda, to Blanche, daughter of Louis IX of France and his wife Marguerite of Provence. Alfonso treasured his relationship with the French king, who—with Marguerite's close collaboration—led the Seventh and Eight Crusades and was eventually canonized as Saint Louis.

The most dazzling of all Alfonso's contemporaries was the Holy Roman Emperor, Frederick II (r. 1220–1250), known as the *stupor mundi*—the wonder of the world—for the sophistication of his itinerant court, based primarily in Sicily and southern Italy. Here, in another part of the Mediterranean world long suffused with Islamic culture, Frederick gathered a multiethnic array of scholars, scientists, musicians, and falconers, among them Muslims, Jews, Greek Orthodox Christians, and Roman Catholics. To Jacob Burckhardt, the nineteenth-century historian and godfather of Italian Renaissance studies, the emperor's intimate knowledge of "Saracenic" government and culture was one factor that enabled him to become, for better or worse, "the first ruler of the modern type who sat upon a throne." But if Frederick II was a model for the young Alfonso, the Spanish prince's wondrous achievements would eventually eclipse the emperor's.

Envisioning himself as a philosopher-king, in line with ideas of rulership circulating widely in the Christian and Muslim worlds at the time, Alfonso X aimed at educating his people using the most commonly spoken vernacular language, Castilian Spanish, rather than the universal Latin of the church. A prolific patron of lyric verses, histories, and works on subjects as diverse as chess, hunting, and the medicinal—perhaps magical—properties of rare and precious stones, he also infused his limitless energy into the compilation of an astonishing spectrum of law codes. The most influential of these codes, the *Siete partidas* (*Seven Divisions*), has been compared in its ambition to those of Justinian and Napoleon and takes the form of 2,700 moral and philosophical essays. It was to have a long afterlife across the Spanish Empire, even shaping civil law traditions in parts of the southern United States. A relief portrait of Alfonso, carved in white Vermont marble, still hangs over the gallery doors of the House Chamber in the US House of Representatives today.

Yet, whereas Alfonso X is a household name in Spain and, indeed, the subject of a television drama series, he remains largely unknown to English-speaking readers. A stereotype of Spain as a fanatically religious and intolerant culture has long obscured the figure of the Wise King and his contributions to global culture. This image, which first emerged in sixteenth-century Protestant Europe and was later absorbed into the Anglo-American imagination, disguises the reality that Spain had long been one of the most richly diverse medieval societies.

For several centuries, Alfonso's name was closely associated with the works of astronomy produced either at his court or under his patronage. The most widely known of the king's astronomical works was the *Alfonsine Tables*, a set of data that made it possible to calculate the relative positions of the sun, moon, and stars. The results revitalized European science; there is no doubt that in this sense Spain played a significant role in shaping the broader European Renaissance. Copernicus relied on the *Tables* in the 1490s as a student at the University of Cracow, and his personal copy still survives. But the tables were just one highlight of an ongoing, cutting-edge scientific program that encompassed the whole of Alfonso's reign. From his de facto capital, Seville, Alfonso monitored this program closely. His fascination with the study of the stars is important in ways that go far beyond its immediate scientific significance. It speaks to his conviction that human intelligence could discern the mysteries of the universe, a conviction that we might usually associate with the Italian Renaissance. His contributions to astronomy and astrology alone would have ensured his immortality: on the surface of the moon, the crater Alphonsus lies adjacent to a second crater called Ptolemaeus, after the brilliant astronomer and mathematician of ancient Alexandria. (In the modern space age, Alphonsus was considered as a potential site for the Apollo 16 moon landings, although NASA eventually opted for Descartes).

Today, however, the king is more widely known for his musical projects. Lovers of early music treasure his *Cantigas de Santa María* (Songs of Holy Mary), a cycle of 419 songs of devotion to the Virgin. The songs were written in the lyric language of Galician-Portuguese, recounting the many miracles performed by the Queen of Heaven. Some of the miracles they celebrated were very recent and very local, while others—particularly the earliest—drew on "international" Marian tales from beyond the Iberian Peninsula. Alfonso himself is thought to have written roughly twenty of the songs and some of the musical settings. Adopting a role as personal troubadour to the Virgin and intermediary between her court and his kingdom, he hoped to enhance an aura of majesty that accentuated his authority as ruler of the realm.

The illuminated images that accompany the text (and sometimes the musical notation) of the surviving *cantigas* manuscripts offer an extraordinary window onto private and public life in medieval Spain. In the *Códice rico* (Rich Codex), above all, we encounter a dazzling array of colors. The images feature, for instance, the deep blue tint derived from lapis lazuli—the semiprecious stone, imported to the western Mediterranean from mines as far

away as Afghanistan, that would become such a prominent feature of Renaissance art. But these songs were not designed for
purely private enjoyment; they were meant for public, theatrical
performance. The illustrations in one manuscript—the so-called
Códice de los músicos (Musicians' Codex)—feature a dazzling variety of instruments, including fiddles, zithers, and bagpipes, played
by both Muslims and Christians.

The songs are embedded in a wide range of real-life social contexts across Spain and other parts of western Europe. They all
bear witness to the compassionate intervention of the Virgin,
whom—as a good stargazer—he describes variously as the Star of
the Morning (*Strela Madodinna*), Star of Day (*Strela do Día*), and
Star of the Sea (*Strela do Mar*). This was a medieval multimedia
project extraordinaire. The songs' words and music alike envelop
modern listeners in the rich fabric of thirteenth-century culture.
Audiences are still treated to performances across the world, allowing the voices and values of Alfonso's court to reach us with
unparalleled immediacy.

The *cantigas* remind us of how medieval Christianity—far
from being a repressive and intolerant foil to the Greco-Roman
world, a barbarous enemy of culture, as the sixteenth-century
Renaissance art historian Giorgio Vasari would claim—often
provided a framework for creative innovation. Vasari, who first
coined the term *rinascità* (renaissance) to describe the rebirth of
the arts after what he imagined to have been a 1,000-year period of darkness, helped to propagate the long-lived and resil-
ient myth that this rebirth had originated in Italy—and above
all in Florence. "Towards 1250," he wrote, "Heaven, moved to
pity by the noble spirits which the Tuscan soil was producing
every day, restored [the arts] to their primitive condition." In
reality, the Italian Renaissance was just one spectacular stage in
a longer process of cultural revitalization, encompassing much

Muslim and Christian lute players in the *Cantigas de Santa María*, no. 120, *Códice de los músicos* (Musicians' Codex), Real Biblioteca del Monasterio de El Escorial, Ms. B.I.2. Reproduced courtesy of Archivo Oronoz.

of the Mediterranean world, including both its southern and far western shores, as well as the north.

In this story, Spain played a vital role. From Barcelona south to Almería, the coastal cities of Iberia had experienced a long economic and cultural revival since the eleventh century. Seville, deeply enmeshed in Mediterranean trade, had become one of the two pillars of a great Islamic empire extending far into North Africa, and a subtle alchemy had been set in motion across the peninsula. It was in Spain that close contact with generations of sophisticated Muslim thinkers, poets, writers, scientists, mathematicians, and architects infused new vitality into the heart of Western culture. But in order to understand the dynamic, hybrid world within which the life of Alfonso the Wise would play out, we need first to turn back the clock to a moment half a millennium before his accession to the throne.

In 711, a decisive military occupation by Berber and Arab forces had brought most of the Iberian Peninsula—all but a sliver of territory in the mountainous north and northwest—under the control of Muslim rulers. The newly occupied territory, whose geographical extent would wax and wane over the coming centuries, came to be known as al-Andalus. It is often convenient to refer to this territory as "Muslim Spain," although the value of this term is limited in two ways. First, at its height al-Andalus included the entirety of what is now Portugal: it stretched far beyond the modern region of Andalusia (making it necessary to use the adjective "Andalusi," not "Andalusian"). Second, al-Andalus was by no means purely Muslim. Andalusi society was vibrantly multiethnic and pluralistic. The majority of the population remained Christian as late as the tenth century, while gradually adopting the Arabic language and adapting to the new cultural forms of their conquerors. The Jewish cultural contribution was also profound; there had been substantial Jewish communities in Iberia since the days of the Roman Empire. The absorption of this Andalusi Jewish population would prove transformative when—from the eleventh century—the Christian colonization of the peninsula accelerated.

Territorial motives rather than ideals of holy war or jihad usually drove both Christians and Muslims at this stage; only in the twelfth century would this change significantly. Military offensives by the emirs of Córdoba, who declared themselves caliphs in 929, overlaid and rebuffed the gradual expansion of petty Christian kingdoms in the north—among them León and, later, the frontier kingdom of Castile. The fragmentation of the caliphate in the early eleventh century allowed the Christians to gain the upper hand for the first time; yet the Castilian recapture of Toledo (1085)—a moment of Pyrrhic triumph—was followed the very next year by an incisive counterattack led by a militant group known as the Almoravids, with their center of operations deep in the Maghreb, in Marrakech. For the next century, the fate of Iberia hung in the balance.

But as armies marched north and south and launched lightning raids deep into enemy territory, new cultural forms also crystallized. More than a place of tolerance, the peninsula became an arena of hybridity and overlapping influences. This was the phenomenon that some modern scholars have termed *convivencia*: a dynamic and pragmatic coexistence among people of different faiths. Not to be confused with multicultural harmony, this coexistence unfolded within a deeply colonial context. Shaped by competing forms of expansionism—both Islamic and Christian—Iberia acquired the cosmopolitan diversity that is often a product of empire. In Christian kingdoms across the peninsula, delicately carved works of ivory from al-Andalus were transformed into reliquaries to hold the bones of Christian saints. Dozens of

Christian churches across the north replicated the architectural forms of the great mosque of Córdoba, and on a broader level still, contact with Muslims permanently reshaped both the language and the diet of ordinary Castilians.

For northern Christians, Andalusi culture enjoyed a magnetic appeal. Like the global projection of American popular culture today, this kind of appeal owed a great deal to the economic power of al-Andalus and permeated society at all levels. There was deep admiration for the cultural advances of the Arabic-Islamic world and the storehouse of knowledge that it embodied. Indeed, the "Scientist Pope" Gerbert of Aurillac had traveled to the monastery of Ripoll in northeastern Spain at the end of the tenth century in search of mathematical and astronomical knowledge from al-Andalus—an attitude that differed entirely, of course, from respect for the religion of Islam itself.

Alfonso inherited this admiration. A decade after he opened the *Book of the Twelve Wise Men*, he stood awestruck before the walls of "Ishbilya"—Seville, the glittering capital of the Muslim realms of the south—while his father, Fernando III, prepared his final assault on the city. As he stood in the vast Christian encampment, besieging the town, he marveled at the architecture before him: at the fortification called the Tower of Gold, radiantly perched on the banks of the Guadalquivir River, and, above all, at the svelte minaret that almost exactly mirrored its twin in Marrakesh and that, in a later age, came to be known as La Giralda, the most iconic structure in Seville.

The prince who stood admiringly at the gates of Seville also inherited a desire to conquer and dominate al-Andalus. This desire stemmed in turn from a haunting fear—one that proved well founded later in his reign—that Islamic forces might reverse and overturn his father's recent conquests in the south. The *Cantigas de Santa María* underscore his belief in the superiority of

Artist's impression of the principal Almohad minaret in Seville (Giralda): Alejandro Guichot y Sierra (1910). Reproduced courtesy of Archivo Oronoz.

Christianity over all other religions, and while they may on occasion have served as an instrument of voluntary conversion, they sometimes call bluntly for the complete elimination of Islam from Iberia. Mary herself, the subject of Alfonso's undying devotion, had already become an emblem of Christian holy war, as well as of protective motherhood. Yet within this colonial context, in which tolerance was neither an explicit concept nor a well-developed reality, it remained possible to be deeply and genuinely impressed by the cultural and scientific achievements of Muslim Spain.

As he prepared to lead his kingdom, Alfonso was transfixed by al-Andalus. Far more than his military-minded father, he would draw on a legacy of lively, long-standing interactions between Castile and its Muslim allies and vassals. In this sense, he anticipated the way in which—in the fifteenth and sixteenth centuries—Italian city-states would later become interlinked with Ottoman Turkey and the Egyptian Mamluks.

Alfonso's powerful engagement with al-Andalus was a vital catalyst. It would shape his pursuit of knowledge of the stars and their impact on human affairs. Ever since Muslim kings had ruled the city in the eleventh century, Toledo in particular had been a hub of astrology: that is, "applied astronomy," or the highly advanced science of the stars as they affected human life. Equally, it shaped his sustained interest in medical science, his appreciation of chess and hunting as markers of courtly sophistication, and his surprisingly open embrace of sexuality. Andalusi contact would heighten his awareness of the importance of personal friendships. He was deeply influenced in this respect by his reading of Aristotle, whose works had been recently translated from Arabic into Latin. Even his devotional songs, the *Cantigas de Santa María*, reflect the influence of Andalusi lyrical forms.

Alfonso also acquired the ideal of the wise king, leading his people as much in culture and reflection as in war, in part from Andalusi culture. This model of kingship, he was sure, might bring contentment both to himself and to his people. His quest for his own happiness and that of his subjects was unrelenting in the face of constant obstacles. For the road that lay ahead of the young prince would be extraordinarily hard, challenging the limits of his skills in rulership, his emotional strength, and his wisdom as a human being. In the cultural renewal of his realms, Alfonso's attempts to transcend personal setbacks, national calamities, and physical and emotional pain would ultimately prove the most powerful catalyst of all.

I

Players

Jupiter has power over the Christian Spaniards. Mars
has power over the Arabs. Saturn has power over the
Berbers. The man who wishes to battle against any of
these peoples should ensure that the planet we have
indicated here is in decline.

—Yehuda ben Mosé, Book of Crosses, 1259

A young king and his soldiers were riding toward the
frontier, across the plains of Castile. It was the autumn of
1221. Fernando III would have cut a fine figure as he traveled.
Born to a long line of warrior kings, he knew the importance of
chivalric prowess and was, as his eldest son later wrote, "adept at
all the arts a good knight should possess; he was skilled at throwing short and long lances in tournaments, and at taking up and
bearing arms in an elegant way." Fernando was to become one of
the most powerful players in the checkered history of his kingdom: the ruler who would later conquer the Muslim-dominated
Spanish cities of Córdoba and Seville, who would be depicted
with sword in hand on his tomb, and who would eventually be

acknowledged as a saint of the Catholic Church, performing posthumous miracles for the humblest members of Spanish society. But all this lay far in the future. For now, Fernando was living in a moment of crisis and rebellion.

All the world's a chessboard, ran the thirteenth-century refrain, and in medieval Spain's complex game of power politics, anything could happen. One false move could spell disaster, and superiority in the social hierarchy was no guarantee of victory. In the pages devoted to chess in the *Book of Games*, which Alfonso the Wise commissioned toward the end of his life, a Muslim player might defeat a Christian, and a black player might defeat a white one. On the chessboard itself, a small piece could always capture a more powerful piece or corner a king.

On the metaphorical board of the realm, the pieces might even revolt against their own king, defecting to another side. That autumn, a member of the most powerful aristocratic family in the land—Gonzalo Núñez de Lara—had turned renegade, orchestrating a rebellion against the king. The roots of the crisis lay in the brief, unhappy reign of the previous king, Enrique I. When ten-year-old Enrique had inherited the throne seven years before, in 1214, his older and politically masterful sister Berenguela had at first acted as regent, but Gonzalo and his brothers had edged her out, using their power to advance their family's interests. When Enrique had died suddenly in 1217, Berenguela—aged thirty-seven—had inherited the throne, assuming the title of Queen of Castile and Toledo. From that point onward, she had co-ruled with her son, Fernando, often as the dominant partner. As the realm descended into civil war, the three Lara brothers had turned for support, in desperation but in vain, to the ruler of the kingdom to the northwest, Alfonso IX of León. Their luck had run out. The eldest was captured, tortured, and—after his release—killed in battle. His younger brothers sought exile in

León but seem to have outstayed their welcome. The second fled south to Morocco—land of the Almohad Empire, the greatest Muslim power in the western Mediterranean—where he died in exile.

It was thus that in November 1221, the last remaining brother, Gonzalo Núñez, was instigating an uprising against royal authority at Molina de Aragon. A contingent of royal soldiers, under the command of the king, was heading at high speed over the plains to confront the rebels.

Riding alongside the king was his young and heavily pregnant queen, the sixteen-year-old German princess Beatrix of Swabia. The queen mother, Berenguela, had chosen her son's bride carefully. Beatrix's lineage could not have been more illustrious. Born into the powerful Hohenstaufen dynasty, she was daughter of Philip, duke of Swabia, who had been assassinated in 1208, in the midst of civil war in Germany, when she was roughly three years old. Later, she had been raised in the household of her father's erstwhile rival Otto IV of Brunswick, whom her elder sister had married as part of a peace agreement with the Hohenstaufens. Otto was named Holy Roman Emperor the following year and would retain this title until his murder in 1215, so for a half dozen years, Beatrix had lived at the imperial court. She was also cousin to the Italian-born Hohenstaufen prince who would succeed Otto as emperor, Frederick II, and had been living alongside him in the years before her wedding. Beatrix had similarly glamorous—and equally turbulent—roots on the other side of the family; her maternal uncle had been the Byzantine emperor, Alexios IV Angelos, and her mother the princess Irene Angelina.

Beautiful and refined, Beatrix—who came to be known in Spanish as "Beatriz"— brought new finesse to the Castilian court. She had arrived for her wedding in the royal city of Burgos almost exactly two years earlier; it had been a solemn occasion, attended by the "leading men of the cities" as well as by the bishops and magnates of the realm. In the upper cloister of the city's Gothic cathedral, constructed later in the century, a pair of polychrome statues depicts the royal couple. A lightly bearded King Fernando stands to the left, gently offering his bride a ring that he holds in his right hand, his robes lined with scarlet. At his feet, a pet dog—symbol of fidelity—rests peacefully. Beatrix stands to the right, every bit his equal in height and dignity, gracefully holding her fur-lined cloak, protection against the onset of early winter.

Leaving Fernando to continue his military campaign against the renegade brothers, Beatrix now took refuge in the city of Toledo, a suitable place for the birth of a prince. Rising majestically above the plains, Toledo—recaptured by the Castilian king Alfonso VI in 1085—was steeped in historical memories. Some were painful. In the eighth century all-conquering Muslim armies had seized the royal city, the spiritual capital of the Visigothic kingdom. Others were violent. The Christians crushed an Almoravid army in 1143, after which they impaled the heads of enemy leaders on Christian spears and led Muslim captives into the city in chains. But the winding streets of the city into which the young queen's cortege now rode also evoked other, happier memories of the past, when this had been a place of intimate (although not always harmonious) coexistence between different religious communities.

Here in Toledo an intellectual revolution had unfolded in the twelfth century, as translators brought to light a world of ancient wisdom, preserved in Arabic, as well as the works of recent Muslim thinkers, setting aflame the imagination of Christendom. Even now, Muslims continued to live alongside Christians. A significant proportion of the Christian community in Toledo spoke Arabic. These "Mozarabs," who had been permitted to live under

Royal couple, probably Fernando III of Castile and León and Beatrix of Swabia: upper cloister of Burgos Cathedral. © Author.

Muslim control, played an important role in the process of cultural translation, facilitating this Spanish "renaissance of learning." So did the city's vibrant Jewish community, which lived mostly in the walled quarter known as Madinat al-Yahud.

One wise and learned ruler of Toledo, al-Mamun (r. 1043–1075), had overseen a cultural flourishing that had made Toledo famous across western Europe as a center of scientific learning. The city's gardens, watered with high-technology irrigation, were renowned across the Islamic world too. In the quarter of al-Hizam, perched high in the eastern sector of the city, al-Mamun constructed a magnificent palace that long entranced the new Christian rulers. When Beatrix entered Toledo in the autumn of 1221, the "cathedral" building was still the grand mosque in which al-Mamun had worshipped.

Beatrix gave birth to a baby boy, Alfonso, on November 23, perhaps in one of al-Mamun's palace buildings. A love for the legacy of al-Andalus would envelop and swaddle him until the end of his days.

As an infant, Alfonso was entrusted very early to a wet nurse, a common practice among the social elites of thirteenth-century Europe. Parents chose their babies' wet nurses carefully, not least because the high rate of infant mortality was often attributed to deficiencies in their milk. One contemporary writer, Giles of Rome, recommended that a nurse should have similar physical characteristics to the birth mother, because a mother's milk corresponded to the needs of her child. Nurses for royal families were usually married women of high, but not aristocratic, social status. Deep emotional and physical bonds might emerge between wet nurse and child. Wet nurses often used to hug and kiss the babies entrusted to them, singing and whistling them to sleep, evening chewing their food for them. Arabic medical knowledge was an important source of guidance on the subject. The Dominican friar Vincent de Beauvais drew generously on the work of Avicenna (908–1037), proclaiming, "The wet nurse must be of middling age, that is between twenty five and thirty years old, which is an age of youth and health. Also to be considered are her physical appearance, her customs, the shape of her breasts, the quality of her milk, and the length of time that has passed since her last birth." (Vincent went on to cite al-Razi [c. 865–925] and Alí Abbas [d. 994], for whom the wet nurse's sexual self-control was an important criterion.)

The prince was raised largely away from the hustle and bustle of court life, in the countryside just to the southwest of Burgos. His childhood friends included a young boy from the Lara family—Nuño González, son of the rebel Gonzalo. The power, wealth, and influence of this old aristocratic lineage were clearly sufficient to allow the boy's family to be rehabilitated. The crown needed to collaborate with the high nobility in order to govern effectively. Alfonso was soon playing games with his own brothers and sisters too. His mother, Beatrix, seems to have borne at least nine other children: six boys and three girls.

As a young boy, the prince was also assigned a tutor, a former butler of the queen mother named Garcia Fernández de Villamayor. Alfonso himself, writing in adulthood, had no doubt as to the importance of the position of tutor. "The sages," he wrote, "declared that boys learning while they are small resemble white wax when an engraved seal is placed upon it, for the reason that it leaves its mark there." Tutors to the prince were entrusted with the vital task of instilling good manners, long deemed an important quality at court. There are indications that Eleanor of

England—daughter of King Henry II of England and Eleanor of Aquitaine—had added a new gloss of refinement to the warrior culture of Castile after her marriage to Alfonso VIII of Castile in 1170. Eleanor's arrival had ushered in a new fad for troubadour poetry in Castile. One poet described the queen herself entering the court "closely wrapped in a beautiful and well-made mantle of silk cloth. . . . It was red with a silver edge and was embroidered with a silver lion."

In elite circles across Europe, there was particular concern with table manners, even for children. Boys should learn to eat politely, cleanly, and gracefully, Alfonso later wrote, to avoid eating to excess. They should take care not to put "a second morsel into their mouths until the first has been swallowed." Failure to follow this precept was not only rude and ill-bred but could lead to choking. They should not grab a morsel with all five fingers of a hand lest the chunk be too large. Moreover, they should eat slowly because otherwise the food "cannot be well ground up, and necessarily must cause injury, and produce bad humours, from which sickness arises." Tutors "should compel them to wash their hands before eating," and afterward "they should wipe [their hands] on towels and on nothing else; for they should not wipe them on their clothes, like some people do who do not know anything about cleanliness or politeness." Alfonso's tutor would also have been responsible for ensuring that the heir to the throne avoided drinking too much wine at table: "Tumors are produced in the heads of boys who drink much wine, and they are liable on that account to other serious diseases." Besides, "it also blunts their sense and gives them bad habits, for it inflames their blood so that they, necessarily, become ill-tempered and disobedient." Nor should they drink as soon as they wake up, the king later added, not unreasonably, for this might cause dropsy or diseases of the brain.

We might perhaps imagine the young prince Alfonso, full of words and ideas, being told to keep quiet. Polite speech was "not uttered loudly, or in a very low voice, or very rapidly, or very slowly, and . . . it is spoken with the tongue, and not by gesticulation with the limbs, exhibiting boorishness by means of them." Nor was there to be any running in the palace. Royal children should "walk in a graceful manner, not holding themselves too straight, nor, on the other hand, too stooped, nor moving too rapidly, nor too slowly." They should wear fine and elegant clothes at all times, suitable for the seasons.

Medieval childhood was rarely easy, even among the privileged. Once, Alfonso saw his mother brought close to death's door, and the experience marked him for life. "Although I was a little boy," he recalled in one of the most poignantly personal of his *cantigas*, "I remember it happened like this, for I was present, and saw and heard everything." His father, Fernando III, on the verge of an assault on a Muslim-held town near Córdoba, on the dusty southern frontier, had ordered the young queen away to the safety of distant Cuenca. Beatrix had been pregnant again, probably carrying a baby boy who would be christened Enrique. When she reached Cuenca, Alfonso wrote, "you never saw a sicker woman than she was." Not even the court doctors from Montpellier, the renowned center of medical learning, believed they could save her.

The queen, tossing violently with fever, had ordered her servants to bring her a finely wrought metal image of the Virgin. "When I see her likeness," she declared, "I have such strong belief that I shall soon recover from all these afflictions." Kissing the Virgin's hands and feet, with the tactile fervor so characteristic of medieval people's visceral relationship with sculpture and art, Beatrix had recovered entirely. Though the queen was saved, we can imagine how deeply traumatized the little child Alfonso must have been, his mind still soft as wax.

The boy also saw his baby sister Berenguela fall so desperately sick that she was thought to have died. Alfonso later recalled this moment of tragedy too. The girl's death "grieved her nursemaid so greatly all through the night that she thought she would kill herself from sorrow. She informed the child's mother at once, and she became greatly afflicted / at the death of her child." Only after Beatrix had placed her daughter's limp body before a statue of the Virgin Mary giving birth to the Christ child, and sadly closed the chapel door, did the little girl miraculously recover. Hearing her cry, Beatrix flung open the chapel doors and fervently took her baby in her arms.

Tragically, the queen herself was to die young, her body exhausted by the task of childbearing. In November 1235, probably after giving birth to her tenth child, she passed away. She was buried richly clothed, and a bird and a flower were placed alongside her in the tomb. Alfonso was approaching his fourteenth birthday.

Two years later, Fernando remarried. His second wife was Jeanne de Dammartin, a daughter of a French aristocrat, who had once been proposed as a potential bride for Henry III of England. The new couple would have five more children: Fernando, Leonor (the future English queen consort, Eleanor of Castile) Luis, Simón, and—finally—Juan. But their half brother Prince Alfonso never became close to his stepmother. His impassioned attachment to a heavenly queen, the Virgin Mary, was exceptional even in a period of widespread Marian devotion. This may partly have been a response to the loss of his beloved earthly mother and a reflection of Beatrix's own piety.

According to Alfonso's confessor, Juan Gil de Zamora, the prince had spent his youth immersed in pleasures, "as is customary for the sons of kings." From the time of his adolescence, Juan Gil wrote, he proved to be "sharp-witted, alert in his studies, and with a brilliant memory, and as for his external comportment, he was discreet in speech, outstanding in elegance, modest in laughter, honest in his gaze, graceful in his walk, and sober in company."

The prince seems to have become a voracious reader, with a flair for languages. In addition to Latin and the spoken language of the region, Castilian, he eventually learned Galician-Portuguese, Catalan, Arabic, and Hebrew, as well as at least a smattering of French and Provençal. The *Book of the Twelve Wise Men*, commissioned for him by his father, Fernando III, in the mid-1230s, was a capstone in this educational program—a work that fused the insights of Arabic, Western, and biblical wisdom literature.

To all this book learning was added the brutal real-world experience of taking part in his father's military campaigns. From the mid-1220s, Fernando III—in the prime of life, with his lineage now secured—had begun to ramp up the pressure on the Andalusi frontier. His hand was strengthened when, in 1230, Teresa of Portugal (queen of León) and Berenguela of Castile agreed, in the "pact of the mothers," that he would inherit the kingdom of León, thus bringing about the final fusion of the two realms. The following year, at the tender age of ten, Prince Alfonso rode alongside his father's troops as they headed southeast to Murcia under the command of the nobleman Alvar Pérez de Castro. There, they confronted the Muslim leader Ibn Hud, who had emerged as a potent force of resistance in Andalusia. The official chronicle that Alfonso later orchestrated, the *History of Spain* (*Estoria de Espanna*), vividly evokes the prelude to battle: "The shouts and the cries of the Moors, and the noise of their drums and trumpets, were so great that it seemed that heaven and earth alike were collapsing." These campaigns, which clearly left a deep impression on Alfonso, culminated in the capture of Córdoba after a long, bitter siege in 1236. Fernando commemorated the victory for years to come.

As he matured, skill at the game of chess would have signaled the type of refinement the prince was cultivating; an illustration from the *Book of Games* shows a young man with flowing blond hair—quite possibly Alfonso—playing the game with an older opponent dressed as a scholar, perhaps his tutor. In Castile, the game was intimately associated with the Islamic world and bore all the prestige and mystique that it had long enjoyed in elite and courtly circles there. Seville, in particular, enjoyed fame as a center for chess. One manuscript by the contemporary chess master Abu al-Abbas b. Turayj (d. 1232) mentions a game-playing party at his house there, attended by players from al-Andalus and beyond. Skill in chess lay at the very heart of courtly culture as a symbol of status and a prestigious marker of grace, intelligence, and sophistication.

As he studied the pieces on the chessboard, Prince Alfonso may not have seen spiritual meaning, as Christians elsewhere did in the thirteenth century. In Castile, as in al-Andalus, the game's significance was entirely secular. But no medieval player could have missed its political and military echoes, least of all a prince at the height of his apprenticeship in the arts of warfare.

The game of thrones, in which Alfonso himself was a major player, was a strange and elaborate one, with many more than two competing sides. In some ways it resembled the medieval variation called "Four Seasons Chess," in which four players vied for control of the board from their respective corners. In this variation, play began with the green player, whose pieces corresponded to the spring, and passed counterclockwise around the board to the red, black, and white players. The seasons thus

Four Seasons Chess: *Libro de los juegos* (*Book of Games*) fol. 88v. Reproduced courtesy of Archivo Oronoz.

passed from spring to summer, autumn, and finally winter. On the first move, each player was obliged to attack the player whose season followed his, but on subsequent moves they might choose to attack any competing color.

But Alfonso's game was more complicated still. At the dawn of the thirteenth century, there were not four but at least half a dozen competing players on the Iberian Peninsula (see map). To begin with, no fewer than five Christian kingdoms sought survival or predominance. To the west, the kingdom of Portugal, having struggled to remain on the board, was now eyeing the possibility of expanding southward into the sun-soaked lands of the Algarve, as well as consolidating its northern frontier. These aspirations brought it into conflict with the larger kingdom of León, in the northwest, which now included the whole of Galicia and therefore the important pilgrimage center of Santiago de Compostela, where it was believed that the body of Jesus's disciple Saint James was buried. Pilgrimage to Santiago—by sea as well as by land—was vital in forging links between Spain and northern Europe.

Meanwhile, the mountainous realm of Navarre had been gradually whittled away by its two powerful neighbors. The crown of Aragon, which included the old county of Barcelona, had been on the rise throughout the twelfth century and established a foothold in southern France, although defeat at the battle of Muret in 1213 had thwarted its rulers' aspiration to create a larger state beyond the Pyrenees. Its great rival, spreading southward from the Burgos region across the Spanish Meseta, was Castile, the land of castles, once a frontier zone of the kingdom of León but since the tenth century an independent realm. In terms of size and population, Castile had become the largest of the Christian territories. It was fitting that, in 1188, Alfonso VIII and Eleanor of England should have sought the most glamorous of matches for their daughter, Berenguela: she was betrothed to Prince Conrad of Hohenstaufen, eldest son of the Holy Roman Emperor. The dream of fusing the Castilian crown and the Holy Roman Empire would later become Alfonso's own obsession.

The five Christian realms had been at each other's throats for generations. Castile and León, in particular, had been locked in a series of fierce conflicts. In the late 1190s, the Leonese had laid waste to Castile with the help of Muslim reinforcements, an event that left a deep mark in Alfonso's family's memory. Nevertheless, the world into which his father was born was intensely dynamic. A number of positive developments, including a new prosperity, cultural vitality, and concern for the inner life of man, had characterized the twelfth century across western Europe. The systematic and violent exploitation of the European peasantry, it is true, continued unabated. But the invasions that had menaced and reshaped the continent in an earlier period—among them, the great waves of Viking incursions into Spain as well as the British Isles and Normandy—had come to a close. The turbulent consolidation of feudal kingdoms in England, France, and Iberia, imposing royal lordship on a disorderly society, had helped to promote prosperity.

The renascent church, asserting its claims to domination over the secular kings and princes of Europe, became a great patron of learning. Cathedral schools and, from the late twelfth century, the first universities—Bologna, Oxford, and Palencia—stimulated a thirst for letters. Sadly, this period also witnessed the birth of a persecuting society, intolerant toward internal dissidence as well as external threats and hostile to belief systems or practices—condemned as "heresies"—that could not be reconciled with official doctrine. We can view the crusading movement, which had first taken shape in the latter eleventh century, as an expression of these accumulated energies. Many of the leading noblemen of

Castile and León participated in crusades in the eastern Mediterranean. The papacy also instilled an ideology of crusade within the Iberian Peninsula, encouraging knights from the vying Christian kingdoms—and their counterparts from England and France—to unite against the Almoravid enemy to the south.

Ironically, it was commercial exchange with the Islamic sectors of the Mediterranean that in large part made possible the Christian kingdoms' cultural rebirth and even their crusading aspirations. For the first time since the decline of the Roman Empire, the great sea became a hub of long-distance trade. Italian cities such as Genoa, Pisa, Venice, and—further south—Naples, as well southern French cities like Marseilles, had begun to flourish in the eleventh and twelfth centuries, profiting from the import of luxury goods from the Levant and breathing new life into the trade fairs of northern Europe, notably in Champagne. But equally vibrant were Barcelona and, especially, the Mediterranean cities of Islamic Spain, deeply enmeshed with the luxury goods trade and ultimately with the Silk Route that spanned the Asian continent. Even the distant city of Merv, in modern Turkmenistan, would be mentioned in a song dating from Alfonso's reign. Ever-larger numbers of ships sailed from Alexandria and Syria into the port of Almería, which the geographer al-Idrisi described as the emporium and shipyard of al-Andalus.

Further west, Seville also benefitted from the upturn in Mediterranean commerce, trading directly with merchants in Alexandria and Genoa, as well as their counterparts in Fez and Marrakech. The city had a *funduq* (exchange house) for foreign traders by the mid-twelfth century, lubricating trade across religious borders. Málaga, Valencia, and Denia were also flourishing, and the emir of Denia is believed to have sent aid to the Egyptian caliph in the mid-eleventh century during a period of famine.

One highly controversial study suggests that he was rewarded with an extraordinary gift, a holy chalice—later possessed by the Castilian king Fernando I and known as the Chalice of Doña Urraca—that the authors of the study identify as the Holy Grail itself. This claim is probably fanciful. It remains beyond doubt, however, that the commercial wealth of the urban centers of al-Andalus injected new life into the economy of the northern Christian kingdoms. Textiles, leather, paper, and spices were exported across the border into Castile, which displayed a growing taste for novelty, and wealthier Castilians of this period enjoyed new, more colorful fashions.

Not everyone celebrated this transformation. The new prosperity of Europe clashed with older Christian sensibilities, and it is small wonder that contemporary observers sensed a gulf between ideals and practice. One French abbot delivered a memorable tirade against what he saw as the moral corruption of the age, which he associated particularly with women: "In all their behavior nothing can be noted but unseemly mirth, wherein are no sounds but of jest, with winking eyes and babbling tongues, and wanton gait and all that is ridiculous in manners. The quality of their garments is so unlike that of the frugality of the past that the widening of their sleeves, the tightening of their bodices, their shoes of Cordovan morocco with twisted beaks—nay, in their whole person we may see how shame is cast aside."

For conservative observers, these shoes were the ultimate embodiment of human vanity and moral decline. Fashioned of Spanish leather and manufactured in Córdoba, they were transported north to France and other parts of Spain. In a Cistercian monastery in León, one such pair of leather shoes survives. They once belonged to a noblewoman named Teresa Pérez, who had withdrawn to the monastery after her husband's death. Her high-soled platform sandals—with their fashionably pointed toes and open heels, decorated with bunches of roses and other formal motifs hand painted in many colors—perhaps served as a valued reminder of her former life outside the cloister.

These shoes of Spanish leather remind us of the thriving market in luxury goods and the long-distance trade routes that converged in Spain. More broadly, they suggest that in accounting for the "twelfth-century renaissance"—from the revitalization of trade to the regeneration of learning and wisdom—we should not underestimate the pivotal role of the Islamic world, particularly the new power that had emerged in the beginning of that century: the Almohad Empire.

If the turbulent life of young Alfonso was a game of chess, the board was not the neat, self-contained geographical square of Iberia; it stretched beyond, in many directions, across Europe and the Mediterranean, all the way to the high Atlas Mountains of Morocco. And it was in the Atlas region, just over a century earlier, that a brutal power play had taken place.

Around 1100, Ibn Tumart, son of a mountain chief, had traveled east to Cairo, and Damascus, and Baghdad. There he had found a world under assault. The first crusade, launched five years earlier, had, by the Christians' own admission, left the streets of Jerusalem ankle deep in blood. A crusader kingdom had lodged painfully in the heart of the Muslim Near East, catalyzing new forms of Islamic militancy against the crusaders and moderate Muslims. Ibn Tumart internalized this spirit and brought it back with him to North Africa. As he traveled through the towns and villages of the Maghreb, he condemned what he saw as lax morality and weak belief. His followers came to be known as the Almohads, a name deriving from the Arabic word for "the oneness of the divine."

In a series of purges, the Almohads consolidated their dominance among the Berber peoples of the Atlas Mountains. Ibn Tumart condemned the belief system of the previous dynasty, the Almoravids, as a weak and effeminate form of Islam and vowed vengeance on all their supporters: "Kill them wherever you may find them," he urged his own followers, "and do not favor among them either companion or ally. All those who refuse to return to the fold will be your enemies until death." Until his own death in 1130, he waged continual war against the Almoravid capital, Marrakech.

The Almohads pursued a spirit of jihad, increasingly strong within the western Islamic world, in which Muslim leaders targeted rivals as much as Christian enemies. Ibn Tumart's successor completed the holy war against the Almoravids—Marrakech finally fell in 1147—and within a few years the Almohads had taken the fight into Iberia itself. By 1160, they had strengthened their presence in Andalusia through a new fortified urban center on the rocky mountain of Gibraltar, *Jebel Tariq*, which took its name from Tariq, the Berber leader who had spearheaded the very first Muslim attack on Iberia in 711. Gibraltar became a well-connected base for major military operations, allowing the Almohads to gain control of much of the southwest of Spain, refashioning Seville as a capital city that would later captivate Alfonso.

The Almohad movement was in many ways intolerant and its interpretation of Islam unusually rigid, abrogating the traditional respect for Jews and Christians as "Peoples of the Book." Its discriminatory policies toward Jews, in particular, encouraged Jewish emigration into the Christian kingdoms of the north. Yet it would be a mistake to imagine, as some have done, that the Almohads were the medieval equivalents of al-Qaeda or the self-proclaimed Islamic State of the early twenty-first century.

The game being played in the early thirteenth century was no simple black-and-white binary. To begin with, the Almohads were—in many ways—pragmatic. They remained important trading partners for both Pisa and Genoa. Military alliances, too, continued between supposed enemies. Alfonso's father, Fernando III of Castile and León, reputedly sent some 12,000 troops to the Maghreb, just as Italian merchants continued to ply their trade in North African ports. More importantly, this was in some ways a cultured and sophisticated regime, living by the word as much as the sword. The central mosque in Marrakech was called the Kutubiyya—a name deriving from the Arabic for "books"—precisely because of the large book market that thrived in the shadow of its minaret. Literacy was highly valued, even in the mountainous regions of the Atlas, and Ibn Tumart himself had underscored the importance of reading and writing as an instrument for spreading the faith.

In al-Andalus, a number of extraordinary philosophical works were composed under the influence of the movement that Ibn Tumart had founded. Among them was the *Guide of the Perplexed*, written at the end of the twelfth century by the great Jewish philosopher Moses Maimonides. Born in Córdoba in 1138 at the end of the period of Almoravid rule, Maimonides lived under the Almohads from the age of ten until his very early twenties and composed his work in high classical Arabic written in Hebrew characters. In 1160, his family migrated to Fez, in the Almohad heartland, where some Jewish communities had survived the onslaught. The family would subsequently settle in Egypt—his life, as one historian has rightly observed, "circled the Mediterranean basin"—but the imprint of Almohad philosophy on his work would remain.

Another of the brightest jewels of Almohad-era literature was a piece of philosophical fiction, set on an imaginary island off the

coast of India, by the Andalusi scholar Ibn Tufayl, a leading figure at the Almohad court during the mid-twelfth century. Written sometime in the 1170s or very early 1180s and named for its
protagonist, *Hayy ibn Yaqzan* traces the dawning religious vision
of its hero, marooned as a baby on a remote island, and his reali-
zation, through the fusion of mysticism and reason, of the oneness of the cosmos. After being translated from Arabic into
Hebrew, the tale passed into the mainstream of late-medieval
and Renaissance European culture and is sometimes thought to
be a source of inspiration for Daniel Defoe's *Robinson Crusoe*.

Ibn Tufayl, in turn, is credited with having introduced to the
caliph a young philosophical prodigy—a Muslim who may possibly
have had Jewish ancestors—named Ibn Rushd, who came to be
known in the Christian West as Averroes and to be regarded as a
giant of rational philosophy. Averroes, convinced that natural reason and science would illuminate the nature of God, has himself
been described as "a Renaissance man before civilization knew the
term." Some have seen him as a foil to the fanaticism of the Almohad regime, but he was in fact part of a wave of cultural ferment
rather than an exception to the rule. Although exiled to Lucena as
the result of a conspiracy that emphasized his supposedly Jewish
ethnic roots, he remained in favor with the Almohad court when
he died in Marrakech in 1198. Averroes's critical engagement with
the ancient philosophy of Aristotle, on whose work he composed a
series of commentaries, would long outlive him, providing a catalyst for intellectual and cultural revitalization in western Europe as
well as the Maghreb. His writings embody a deep reflection on ancient Greek rationalism that has led some modern scholars to
claim that this period marked an apex in civilization, eclipsing
even the cultures of the ancient Mediterranean.

Even battle could not stop the influx of philosophy and literature from al-Andalus. In July 1212, nine years before Prince

Alfonso's birth, a coalition of Christian forces led by his grandfather and namesake, Alfonso VIII, had won a resounding victory over the Almohad army at Las Navas de Tolosa, on the plateau just north of the olive-growing city of Jaén. This unlikely alliance of the warring northern kingdoms was in large part the achievement of one man: Rodrigo Jiménez de Rada, archbishop of Toledo. In some respects, the archbishop, more deeply imbued with crusading ideals than most of his fellow Spaniards, was atypical of his culture. The previous year, he had carried out a preaching tour, aggressively framing the relationship between Christians and Muslims in Spain as part of a cosmic struggle between good and evil. He had gathered the Christian military forces in Toledo, before the march south, and ensured that Pope Innocent III blessed the campaign as a holy war. As the Christian troops rode into battle against the Almohad caliph, a banner fluttered above them in the wind, bearing the image of Mary and her son.

Later generations would commemorate the battle of Las Navas de Tolosa as the victory that prevented Islam from slicing further into the continent and ensured the eventual supremacy of Christianity in Europe. Without doubt, it dealt a huge psychological blow, and the archbishop himself later described the battle as a turning point in history. "This victory was the cause of the collapse and the annihilation of the Almohads," he wrote. The Arabs had been forced to flee from the battlefield, "so that the sword of the Arabs was suffocated and the force of the Goths restored, opening the pathway for Christian retaliation." The realities of this retaliation were brutal. Thousands of Muslim men and women were killed in the aftermath of the battle, and many more were subjected to enslavement or captivity.

Almohad authority in al-Andalus would crumble in the next generation, reaching a symbolic nadir when, in 1230, a popular rebellion led to the hurling of the Almohad governor of Seville over the city walls. For several years, a former Almohad military commander named Ibn Hud clung on to almost all of al-Andalus, but only a pact with Fernando III allowed him to fend off a determined rival: Muhammad I of Granada, known as Ibn al-Ahmar (Son of the Red). When Fernando decided to dissolve the pact, the carpet was pulled from beneath Ibn Hud's feet; in June 1236, the Castilian king captured Córdoba. The Aragonese, too, exploited the rapid decline of Almohad power, occupying both Majorca (1229–1231) and Valencia (1238).

Yet, even as Christian troops from the north overran much of al-Andalus in the second quarter of the thirteenth century, the spirit of the place seems to have conquered the hearts and minds of the conquerors. Dozens of churches in the Christian realms were constructed in an Arabized architectural style, while the design of wooden ceilings replete with bilingual symbols followed Islamic patterns. Pottery inspired by Andalusi models began to proliferate as ordinary Castilians took their dietary inspiration from the Muslim south.

In the sphere of elite literary culture, a tidal wave of translations from Arabic into Latin—a significant number of them by Jewish scholars—washed over Castile, bearing with it the philosophical sophistication of Almohad culture. The archbishop of Toledo became a great patron of this translation movement, which for him, personally, entailed no respect for Islam itself; the knowledge that had flourished in Islamic Spain was simply a treasure to reclaim for Christendom. These cultural borrowings took place within a colonial context: the appropriation of knowledge and aesthetic style accompanied the appropriation of land. But imperialism often breeds hybridity. Iberia was the arena for kaleidoscopic interactions among peoples, in which colonial contact and fusion ultimately enabled the cultural rebirth of the northern Christian realms. On his death in 1247, the archbishop of Toledo

was buried in Andalusi robes—almost two centuries before Fra
Angelico (c. 1395–1455) painted a Madonna and Child in the
church of San Marco in Florence, with Arabic inscriptions woven into the Madonna's dress. These robes, divested of any specifically Islamic significance, expressed a pan-Iberian style that
crossed the boundaries of faith.

Alfonso's world was faster-moving, and more mercurial,
than the ponderous form of chess commonly played in
thirteenth-century Iberia. In this standard version, the *fil*, or
"elephant" (ancestor of the modern game's bishop), moved only
three squares diagonally instead of going as far as it could unim-
peded. The pawn, if it reached the opposite end of the board,
could not be promoted to whichever piece the player wished, as
in the modern game; it simply became a *fers*, a medieval chess
piece somewhere between the earlier Arabic piece called the
firzan—a "vizier" that could move one space diagonally in any
direction—and the powerful modern queen. The invention of
the queen occurred only in the later Middle Ages and may possibly have been associated with the power of Queen Isabella—
Isabel la Católica—at the end of the fifteenth century.

The form of the game that most closely captured the Castilian
political scene in the 1230s—a wildly exotic variation that Alfonso loved to play—was the so-called *Grant acedrex*, or "Great
Chess." Played on a board with 144 squares and featuring a veritable menagerie of birds and beasts, it demanded intense concen-
tration and particular mental skill. The key piece, as usual, was
the king, "who is like the head and lord of his whole army." But
in Great Chess, the king seems to have had more freedom of
movement: he could jump two squares forward or diagonally,
even if another piece occupied the square between; he also had
the option of moving to an adjacent square.

As he looked at this chess piece, Alfonso may have thought of his mighty father, Fernando III, to whom—despite long periods of separation—he felt deeply indebted. We know from his own description of Fernando that his father's good courtly tastes included a love of the game of chess: "He was an expert in all types of hunting, as well as playing board games and chess and other good games of many kinds; he was fond of paying men to sing, as well as knowing how to sing himself, and of troubadours, and of jongleurs who knew how to play instruments well." Alfonso always venerated his father, finding cosmic meaning in the very letters of his name. The *f*, he wrote, signified his great faith (*fe*), the *e* that he was committed (*encerrado*) in his deeds and had a great understanding (*entendimento*) of God, and the *r* that he was robust (*rrezio*) in will and in deed against enemies of the faith and other evildoers. Skipping the first *n*, Alfonso continued: the *a* indicated that his father was a friend (*amigo*) of God and lover (*amador*) of law, the *n* that he had great nobility (*nobleza*) of heart and thus gained great fame (*nonbradía*); the *d* showed that he was just (*derechurero*) in speech and in deed and, finally, the *o* that he was a fine man (*omne conplido*) in manner and in behavior and was therefore honored (*onrado*) by God and all men.

But in the game of Great Chess, the piece next to the king was far more powerful. By his side stood

a bird that has authority over all the other birds. And while this bird has many different names, depending on the languages of peoples, in India specifically, where this game originated, it is called the *aanca*, which means a beautiful and fearsome bird. Because, as wise men tell in their books, wherever this bird flies, no other bird dares to take flight, and the birds in trees and caves dare not leave them but instead try to hide as well as they can, because it is so large that it can carry the elephant and all the other large beasts it finds to its nest. This bird is very beautiful, because its chest and neck shine as though they were made of gold. And its sides and wings are yellow. Its feet, eyes, and beak are red as scarlet and it has very black claws. And it has on its head a round spiked crown, like a diadem.

In this chess variant, the royal *aanca* had greater bite and flexibility than the king. It could move to any adjacent square on the diagonals on which it stood and could then either remain on that square or continue to any square on the same file or rank.

It would not have been surprising if, as Alfonso reflected on the *aanca* and the game of thrones being played out around him, the towering figure of Queen Berenguela came to mind. Throughout the 1230s, the queen mother—still co-ruling with her son Fernando—continued to exert a decisive influence, a reminder that we need to question the presumption that medieval women in general were disempowered and that queens in particular were valued only as child bearers. Official rhetoric attempted to reconcile Berenguela's femininity—her "weapon of choice"—with the reality of her dominance at court and her formative influence over the king. Adapting the words of Rodrigo Jiménez de Rada, archbishop of Toledo, Alfonso's *History of Spain* related how "with breasts full of virtues she gave him her milk in such a way that, even though King Fernando was now a man grown and confirmed in the age of full power, his mother Queen Berenguela did not cease (nor had she ever ceased) from telling him and teaching him diligently the things that please God and men. Everyone considered it good; and she never showed him the habits and matters that pertained to women, but rather those that led to greatness of heart and to great deeds." As queen, Berenguela was an exceptionally successful operator, binding the realm together and enabling it to move beyond the state of fractious civil war. If there were few medieval queens like her, one historian has observed, there were few such medieval kings either. In Alfonso's words, Berenguela was "a very wise lady and a great expert, sharp in political affairs." It was she who had orchestrated Fernando's accession to the throne of Castile in 1217, she who had effected the fusion of the two rival kingdoms—Castile and León—in 1230, and she who in many respects dictated the rhythm and logistics of military campaigning against the Almohads.

In strategizing, a third figure had joined Fernando and Queen Berenguela: the crusader-archbishop of Toledo himself. Not content with having organized the pivotal battle of Las Navas de Tolosa in 1212, Rodrigo Jiménez de Rada assumed responsibility for the defense and settlement of a vast swathe of territory deep in the frontier region and, as early as 1219, led a surprise assault diagonally southeast in the direction of Valencia, designed to limit the expansion of the rival crown of Aragon, as well as to seize territory from the Muslims. Did Alfonso perhaps see a parallel in the Great Chess crocodile, located on the king's right-hand side? The crocodile, he later explained in the *Book of Games*, "is so powerful that, while it has its two hind feet and its tail in the water, there is nothing that it grabs on dry land that can escape, however strong it may be. When it wants to grab something it pretends that it is looking somewhere else to deceive it, and then it turns quickly and diagonally and goes after it until it captures it."

In the company of the king, the *aanca*, and the crocodile, the prince was reaching adulthood. In the late 1230s, he participated alongside his father in new campaigns in Andalusia, and by the end of the decade he had acquired his own household, welcoming his close friend Nuño González de Lara into it. Acknowledging his political maturity, King Fernando now granted him the "tenancy" of a number of towns in the southern part of León:

Alba de Tormes, Salamanca, Toro, and the city of León. He also became lord of Ribadavia, in Galicia, gaining exposure to the vibrant Galician-Portuguese lyric tradition of the noble courts in the region. The prince had become a Great Chess lion, one that "jumps a great distance sideways or forwards, more than any other beast when it wants to capture something." Over the next decade, he would be active in the capture of two vital cities, Murcia and Seville. But the young man's conquests, more than merely territorial, would also be of the heart.

2

LOVERS

Venus always signifies good, and fortune, and pleasures, and joys.

—YEHUDA BEN MOSÉ, BOOK OF CROSSES, 1259

THE STORY OF ALFONSO'S TWENTIES IS IN PART ONE OF youthful military adventure. It is also the story of his betrothal and marriage and a tale of two love affairs: one, a long-lasting premarital liaison, and the other, a complex attraction to the city that had become the supreme object of desire. The prince's relationship with Seville, and with Arabic culture more generally, was steeped in colonial ambition but also served as a spur to the creation of a new, vibrantly humane culture. It is tempting to imagine this phase of Alfonso's life unfolding under the eyes of Venus, a planet that, according to astrological wisdom, brought "good, and fortune, and pleasures, and joys." But, of course, more terrestrial influences were at work—and they were not always so benevolent as Venus. In this world of affections, political considerations were entwined from the very beginning.

In 1241, a proposal reached the Castilian court. Alfonso was to be betrothed to an Aragonese princess, the daughter of the great conquering king of Aragon, Jaume I, and his wife, Yolanda of Hungary. The girl, Yolant (b. 1236/37), was no more than four years old at the time. The Hungarian queen was an astute political player, active in decision making alongside her husband. She would bequeath this political intelligence to her daughter. As for the little princess, some fifteen years younger than Alfonso, Yolant would eventually bear him nine of his thirteen children and come to exert a decisive influence on the political course of his kingdom. In the short term, however, the Aragonese match proved the cause of more headaches than pleasures and joys.

In the upper echelons of medieval society, marriages were frequently arranged for political motives; personal attraction could play no role in such a match. Although Yolant could not wed formally until the age of twelve, the betrothal presented strategic advantages to both sides. Not only did both Castile and Aragon, old sparring partners, have designs on the southeast of the peninsula; Queen Yolanda of Hungary was also anxious to advance her children's interests over those of King Jaume's son by his first marriage. As it turned out, however, the betrothal did little to ease the acute tensions between the two realms. Territorial rivalries quickly soured the relationship between Prince Alfonso and his prospective father-in-law.

In late 1241 or early 1242, as he turned twenty, Alfonso was made *alférez* of the Castilian army—that is, its standard-bearer and ceremonial commander. Fernando III's health was failing, and the prince was entrusted with the task of negotiating the surrender of the Muslim city of Murcia in 1243. As Almohad power declined, Andalusia had begun to disintegrate into a number of smaller emirates. Abuzz with cultural activity but riven by internal conflict and crippled by the 1238 assassination of its ruler,

Ibn Hud, Murcia was a much coveted jewel. The Castilians, the Aragonese, and the rulers of Granada all had their eyes on this prize. But its beleaguered ruler had turned to Castile for military protection, and on May 1, 1243, Alfonso led the army of occupation into the city, taking possession of its fortress. With the signing of a surrender treaty, Murcia became a vassal kingdom, paying tribute to Castile. The treaty authorized the Castilians, in turn, to station a garrison there. Alfonso successfully occupied the northern and central parts of the kingdom, adding luster to his public image; in the following weeks, he occupied the rest of the realm before returning in some glory to the Castilian court at Burgos.

The loss of Murcia was a decisive blow for Muslim Spain. Archaeological evidence suggests that urban centers in the region had all continued to grow in the years after the supposedly pivotal battle of Las Navas de Tolosa in 1212. Now the process was violently interrupted. New Christian settlement led to an exodus of the Muslim population, and many fled southwest to the safety of Granada.

Alfonso's success also generated immediate ripples in his relationship with the Aragonese. Jaume I observed his victory jealously, and his alarm turned to fury as Castilian forces began to encroach on Muslim territories that he saw as rightfully belonging to Aragon. Tensions mounted over the possession of Xàtiva, a Muslim center of paper manufacture, in the rich and fertile lands that lay between Valencia—now in Aragonese hands—and the conquered Castilian vassal kingdom of Murcia. According to Jaume's remarkable autobiography, the *Book of Deeds* (*Llibre dels fets*), Prince Alfonso had the nerve to send a messenger to the Aragonese in 1244, claiming that he was going to Xàtiva simply to buy a tent (a local specialization), when he was really going to carry out negotiations with local Muslim leaders. Jaume proclaimed that anyone who conversed with the Muslims without having asked permission from the Aragonese would be arrested and brought before his court. The messenger himself was hanged from a tree. The king of Aragon expressed his shock that two towns in the area had also surrendered to Alfonso "since it was of our conquest and he had our daughter as his wife." He then described how he laid an ambush and captured seventeen men—implicitly, Castilians or their collaborators—half of whom were hanged and half beheaded. Relations with the man he evidently already considered his son-in-law could hardly have been more strained.

Not for the last time in our story, a queen intervened as peace-maker. After a date had been set for a meeting between Jaume and Alfonso in the frontier town of Almizra, Queen Yolanda of Hungary "asked us that we should allow her to attend the meeting, so that she might help to solve the dispute that there was between us and our son-in-law; and he came to see her as soon as she arrived there." Alfonso seems to have expressed his claims assertively, while Jaume, never short of self-confidence, bridled at the young man's boldness: "He was married to our daughter," Jaume protested, "and he believed that we could not have married her with any man of the world better than him; for which reason he believed he ought to receive, with her, a portion of land for the marriage, and that we ought to give him Xàtiva, which we had assigned to him through Ovieto García, who had negotiated the marriage."

In a calculated display of anger, Jaume ordered his horses saddled and threatened to storm out of the meeting: "There is no man in the world whom you would not make lose his temper, because you do everything with such pride and you think that everything that you want ought to be done." Only the queen's entreaties persuaded him to stay, and at the thirteenth hour, an agreement was reached. Alfonso relinquished his claims to Xàtiva and was granted a number of other towns and villages in the border region instead. "We departed," Jaume concluded unconvincingly, "as good friends."

The occupation of Murcia was already proving a diplomatic challenge for Alfonso. But with it he gained access to a treasury of culture and knowledge. The city, until recently home to the great Muslim mystic Ibn Arabi (1164–1240), had become a hub of Arabic learning; it was in some ways to the thirteenth century what Toledo had been to the eleventh. Alfonso fully recognized the value of this tradition. Muslims, Jews, and Christians alike continued to learn at the famed school of Muhammad al-Riquti until the 1260s. Alfonso's experience in Murcia surely accentuated his fascination with the wealth of the Arabic heritage. As early as 1243—the year in which he conquered the city—he is said to have asked his Jewish physician to begin translation of a book on the healing properties of minerals and gemstones that he found in Toledo. Completed eleven years later, this translation, the *Book of Stones* (*Lapidario*), became one of his most prized resources, and in later life—afflicted by physical ailments, emotional turmoil, and political crises—he would arrange for the production of a luxury edition.

One theme in the *Book of Stones* that surely interested the prince most, in the flush of his youth, was sex. The stone known as *margul* had a particularly desirable effect. "The stone's color is like that of an egg yolk, and when it is broken, a damp substance is found inside, which sticks to the hands and smells very good." It is useful for curing sores or facial discolorations, the passage continues, but "this damp substance has another virtue that is very good for bridegrooms. If, when they lie with their wives, they anoint with it the virile member with which they are to beget offspring, it will make the member grow, so that it will be longer and bigger." Conversely, the "hermit's stone," called *zam-oricaz*, was a valuable prophylactic:

> This stone is highly valued in the land where it is found and it is used in rings and necklaces, for the man who wears it feels no desire for a woman and even if he tried to mount her, he would not [be] able to do anything while having this stone on his person. For this reason, the learned men of old gave these stones to the religious and the hermits, and to those who had taken the vow of chastity. And some gentiles, who wanted to lie with their wives only at certain times, in order to have them get pregnant quicker and to make their sons stronger and more robust, carried this stone on them at all times, save when they wanted to beget.

The prince may well have read these passages eagerly. In the early 1240s, soon after establishing his own household and around the same time that he became *alférez*, Alfonso had become became intimately involved with the noblewoman Mayor Guillén de Guzmán, daughter of a powerful lord from the kingdom of León. For the Guzmán family, which in the following decades rose to become one of the greatest dynasties in Castile, a closer relationship with the heir to the throne was a boon. Although his relationship was sinful, Alfonso acknowledged—paying grudging lip service to ecclesiastical norms—it was the lesser of two evils: "The Holy Church forbids Christians to keep concubines, because they live with them in mortal sin. The wise men of the ancients, however, who made the laws, permitted certain persons to keep them without being liable to a temporal penalty, because they considered it less wicked to have one than to have many."

The church frowned on but tolerated Alfonso's relationship with Mayor Guillén de Guzmán, and the Castilian court widely accepted it. In contemporary terms, Mayor Guillén was a *barragana*, a long-term concubine, although we might think of her more simply as a premarital partner. In the thirteenth century, a widespread cultural expectation held that young men needed to find an outlet for their sexual energies before settling down; this was, in practice, a period of greater tolerance and permissiveness toward male sexuality than the later Middle Ages or early modern period. Churchmen might condemn premarital sex, unless the couple intended to get married in the future, but courtly culture and the secular world more generally saw it as a natural and medically advisable expression of healthy masculinity.

Equally, there was a surprising tolerance for the siring of children before and outside marriage. In mid-1244, Alfonso led a successful military campaign in the kingdom of Murcia against local Muslim forces in a number of towns—Mula, Lorca, and Cartagena—whose leaders had held out, refusing to accept the peace treaty and declared loyalty to the ruler of Granada. But he then returned to Castile, for Mayor Guillén had just given birth to their first child, Beatriz (the name by which Alfonso's mother had been known in Spain). The prince formally granted the town of Elx (Elche), north of the city of Murcia, to the baby girl. In fact, the relationship between father and daughter became one of the most affectionate of all his personal relationships.

In principle, Castilian court culture certainly recognized the need for men to restrain their sexual desires. In the *Book of the Twelve Wise Men*, Alfonso had read, "The people see the chaste Prince or ruler as a mirror; through sexual luxuriousness we have seen many princes and kings be lost." In his *Siete partidas*, he himself insisted that the king should avoid sex with lowborn women because they will "degrade the nobleness of his line," and he will not have legitimate children "as the law directs." Womanizing meant that a man "will sustain great injury of body, and will lose his soul also by this means." Needless to say, the king "should carefully avoid obtaining offspring in improper quarters, as, for instance, by his relatives, or by his sister-in-law, or members of holy orders, or married women." He should also be careful about his consumption of wine. Excessive drinking after eating "impels man to lasciviousness on improper occasions; and great injury will result to him who practices it at such times, for it weakens the body, and if any children are born to him, they will be small and weak."

The romantic, sometimes raunchy, lyrics of the troubadours were one sign of the era's generally greater permissiveness. Alfonso's *Cantigas de Santa María*, which were composed from the 1260s onward, were colored by the more noble of these lyrics, sublimating the celebration of courtly love in his veneration of the Queen of Heaven. Some influential churchmen were also reconciled to the idea that there might be some good in human sexuality as well as in marriage. Bartholomew the Englishman, who was writing at almost exactly the same time that Alfonso was sharing his bed with Mayor Guillén, wrote of the ideal husband that "whatever he is asked to do or make for her love, he does immediately with vigor; he denies nothing [to anyone] who asks him to do anything in the name of his bride; he addresses her flatteringly with ardent eyes. At last, finally agreeing with her, he takes her into marriage." The Dominican friar Vincent de Beauvais, whose encyclopedic *Speculum maius* (*Great Mirror*) is known to have become an important influence on the Wise King's later thinking, wrote that "marriage was instituted in paradise." Having been "ravished by ecstasy," he wrote, "man will abandon his father and mother and will cling to his wife, and the two will be one flesh."

Alfonso's own *cantigas* express competing attitudes toward men's sexuality. One pious song tells of the story of a pilgrim who, before setting off for Santiago de Compostela, has sex with a "dishonest woman to whom he was not married." At the instigation of the Devil, who has taken the form of Saint James himself, he first cuts off his penis and then slits his own throat to gain salvation. Eventually the Virgin Mary restores him to life, but he "never recovered the missing part with which he had sinned." In the end, however, the *cantigas'* tolerance—sometimes even their explicit embrace of sex—is the most striking, particularly in a work of spiritual devotion. In another song, a certain abbess has had an affair with her steward and become pregnant. The nuns, over whom she had ruled with an iron fist, happily report her to the bishop. Summoning the abbess, the bishop tells her that she has made an awful error of judgment. But precisely as he is speaking, the abbess prays to the Virgin, and "as though in a dream, Holy Mary had the child removed and sent it to be reared in Soissons." After she awakes from her swoon, the bishop asks her to undress; he examines her naked body, sees no sign of pregnancy, and promptly declares her innocent.

If, on the surface, the lyricist sings of human transgression and divine mercy, there is nonetheless a palpable, good-humored delight in the abbess's sexual misdemeanors. While giving a cursory nod in the direction of ecclesiastical norms, the song's real spirit is one of winking indulgence. Another *cantiga* tells of an oversexed French priest who "set out to have his sinful pleasure and got into a boat and crossed the Seine, which runs through Paris." The boat is overturned, and he lies in the river for four days, but the Virgin comes to his rescue, overlooking his very human dalliance.

These episodes would hardly be out of place in the pleasure-loving world of Giovanni Boccaccio's *Decameron*, written in the aftermath of the Black Death, which devastated the city of Florence between 1348 and 1351. Boccaccio framed his stories as a response to this human catastrophe, and many of them embody the debauchery that, he suggested, was a common response to the plague. Many men and women, he wrote, "maintained that an

infallible way of warding off this appalling evil was to drink heavily, enjoy life to the full, go round singing and merrymaking, grat-
ify all of one's cravings whenever the opportunity offered, and
shrug the whole thing off as one enormous joke." His tales of lascivious men and women, among them nuns and even hermits,
reveal a culture that accepted heterosexual dalliances with a nod
and a wink.

But this particular culture of tolerance long predated the
plague and had flourished under Andalusi influence. Al-Andalus
may not have been a paradise of sexual tolerance, as supposed by
the Orientalist imagination; yet the poetry of Ibn Quzman (d.
1160) illustrates the graphic embrace of heterosexual male wish
fulfillment that thirteenth-century Castile absorbed by osmosis.
One poem sings the praises of a Berber girl's beautiful body:
"Hardly had I beheld that leg / And those two lively, lively eyes /
When my penis arose in my trousers like a pavilion / And made a
tent out of my clothes."

While still far removed from this degree of frankness, the illustrations to the *cantigas* reveal an interest in human sexuality that
goes far beyond any straightforwardly pious desire to condemn
sinfulness or to illustrate the miraculous healing powers of the
Virgin. The miniatures accompanying one song show a husband
who, urged on by black devils, is unable to keep the vow of chastity he has made with his wife; he hurries toward her bed, where
he lets the sheet fall from his naked body and reaches out for his
topless partner (who appears significantly less distressed than the
words of the song itself would have us believe). The final miniature of another song delights in depicting two blond-haired lovers lying in bed. The young man, right arm around his lover, cups
her breast, while she reaches across his waist. The two recline
beneath pink-purple silk sheets, under a luxuriant canopy whose
design suggests Andalusi inspiration.

The devil leads a husband to break his vow of chastity: *Cantigas de Santa María*, no. 115, *Códice rico* (Rich Codex), Real Biblioteca del Monasterio de El Escorial, Ms. T.I.1. Reproduced courtesy of Archivo Oronoz.

The theme of sexual desire persists in many of Alfonso's other works too. In the *Book of Games,* a royal figure, emblazoned with the heraldic symbols of Castile and León, reaches toward one of two women, scantily clad in diaphanous dresses and playing a game of chess. The woman wears gold bangles, her legs are splayed open, and she directly faces the viewer. Later, more puritanical censors appear to have attempted to smudge this risqué image, unintentionally making the royal figure appear as if he is touching the woman's breasts. It is unlikely that the figure is Alfonso himself or that the woman is his lover, Mayor Guillén. Such a highly sexualized image would have tarnished her prestige and standing at court. It is less plausible still that the woman's opponent is Alfonso's first-born daughter, Beatriz. These women are probably courtesans or concubines, Andalusi in origin or at least cultural style. But the image speaks to the culture of eroticism that, seeping across the frontier, had begun to pervade the Castilian court.

If Muslim Spain was the source of a culture celebrating male sexual desire, its most prominent city, Seville, was itself an idealized object of *colonial* desire—a place to be possessed and dominated. In the imagination of its conquerors, sex and power converged. The image of Seville as a beautiful woman, in fact, had a long history in Arabic literature. Around the turn of the thirteenth century, Abu 'l Walid Isma'il ibn Mohammad al-Shaqundi (d. 1231/32) had written an elegy to the city and its rich, fertile hinterlands, the Aljarafe, recalling in turn the words of the poet-king al-Mu'tamid ibn Abbad (1040–1095), who had serenaded the place that formed the heart of his realm: "Seville is a bride / Whose groom is Abbad / The Aljarafe is her crown; / Her necklace the river."

Alfonso had surely been exposed to the bride's wealth and beauty and the wonders of the Aljarafe. "Its products travel to all the regions of the earth, and the oil pressed from its olive trees is exported as far as Alexandria," al-Shaqundi had written. "Its villages surpass all other villages in the beauty of their construction and the zeal with which their inhabitants care for them both inside and outside, to the point at which they appear, from their whitewashed walls, white stars in an eternal sky. A man who had seen Cairo and Damascus was asked, 'Which do you prefer: these two cities, or Seville?,' and he answered that he preferred Seville, adding: 'Its Aljarafe is a forest without lions, and its river is a Nile without crocodiles.'" Its women, like its citrus fruits and its architecture, were peerless. Its learned men, experts in every branch of knowledge and culture, both serious and comic, were countless. And as for the numberless poets to be found there, they gained endless favors and gifts from the grandees of the city.

Al-Shaqundi's eulogy responded in part to the ascendancy of the Berbers of North Africa, whom he generally regarded with disdain. His contempt and local pride may have been mixed with anxiety about a shift in the center of gravity in the Islamic world. The twelfth century had witnessed the apogee of two Berber dynasties, the Almoravids (whom he particularly despised) and later the Almohads. Political, military, and economic power had begun to shift away from al-Andalus and toward the Maghreb. Reflecting this change, cities such as Sijilmasa, Fez, Tlemcen, Sabta (Ceuta), and especially Marrakech had experienced a spectacular phase of growth, benefitting from the development of trade across the Sahara. Al-Andalus, once the fulcrum of the western caliphate, had lost some of its protagonism; the new cities across the strait had definitively and permanently eclipsed Córdoba. Al-Shaqundi was in this sense articulating a distinctively "Spanish" sensibility and pride of place that Alfonso later inherited.

But the city that the Castilians so coveted had, in some ways, been enriched by her North African suitors. Under the leadership of Abu Ya'qub Yusuf (1163–1184) and his son and successor Abu Ya'qub al-Mansur (1184–1199), Almohad government in al-Andalus had reached its pinnacle, and Seville, which had occupied a key role ever since the first Almohad incursion in 1146, became a second, de facto capital, mirroring Marrakech, their stronghold in North Africa. According to an exceptionally useful source—the descriptions of the twelfth-century Andalusi historian Ibn Sahib al-Sala—the caliph Abu Ya'qub first made "Ishbilya" (Seville) the capital of his realm; he rebuilt the city walls, aqueduct, and *alcázar* (fortress) in the aftermath of a catastrophic flood in 1168 or 1169 and an earthquake the following year. Early in the process, the caliph constructed a new palace and botanical gardens at the Buhayra, on the outskirts of the city, ordering that the grounds be planted with olive trees, vines, and exotic fruit trees. "Orders had been given to the governors of Granada and Guadix to send to Buhayra apples and various kinds of the pear the doctors called Kumizri," Ibn Sahib writes. "Thus they arrived, mule train after mule train, with all the fruit trees that had been chosen for planting and fruition."

This was the prelude to the most spectacular construction project of all: the building of a new mosque. The caliph gave the supreme order to begin construction in the month of Ramadan of the year 568 (May 17 to 26, 1172), Ibn Sahib reports, in order to provide the people of Seville with a proper space for prayer; no mosque in al-Andalus, he claimed, equaled it in size or number of naves. The building was clearly intended as a display of power; construction continued unabated for four years. The following decade, the mosque's soaring minaret was added. It "rises up in the air and into the sky," wrote the Muslim historian, "seeming to an observer several days from Seville as if it is among the stars of the Zodiac." In 1198, the four golden balls known as a *yamur* were placed on its pinnacle.

Here was a cityscape that, in 1247 and 1248, dazzled Alfonso and the besieging Castilian troops. His lavish description of Seville, the beautiful object of his longing, breathlessly echoes the admiration of generations of Muslim authors. Alfonso begins his description with a eulogy to one of the most recent additions to the city: the Tower of Gold, the brightly painted edifice that, since its construction around 1220, had stood guard over the Guadalquivir River. But the minaret, La Giralda, left the prince spellbound:

> With such mastery was it made, and so fine is the staircase by which they go up to the tower, that kings and queens and important men who want to go up there on horseback can go up to the top when they wish. On top of the tower there is another tower, which is about forty-eight feet high, made most marvelously. On top of this there are four spheres placed one on top of the other; they are made so large and with such great labor, and with such great nobility, that in the whole world there cannot be any so noble, or any equal.

Echoing al-Shaqundi's paean to the commercial dynamism of Seville, Alfonso went on to enumerate the impressive array of places—both Muslim and Christian—with which the city's merchants regularly traded. Ships and galleys brought all the merchandise of the world to Seville, he wrote—from Tangier, Ceuta, Tunis, Bejaia, Alexandria, Genoa, Portugal, England, Pisa, Lombardy, Bordeaux, Bayonne, Sicily, Gascony, Catalonia, Aragon, and France. The list underscores how the merchants of Seville, enmeshed in a pan-Mediterranean commercial network, matched their counterparts in the northern Italian cities with which we have conventionally associated the idea of "rebirth." In economic terms, as well as in the realm of culture, al-Andalus had long been ahead of the game.

It was not easy to capture such a bride, or, to put it more bluntly, to seize such a valuable and well-defended bastion. Besides, there were distractions. Having begun to prove his military mettle by capturing Cartagena in 1245, Alfonso then embarked on a somewhat quixotic incursion into Portugal. The Portuguese king, Sancho II, had fallen foul of his bishops, imposing heavy taxes on them to pay for his conquests in the south, and Pope Innocent IV (1243–1254) had roundly condemned him. In June of that year, Innocent had angrily deposed no less a ruler than Holy Roman Emperor Frederick II, giving rise to a renewed phase of conflict in Italy between supporters of the empire and supporters of the church. The very next month, he imposed his will on Portugal, naming Sancho's brother regent of the realm.

Across the frontier, the Castilians would have reacted with nervous uncertainty; Fernando III had long tried to steer a diplomatic course between Guelphs and Ghibellines—that is, between the pro-papal party and the pro-imperial party—and Sancho sought his support without success. But Prince Alfonso was more impetuous. Perhaps motivated by a desire to make his name as a young warrior-prince, he rushed to the defense of the beleaguered king of Portugal in late 1246. On November 26, before leaving, he signed a nuptial agreement with the Aragonese princess Yolant (who was now roughly ten years old) in the royal chapel at Valladolid. The ceremony appears to have been a small and passionless affair. Only a few people were present: a handful of clerics and friars, a sampling of Yolant's retinue, and—on Alfonso's part—two of the women who had raised him as a child.

By December, Alfonso was in Sabugal, on the Portuguese border, where he wrote to thank Jaume I for sending military support. His Franciscan confessor Gil de Zamora—author of a brief biographical sketch—picks up the tale, presenting the prince as an incisive and daring figure. "Since King Sancho was lenient, negligent and remiss in doing justice," he writes, "the princes and knights and other people carried out robberies and brigandage, striking against the churches and monasteries. So the infante [prince] Alfonso entered stealthily into the kingdom of Portugal with a substantial militia from León and Castile . . . until he reached Leiria." Alongside him, in the thick of the action, was his childhood friend Nuño González de Lara: "Lord Nuño González, a noble Prince and strong Baron, whom the people of Leiria wished to serve, attacked manfully and boldly, striking some men down with lances and swords, and capturing others to be released on mercy." In March 1247, Alfonso returned to Castile, bringing the Portuguese king with him; Sancho had made him his adopted son and heir.

We can only speculate about the prince's motives. Opposition to Innocent IV's assertion of papal power across Europe may have been an important factor. But the incursion had little support within Portugal and brought scant reward. Sancho had been unable to save his kingdom and died in exile, in Toledo, the following January. Alfonso's father, Fernando III, was not pleased by the prince's actions. He unquestionably realized that they threatened to tarnish the reputation of the Castilian dynasty at the papal court and jeopardized the chance that Alfonso or another member of the dynasty might gain the imperial title.

Fernando also knew that Alfonso's actions undercut preparations for the climactic assault on Seville. The Castilian king had already made vital inroads toward this goal. In 1246, after a long siege that had left many of the city's inhabitants dying of hunger,

Fernando had gained control of Jaén. Muhammad I, ruler of Granada, negotiated the surrender of the city on reasonably favorable terms, gaining Castilian recognition of his kingdom for the first time and avoiding the humiliating fate that Murcia had experienced in 1238: the garrisoning of Castilian troops in his territory. According to the terms of the treaty, he consented to pay 150,000 *maravedís* each year—a payment that immediately became the most important source of income for Fernando—and agreed to provide military aid and counsel (*auxilium* and *consilium*) to the crown of Castile. For now, at least, both rulers were contented, and Fernando III could turn his sights to the supreme prize.

The siege of Seville began in August 1247, and at the end of the year, Fernando III summoned Alfonso to join the campaign. The prince arrived with a substantial force, including a number of exiled Portuguese noblemen, and encamped in the exotic surroundings of the Buhayra palace. His *History of Spain* provides a rich description of the vast encampment of the besieging army: "It had streets and squares for every craft, one right next to another. There was one street for tailors and moneychangers; another had spice merchants and pharmacists for the medicines needed by the wounded and sick; another had armorers and bridle-sellers; another had butchers and fishermen; and so on for every craft in the world." In the prince's imagination, the wonders of Seville—the besieged Muslim capital—had permeated the Christian camp itself.

The city fell on November 23, 1248, Saint Clement's Day and Alfonso's twenty-seventh birthday. The date cannot have been a coincidence; the aging king, Fernando III, had recognized an opportunity for political theater. The royal standard of Castile and León now flew from the great Almohad mosque. On the following day, the king wrote to his Aragonese counterpart, Jaume I, to arrange the formal celebration of Alfonso's wedding to Yolant, who must now have been approaching the marriageable age of twelve. The prince wrote too, addressing his bride's mother, Yolanda of Hungary, to confirm receipt of a letter that she had sent through the bishop of Huesca and to ask that a date and place be established for the formal wedding ceremony. In the following weeks, the parties seem to have agreed that it should take place in the north of Castile, in Valladolid.

After one month's grace period, during which they were allowed to sell the possessions they could not take with them, the city's Muslim inhabitants were forced to evacuate Seville. The official account in the *History of Spain* suggests Christian triumphalism, inspired by a conviction that the realm of the Visigoths, overrun by Muslim forces in 711, was finally being reconquered. The archbishopric once held by the great Visigothic intellectual Isidore of Seville (d. 636) was restored. The chronicle tells us that in the final years of his reign, Fernando III "organized his city very well and nobly; he settled it with very good people, he allowed it to be shared, he gave property to the military orders and many good knights, and to princes and nobles, and he gave them great estates and many rich dwellings there. . . . He also redistributed the Aljarafe, and had it settled and worked by many people who came from all parts of the land to settle because of the renown of the great splendors of Seville." Yet the description is disingenuous, shaped by Alfonso's wish to promote an image of his father, and of the monarchy itself, that served his purposes in a period of growing political division.

After the expulsion of its Muslim inhabitants, Seville was reduced to a ghost of its former self. Furthermore, the partition of lands proved deeply contentious. There was already acute tension between Alfonso and his stepmother, Jeanne de Dammartin, over the extent of the lands that she had acquired in Andalusia.

This became aggravated when Carmona—in the hinterland of Seville—was added to her list. At court, two blocs emerged: on the one hand, the infante (prince) Alfonso and his old friend Nuño González de Lara; on the other, the rival noble houses of Haro and Girón, the queen, and the infante Enrique, one of Alfonso's younger brothers. Enrique was infuriated by Alfonso's proposal to their father, the king, that the vast lands and other properties acquired in the conquest of Seville should be granted as fiefs and that the new landowners should pay homage to him as heir. He believed that they should instead be given freely in return for military service. The tension was palpable in a letter that Prince Alfonso sent to Jaume I on January 13, 1249.

By this stage, Alfonso had begun a long, crescent-shaped ride north to Valladolid, planning to meet the Aragonese king en route at Uclés. The same week, two papal bulls sided with the queen's camp; Innocent IV had perhaps not forgiven Alfonso for his intervention in Portugal. Alfonso was correspondingly anxious to smooth over his relationship with the king of Aragon. He began by apologizing for a delay in his journey. He had been waylaid in Seville for three or four days, he suggested, because his father had wished to take counsel with his aristocrats and with the military orders regarding the distribution of lands, and he had demanded their loyalty to his heir. The king had ordered Enrique to perform homage to Alfonso, but Enrique had refused. Alfonso's advisors, the letter continued, had urged him to stay and take revenge on his enemies, but instead, he assured King Jaume, "I am going to Valladolid to receive the blessings with your daughter."

The wedding was celebrated at the end of January. Alfonso's new queen was scarcely out of childhood by modern standards. But in the course of her long life, she grew into her position and would defuse major political problems for her husband on more than one occasion. The only certain portrait of Queen Yolant, a manuscript illumination in a collection of charters from the monastery of Tojos Outos (in Galicia), shows the royal couple with their first-born son, Fernando de la Cerda. Yolant, elegantly seated upon her throne and wrapped in a deep blue cloak, takes center stage, and her figure is marginally taller than the king's.

Alfonso later had cause for great gratitude to Queen Yolant, and the fact that she bore nine of his children also suggests that he found her attractive. It is impossible to go further; we do not know if love blossomed in this arranged marriage. The *Siete partidas* suggest a view of matrimony as a functional matter, although the emphasis on the desirability of a beautiful bride hints that the marriage bed might also be a place of pleasure. "First," one law stipulated, the ideal wife "should come of a good family; second, she should be handsome; third, she should have good habits; fourth, she should be wealthy."

Given the difficulty of finding women that might fulfill all these criteria, some qualities are more important than others. If a man "cannot find anyone of this kind, he should see that his wife is of good family and of good habits, for the benefits which result from these two qualities, will all abide in the line which descends from her; but beauty and riches pass away more easily." The ensuing passage of the *Partidas* further stipulates that "she alone should be, according to law, his companion in joys and pleasures" and that "he cannot have more than her according to law." Her fidelity should be faithfully guarded so that "the children she may have may be the more certain." The *Partidas* also express a view of the queen consort as an active partner in government, a role that in due course Yolant would fulfill.

Even after his marriage, Alfonso's long-term *barragana*, Mayor Guillén, appears to have remained at the royal court, and it is possible that this relationship lasted until the birth of his first legitimate daughter, Berenguela, in 1253; only then did Alfonso seek an honorable exit for her. Doña Mayor was granted a specially created lordship at Alcocer, east of Madrid, where she could live comfortably for the rest of her life in a convent of Poor Clares. Alfonso married off his first-born child, Beatriz, to the new king of Portugal, although he would maintain a very close emotional and political bond with her until the end of his life.

All the while, Alfonso's devotion to Seville continued unabated. Having returned to the city in early 1250, he spent almost all of the next two years there, and as his father's health began to deteriorate, the prince attended more and more to the government of the realm, making Seville a de facto capital of the Christian realm, just as it had been for the Almohads. The haunting presence of the Muslim emirs and caliphs who had governed the city and their model of wise leadership would entrance him, just as the aesthetic style of Almohad Seville would influence cultural production under his rule. From the very first years of his reign, he adopted a style of leadership that was not only informed in its details by Arabic learning and scholarship but also shaped in its contours by the model of his Almohad predecessors.

On the last night of May in 1252, Fernando III of Castile and León passed away, either in the *alcázar* or perhaps—as new archaeological work suggests—at the site of a former Almohad palace, now the monastery of Santa Clara. According to one late-thirteenth-century account, he addressed his eldest son in weighty, prophetic language:

"My son," he is said to have declared, "you are richer in lands and good vassals than any other king in Christendom. Strive to do well and to be good, for you have the ability to do so. . . . If you know how to preserve in this state what I leave you, you will

Scene from a garden in Seville during Almohad rule: *Tale of Bayad and Riyad* (early thirteenth century). Reproduced courtesy of Archivo Oronoz.

be as good a king as I; and if you win more for yourself you will be better than I; but if you diminish it, you will not be as good as I."

Some historians have suggested that his father's memory bore down on Alfonso like a nightmare and that Fernando was a daunting model, whom the king unsuccessfully attempted to imitate throughout his life. Yet the deathbed scene, composed in the reign of Alfonso's own son and successor, Sancho IV, was a transparently self-interested text designed to suggest that Alfonso had failed to live up to the high standards of his saintly warrior father.

In addition to his military conquests, Fernando had been an innovative ruler, the first to introduce the most widely spoken vernacular language of the realm, Castilian, as an instrument of government. Alfonso would in fact build on these legacies, but there was an important temperamental difference. The son was far more impassioned by the life of the mind than his father had been and more in thrall to the inheritance of Seville, Toledo, and the other great cities of al-Andalus, cities that we might consider among the original birthplaces of the Renaissance.

It has been said that Alfonso so deeply valued the minaret of the great mosque of Seville—the soaring tower of La Giralda—that he vehemently opposed plans for its destruction and even threatened with death anyone who dared so much as destroy one brick. After his father's death, the friar Juan Gil de Zamora tells us, Prince Alfonso ordered a tomb built out of gold and silver; next to it he placed candles that burned continuously. He then "privileged and enriched the church of Seville above all others." Some of the doors of the mosque were covered to create a somber place of Christian worship, and its pillars were repainted with Gothic images. But the sepulcher that Alfonso commissioned for his father, here in the city of desire, bore an epitaph in all four languages of Andalusia: Latin, Castilian, Hebrew—and Arabic.

3

STARGAZERS

When Mercury is conjoined with Jupiter, men will seek
knowledge, the sciences and writing.

—ALY ABEN RANGEL,
PERFECT BOOK OF THE JUDGMENT OF THE STARS

THE COOL WATER RAN IN CRISSCROSSED RIVULETS THROUGH
the courtyard in the old palace gardens of Seville. Here amid
the quiet galleries and the citrus trees, the Almohad rulers, too,
had found shelter from the heat of the Andalusian summer. It
was Sunday, the second day of June 1252. Prince Alfonso, thirty
years old, was no longer the young lion but now king. The previous day, mounted on horseback, he had ceremonially girded himself with his arms in the great mosque—a cathedral of Saint Mary
in name more than nature—whose grandeur he so deeply loved.
He had not yet been formally crowned, an occasion he was saving for a journey to Toledo, ancient capital and supreme symbolic center of Christian Spain. But as he rode out into the streets
of Seville, the cries of the people had proclaimed him the new

ruler of the realm. Within twenty years, the astronomers who produced the *Alfonsine Tables*—one of the king's great legacies to Renaissance Europe—were to present this moment as the dawn of a new age, the "Alfonsine era." "Our king, Don Alfonso," they wrote, "outdid all other wise kings in knowledge, intelligence, and understanding, justice, goodness, piety and nobility. We therefore deem it fitting that the era be judged to begin with the year in which this noble king began to reign."

From the outset, Alfonso needed to project the mystique of monarchy. He could not rely on the saintly pretensions of the French kings, who claimed to be able to heal scrofula with the power of their touch. Instead, he would increasingly turn to a source of royal prestige that had long been especially significant in the frontier kingdom of Castile—military leadership and territorial expansion—while seeking to fill the glorious role of Holy Roman Emperor. But throughout the reign he also drew deeply on the ideal of the ruler who mastered and breathed new life into his realms through his wisdom. Alfonso envisioned the reinvigoration of an entire nation through culture. As teacher to his people, he might ensure not only their political unity but also their happiness and well-being. There was, unquestionably, a practical dimension to this project: that is, he aimed to revitalize and give coherence to his kingdom. At the same time, he was immersed in a cultural environment where the value of wisdom, emanating from God and permeating both the private and the public realms, was held in the highest esteem.

In modern rulers—presidents and prime ministers—intellectual accomplishment can sometimes become an electoral liability. For their medieval counterparts, however, wisdom had long been a desirable attribute, and the deepening of learning in the twelfth-century Renaissance had enhanced its value. "An unlettered king is like an donkey with a crown," John of Salisbury (longtime secretary of Thomas à Becket, archbishop of Canterbury) had averred in 1159. Across Europe, the royal court came to be perceived as a place where the children of noble families might be properly educated. "It was always a custom, in Spain," Alfonso wrote, "for men of rank to send their sons to be brought up at the courts of kings, that they might be polite and well-informed, and free from wickedness and faults, and might acquire good manners in speech as well as in action, so that they would become good." Sancho VI of Navarre (r. 1150–1194), with his court in Pamplona, had been the first Spanish king known as El Sabio, and Rodrigo Jiménez de Rada, future archbishop of Toledo, had first been educated there. Fernando III himself had overseen a new flourishing of historical writing, patronizing the bishop of Tuy, Lucas, author of the great *Chronicon mundi* (Chronicle of the world). He had also begun the sea change toward literary production in the most widely spoken language of the realm, Castilian. The *Book of the Twelve Wise Men*, which he commissioned for the young infante Alfonso, was written in the vernacular and made the lesson clear: "Wisdom is the love of all loves, the water of all fountains, and the memory of all peoples."

Alfonso had absorbed this lesson deeply. In learning, as in all things, he wrote, kings themselves resemble a mirror in which men view their own images. The new king saw himself as a Solomon to his father's David—as the inheritor of a great royal lineage, bequeathing his wisdom to his subjects and to future generations. A king must be able to read, he stated, for reading is the key to secrecy and a means of self-mastery: as King Solomon observed, "He who places his secret in the power of another becomes his slave; and he who knows how to keep it is the master of his own heart." Alfonso was also convinced that history held its own secrets. A king should learn from the wise men of the past, for by reading he will come to know "the remarkable events that transpire, from which he will learn many good habits and examples." Alfonso saw in the recounting of the past a story that could also serve to bind his people together. He soon became personally involved in the writing of the *History of Spain* (*Estoria de Espanna*), which casts human agency and motivation—rather than divine providence—as pivotal factors.

But Alfonso was no mere historian. Living long before the modern divide into "two cultures"—the sciences and the humanities—he was a renaissance man *avant la lettre*, multifaceted and as committed to the sciences as to the arts, and it is here, above all, that the deepest roots of the image of the Wise King are revealed. Muslim models of rulership largely inspired his fascination with the "philosophy of nature," especially with the related fields of astronomy, astrology, and magic. Some of these models were very old, harkening back to the golden days of the caliphate in Baghdad. There, in the ninth and tenth centuries, the caliphs of the Abbasid dynasty—anxious to soak up the ancient Greek learning of the Hellenistic world that they were conquering—had founded a school of translation that came to be known as the House of Wisdom.

This model had passed down to the Spanish-Muslim rulers of al-Andalus: to the caliphs of Córdoba, whose library had dwarfed any in medieval Christendom, and later to the *taifa* kings of the eleventh century. In the *taifa* period, the city of Toledo had become a hub of medieval science, an epicenter of rational, empirical inquiry. A stellar circle of scholars had clustered at the court of al-Mamun, who had ruled between 1043 and 1073. Ibrahim ibn Said produced two brass celestial globes, while the polymath Ibn al-Wafid wrote some of the most important medical texts to emanate from al-Andalus, as well as a treatise on astronomy. And here, the astronomer al-Zarqali (known as Azarquiel to Christian Spaniards) had refined the astrolabe and built a water clock that emptied and filled in harmony with the stages of the moon. Columbus reached America, it has been said, in part because al-Zarqali created the instruments with which his ships navigated the oceans.

At the very heart of the scientific wisdom bequeathed by the Arabs and translated by Jews lay astrology—that is, astronomy applied to questions of human happiness. Far from an occult form of faith in the supernatural, astrological thinking was a highly developed form of rational inquiry and enjoyed immense prestige at the courts of the Muslim rulers of Córdoba and the caliphs of Baghdad. The Umayyad emirs of al-Andalus had employed an official astrologer appointed since the reign of al-Hakam I (r. 796–822). Its critics rejected it not on scientific grounds but because it limited human and divine agency and therefore infringed on religious principles. In fact, the astrologers' conviction that immutable laws of nature linked men to the rest of the cosmos bears much in common with modern scientific assumptions. The important distinction, for Alfonso, was not between astronomy and astrology but between science, on the one hand, and misguided folk belief, on the other. He drew a sharp line between "divination accomplished by the aid of astronomy which is one of the seven liberal arts" and the malpractices of fortune-tellers, soothsayers, and magicians, "who investigate omens caused by the flight of birds, by sneezing, and by words called proverbs; or by those who cast lots, or gaze in water, or in crystal, or in a mirror, or in the blade of a sword, or in any other bright object."

In his pursuit of wisdom, Alfonso also owed a great deal to his immediate North African predecessors. Despite their reputation for intolerance, the great Berber empires—the Almoravids and especially the Almohads—had perpetuated the tradition of wise rulership. The Almohads, seeing one of the caliph's key roles as promoting and guaranteeing all forms of knowledge, had deliberately fostered the cultivation of philosophy, medicine, and natural sciences. Not without reason has Alfonso been playfully termed "the last Almohad caliph."

Yet, as he paced the galleries and corridors of the Almohad palace in Seville, the Wise King would have been conscious of the acute challenges he faced. The city itself had become an empty shell—a frontier town inhabited largely by memories of the past, headquarters of a vast and restive occupied territory. Some former Jewish inhabitants of the city had remained after the conquest and were allowed to convert the three mosques in the Jewish quarter to synagogues. Besides the modest number of Christian courtiers and other settlers, there was certainly a modest influx of Jews from Toledo and elsewhere in Castile. These newcomers included a small number of Jewish court officials (including ambassadors, astronomers, and one secretary). Most were small-scale artisans and tradesmen, day laborers, or owners of small agricultural properties. There was also a small community of foreign merchants—most conspicuously, traders from Genoa. Soon, at least two members of the old Muslim nobility joined them: the son of the king of Baeza and the deposed petty king of Niebla. But this was no compensation for the mass expulsion of the city's Muslim inhabitants.

The city remained woefully underpopulated. As late as 1263 Alfonso lamented, "The noble city of Seville has been depopulated and ruined, and . . . many houses are being destroyed by the fault of those to whom they were given, or by their men." Within the *alcázar*, he began to construct a new Gothic palace, superimposed on the old Almohad structure, while maintaining the gardens and galleries in which he had walked, along with the adjoining Palacio del Yeso. But beyond the palace walls, Seville—the beautiful bride of Muslim Spain—was fading, her roads unpaved, dusty and muddy, her water supply and sewage system falling into disrepair, while garbage accumulated amid several pestilential lagoons.

Nearby, several Muslim enclaves—Jerez, Niebla, and Tejada—presented a serious threat to Seville. This motivated the first preemptive strike of the new reign, the capture of Tejada, just to the west of the city, in late 1252 or early 1253. A deep sense of insecurity, as much as any hope of expanding his father's empire, catalyzed the development of new royal shipyards (*ataranzas*) on the banks of the Guadalquivir River. Yet neither this project nor military victory at Tejada could disguise the deeper, underlying problems. Aside from the question of underpopulation, bad weather across the realm compounded economic stress and inflation. As harvests failed, there was a shortage of bread, and as the vines froze, the price of wine increased sharply.

There was also unfinished business on the international front in Navarre, once the realm of that first "wise king," Sancho VI. At the age of thirteen, Alfonso had been engaged to the heiress of Navarre, but Thibault I had broken the agreement. Thibault's death on July 8, 1253, rekindled the Castilian king's aspirations to the northern kingdom. He seems to have contemplated a marriage between his half sister Leonor and the new Navarrese king, Thibault II, in order to extend his sphere of control, but a new alliance between Navarre and the powerful kingdom of Aragon frustrated his ambitions. With war on the horizon, and in pressing need of financial and diplomatic support, Alfonso summoned a Cortes (a representative assembly). It was to meet, early in 1254, in Toledo—his birthplace and the hub of Arabic science.

As the royal cortege approached Toledo across the plains of La Mancha that winter, the king would have seen the majestic new Gothic cathedral, its spire piercing the blue skies. The Roman and Visigothic masonry in the new construction, begun

in the first third of the century, pointed triumphantly to a period
before the Muslim conquest, when Toledo had ruled over a
united "Hispania"; this was the architectural cornerstone of
Archbishop Rodrigo Jiménez de Rada's project. Yet, even here,
the ghosts of the Muslim caliphs flitted among the arches of the
chancel, which, remarkably, echoed the design of the great
mosque of Córdoba. Even the archbishop and his masons were
under the influence. Across the city, contact with Islam had permanently altered artistic taste. In the tower of the Church of San
Román, the hallmark horseshoe-arched arcade brought to mind
the elegance of Islamic palaces, and Almohad aesthetic motifs
and Arabic inscriptions suffused the synagogue now known as
Santa María la Blanca.

By late February, the great gathering of the Cortes was in full
swing. At the royal palace in Toledo, before his assembled vassals, Alfonso projected an image of majesty in keeping with the
city's ancient echoes. It was probably here, two years into the
reign, that he had himself formally crowned. This great gathering
of noblemen and urban delegates was the first meeting of the
Cortes attended by his vassal Muhammad I of Granada. Here,
amid great ceremony, he would have ostentatiously assured Alfonso of his loyalty and renewed his commitment to provide annual tribute of a quarter million *maravedís*. Taking advantage of
the setting, Alfonso ensured that his vassals—both Christian and
Muslim—rendered homage to his infant heir, Berenguela, his
first daughter born within marriage. Queen Yolant, aged about
sixteen, had given birth on December 6, 1253. Wrapped in swad-
dling clothes, Berenguela was less than four months old. In 1255,
before she reached the age of three, she was betrothed to a French
prince, Louis, who died before a wedding could be celebrated.
But for now, Alfonso's diplomats were reaching out in another
direction: toward England.

One of Alfonso's most pressing tasks in Toledo was to meet an Englishman who had made a much longer journey to reach the city: John Maunsell, Henry III of England's lord chancellor and one of his most trusted advisors. Maunsell had been sent on a twofold mission designed to make sure that Alfonso did not press his dynastic claims to Gascony in southwestern France. On the one hand, he was to promise English assistance to Alfonso in his efforts to claim Navarre. He was also entrusted with beginning negotiations for the marriage of Prince Edward (b. 1239), Henry's eldest son, to Alfonso's half sister Leonor (b. 1241), daughter of Fernando III and Jeanne de Dammartin.

Thirteenth-century Englishmen did not generally have much love for the Spaniards. Gervase of Tilbury, writing at the beginning of the century, had claimed that Spaniards were distinguished most by tightness of their trousers. Some fifty years later, Matthew Paris characterized them as the scum of mankind. Medieval Spaniards were quite aware of the peculiar nature of the island nation. "The English," wrote the fifteenth-century biographer Diego de Games, "have a liking for no other nation, and if it happen that some valiant knight visits them . . . the English try to seek some way of dishonoring them or of offering them an affront." But love of power, at least, is blind. King Henry feared that the Spanish might also lay claim to Gascony, whose noblemen were in revolt against their English overlords. The treaties were signed in the fortress of Toledo between March 31 and April 1. Alfonso renounced all claims to Gascony and agreed to knight Prince Edward. The English pledged support in the war in Navarre, and Henry agreed to accompany Alfonso on a campaign in North Africa. A spectacular copy of the marriage agreement, replete with a gold seal of "Alfonso, the illustrious king of Castile and León"—castle on one side, lion on the other—survives in the National Archives in Kew (London). The document—once held in a cylindrical oak container traditionally believed to hold the will of Henry VIII—is now faded, but the gold leaf that illuminates the names of King Alfonso and Queen Yolant remains radiant to this day.

Despite this diplomatic success, Alfonso must have remained anxious about the future and would have sought answers wherever they might be found—notably, by means of judicial astrology. At precisely 6:28 a.m. on March 12, 1254, one of his most accomplished translators, Yehuda ben Mosé, set to work on a compelling work titled the *Perfect Book of the Judgment of the Stars* (*Libro conplido en los iudizios de las estrellas*). Yehuda, born around 1205 into a prominent Jewish family from Toledo, was approaching the age of fifty. In his youth, he had produced a Latin version of a book by the astronomer al-Zarqali. By his early thirties—at the time when Alfonso had occupied Murcia—he had become the infante's physician, and unsurprisingly the prince had entrusted him with the translation of the *Book of Stones*.

Yehuda's role underscores the importance of Jewish intellectuals in shaping the Castilian Renaissance. Thirteenth-century Spain has been described as the "heart of European Jewry, a kaleidoscope of jostling and interacting Jewish subcultures." This community included Arabized Jews and, later in the century, waves of Jewish immigrants expelled from northern Europe. In Castile, Jews retained the relatively stable position they had experienced in al-Andalus. Alfonso's legislation regulated the position of the Jewish minority in a way that, while discriminatory, resisted the more vehemently anti-Semitic spirit of the Fourth Lateran Council. In practice, he allowed for ample Jewish self-government and legal autonomy. As a minority that did not represent a military threat, the Jews benefitted from pragmatic royal policies, including tax exemptions and land grants in return for loyal service, and exerted a powerful influence on Spanish culture. Alfonso had a number of Jewish courtiers and financial administrators. One of the courtiers, Todros ben Judah Abulafia, sang the ruler's praises and in one epigram recounts, "When I went to the king to enter his service I gave him a finely crafted goblet engraved with this inscription: 'Truth beheld revenge on falsehood / when Alfonso became king.'"

Many Castilian Jews were trilingual, crossing easily between linguistic codes and adapting to the dominant society while retaining strong links with al-Andalus. For them, Hebrew was a sacred language, Castilian a commonly spoken one, and Arabic the language of scientific learning. Castilian Jewish scholars had already played a vital role in the tsunami of translations from Arabic that washed over Spain in the twelfth and early thirteenth centuries. These men had typically translated from Arabic into Castilian and often appear to have passed the text on to a local cleric who could translate into Latin. Only now, in the thirteenth century, had the vernacular language, Castilian, become the end point in the translation process.

In the twelfth century, the Navarrese Jewish intellectual Abraham ibn Ezra (1089–1164) had introduced Europe to the work of al-Sufi (903–986), a Persian astronomer and mathematician. Al-Sufi's book on the constellations, the *Book of the Fixed Stars* (964/65), had built on and critiqued the ancient Alexandrian scientist Ptolemy. It had recorded the Arabic star names in each constellation, along with two drawings of the constellation, one as seen on a celestial globe, one as seen in the sky. Al-Sufi had also provided a table of the stars making up that constellation, with the longitude, latitude, and magnitude of each. Ibn Ezra had referred to him as Azophi, and the Persian was often known as such in Europe. When the Renaissance artist Albrecht Durer published two maps of the night sky in 1515, including portraits of astronomers from four cultures, he depicted Azophi Arabus in the lower right-hand corner. From the thirteenth century onward, Latin versions of the *Book of the Fixed Stars* began to multiply across Europe, and one lavishly illustrated manuscript, based on a Sicilian original, was produced in Bologna during Alfonso's reign. Al-Sufi's work became a powerful influence on the astronomical studies being conducted in Toledo.

In at least two respects, Alfonso was following the model of archbishop Rodrigo Jiménez de Rada: he, too, had also used Jewish collaborators in the process of translation and had also done a good deal to protect the Jewish community within his jurisdiction from the aggressive legislation emanating from the papal court. Neither man, of course, was a modern multiculturalist. Rodrigo Jiménez, after all, had summoned the crusading armies who had won the battle of Las Navas de Tolosa in 1212, and he deeply disliked the Arabicized Christians of Toledo (the Mozarabs), who had also played a fundamental part in the translation of Arabic texts. Alfonso was no self-conscious protector of the "Spain of Three Cultures." This was a society in which religious minorities remained under strict conditions and as second-class citizens. The *Cantigas de Santa María* sometimes draw on anti-Semitic stereotypes, partly in order to encourage conversion. Social and sexual boundaries, ensuring the "purity" of Christian women, were carefully policed. Jewish people, like Muslims, were technically—but only technically—forbidden from exercising any administrative authority over Christians. Yet, in view of Spain's later reputation for fanatical intolerance, it is worth underscoring that there was no interest in casting Jews out of the kingdom, such as occurred in England in 1290. Even two centuries later, the expulsion of the Jews from Iberia must have looked unlikely. Fanatical intolerance was largely—like the Spanish Inquisition—a late-medieval and early modern development and a betrayal of the spirit

Astronomer: al-Sufi, *Liber de locis stellarum fixarum* (*Book of the Fixed Stars*) ['Sufi latinus'], Bibliothèque National de France, MS 1036, fol. 71r. Courtesy of BnF.

of Alfonsine culture. The Wise King employed many Jews in his administration, and many participated in his cultural project.

Both in Toledo and across Castile, Jewish thinkers, writers, and translators exerted influence far beyond the limits of the Jewish quarter. The involvement of elite Jews in Alfonso's court was sufficient to cause anxiety among some of their more pious contemporaries, like the Castilian Jewish polemicist, physician, and kabbalist Ibn Sahula (b. 1244), who designed his *Fables of the Distant Past* (*Meshal ha-Qadmoni*, c. 1281) to combat spiritual, social, and sexual error. For Ibn Sahula, the Spanish Muslim courts and the Christian courts that imitated them were rife with dangerous, foolish pursuits, such as poetry, philosophy—and science. Most thirteenth-century intellectuals, however, would have seen the *Perfect Book of the Judgment of the Stars*, which Yehuda ben Mosé was busily translating, as a sophisticated work of science, entirely fitting as an indication of the king's wisdom.

The translation begins with a resounding paean to the greatness of God and the ruler he has chosen to place on the throne: Alfonso, an earthly lord deeply in love with the truth and expert in sciences, who gathers around him wise men who can explain their knowledge and translate masterworks into Castilian. It provides a highly complex guide to penetrating the secrets of the cosmos and the hidden connections between the heavens and the earth. The anthropomorphized description of "planetary" influences, which appears very early in the text, provides merely the simplest threads in a richly patterned fabric of meaning. The sun, we read, is governor of the world and maker of time; like all planets—for so the sun was understood—it empowers and gives life to all the signs of the zodiac. Correspondingly when it moves beyond a certain zodiacal sign, that sign becomes dead and lifeless. The moon most closely resembles mankind in its waxing and waning. Saturn, for its part, is the old tired planet of scorn, cares,

sadness, and long illnesses, while Jupiter is the planet of goodness, improvement, understanding, intelligence, and piety. Mars
is the hot, dry, fiery planet, favoring killing, battles, and conflicts,
while Venus is "nocturnal, happy, joyful, smiling, good-looking,
beautifully made up, clean, attractive," loving to sing, eat, and
drink. Of all the planets, Mercury is most closely associated with
the tasks of the wise ruler: teaching, writing, and studying mathe-
matics and sciences.

The *Perfect Book*—first written in Kairouan (in modern Tuni-
sia) between the 1020s and 1040s—bears the unmistakable hallmark of its origins. Its geographical scope remains largely rooted
in the Islamic world. One chapter, devoted to the correspon-
dences between climates and planets, suggests that the climate of
India corresponds to Saturn, Babylonia to Jupiter, Turkey to
Mars, Rome to the sun, Mecca to Venus, Egypt to Mercury, and
China (Çim) to the moon. Passages about the astrologically preferred times for bathing (generally when the moon is in one of
the houses of Mars) and for nail cutting also yield glimpses of a
society quite different from the one into which Alfonso had been
born. But other passages had a more universal human interest:
the *Perfect Book* tells us when it is best to move from one house to
another, when to sow and plant trees, when to remove a phan-
tom or other frightening presence from your home, when to conceive a child or enjoy sexual pleasure, when to make wine, when
to get married, and how to tell the future.

Some chapters must have been of pressing interest to the
king in the mid-1250s. We can imagine Alfonso poring over
the sections discussing how to determine the fate of a king: how
long he was to rule, whether he would be killed by his enemies,
imprisoned, or die of disease, how many kings of his line were to
rule and for how long, and whether another people would dis-
place his own. What of the fate of his program to revitalize

Castile through culture and learning? When Mercury is conjoined with Jupiter, men will seek knowledge and sciences and
writing, but wise men will be scorned when it is joined with
Mars, and when it is joined with the sun, sciences and knowledge will be obscured. Alfonso perhaps gazed at the night sky
with particular anxiety about the conjunction of Mars and Jupiter, which foretold many battles, crusades, and wounds—and
the death of a king.

The *Perfect Book* was translated into Latin, the lingua franca
of Europe, and proved one of the most widely respected astrological treatises in later medieval Spain and beyond. The fifteenth-
century French astrologer Simon de Phares considered it
alongside Ptolemy's *Almagest* as one of the two great authorities
in the realm of astrology. It survives in at least four manuscripts.
One contains many marginal notes in Hebrew, suggesting that its
owners were Spanish Jews. Another is written in Portuguese, but
in Hebrew characters, and seems to have arrived in the Low
Countries with a Jewish family after their expulsion from Portugal in 1496. The English astronomer, astrologer, and mathematician John Dee—a close personal advisor to Elizabeth I of
England—purchased this copy at Louvain (in Belgium) in 1563.
He, too, aimed to penetrate the mysteries of the cosmos and to
unlock its assistance as England's star began to rise.

Having completed his Castilian version of the *Perfect Book* in
1256, along with another rendering titled the *Book of the Eighth
Sphere*, Yehuda ben Mosé was soon engaged in a translation of
the *Picatrix*, a twelfth-century Andalusi text that ventures more
clearly toward the occult. Aiming to provide a means for people
to harness the heavens through "suffumigation" rituals, the *Picatrix* gave itself to a growing perception of Spain, among traditionally pious Europeans, as a "shadowy land of magic." But it, too,
should be seen against the backdrop of Alfonso's search for

human happiness on this earth and the rational, scientific conviction that the whole cosmos was interconnected. Certainly,
this was no manual of dark arts; its opening pages insist that the
book should be used only for good. The stars were to be harnessed
only for beneficial ends, such as healing, repelling bad weather,
ensuring loyalty to a lord, or establishing lasting love between
two people.

In the early years of his reign, Alfonso would find many tempting uses for these valuable techniques.

Preparations for the English wedding were finalized in the summer of 1254, and in October Alfonso rode north toward Burgos. There, he and his courtiers lodged in the castle above the
city center. Beneath them, a Gothic cathedral was under construction: a pinnacled masterpiece that mirrored French cathedrals such as Bourges. The French connection, always strong in
Castile, had been strengthened in the 1230s by Fernando III's
marriage to Jeanne de Dammartin. Their daughter Leonor had
now reached the marriageable age of twelve. She had been raised
with her mother in the sophisticated courtly circles of Córdoba
and Seville and as an adult would show much the same literary
passion and cultural imagination as her half brother Alfonso. The
groom, Prince Edward of England, some two years older, was less
intellectually minded but destined to transform his own kingdom
during his reign.

The English chronicler Matthew Paris gives a vivid account of
the wedding, telling us that people in the streets commented on
the tall, handsome young prince as he arrived in the Castilian
city (probably on October 18). A few days later, the English royal
entourage made its way to the Cistercian convent of Las Huelgas,
a mile outside the city. There, in the monastery church, Edward
would have undertaken the vigil of arms for his knighting. The

wedding itself was an occasion that Alfonso long commemorated in his charters, and the marriage prospered. While some of her English subjects mistrusted her Castilian advisors and her foreign tastes (including her fondness for chess), Leonor—"Eleanor of Castile"—became an influential patron of artists and the first English universities. Edward would never have a mistress, and the twelve "Eleanor Crosses" that he commissioned after she passed away in 1290 still dot the land from Lincoln to London, a permanent reminder of a queen who injected new continental flair into the culture of the island nation.

Yet, behind the scenes at the wedding, all was not well. In a pattern repeated fifteen years later, when Alfonso and Yolant married their eldest son to a French princess, the gathering was also an occasion for scheming and plotting. Two powerful members of the king's family—his younger brother Enrique and his stepmother Jeanne—were mired in resentment. Both were convinced that Alfonso had been maneuvering to deny them the estates that were theirs by right. The tension between the two brothers stretched at least as far back as 1248, when Alfonso—still heir to the throne—had proposed that all the nobles of the realm perform homage to him in return for the properties that they received after the conquest of Seville. Enrique had refused, storming out of the court, as Alfonso had related in a letter to Jaume I of Aragon. Writing on January 8, 1249, he had described how Fernando III had "agreed with all the *ricos omes* (aristocrats) and the men of the military orders who were there that they would wage war or peace, in return for those lands, for me or whoever might be king of Castile and León after the days of the king, my father. He ordered Enrique that he perform homage to fulfill this. Enrique did not want to do anything of what the king ordered, and kissed his hand and took his leave of him."

Enrique had become even more furious when in 1253, shortly after Alfonso's accession, the king finally distributed the lands of Seville and granted the Andalusian lordships of Jerez, Lebrija, Arcos, and Medina Sidonia (which Enrique believed should have been his) to the military order of Calatrava. While the Castilian court was in Burgos, the prince appears to have met in secret with a number of coconspirators, probably including Diego López, head of the aristocratic Haro family, who in turn was bitterly aggrieved by the favor that Alfonso was showing toward the rival Lara family. Jeanne, too, may have attended one such meeting, and—perhaps as a sign of her alienation from Alfonso and his strategies—did not even stay in Burgos for the wedding itself. Her closeness to Enrique gave rise to rumors that the two had become lovers.

Over the following months, relations between Alfonso and Enrique deteriorated further. After his ally the lord of Haro sought to build links with Jaume I of Aragon early in 1255, Enrique seems to have sounded out the possibility of marrying the Aragonese princess Constanza—Yolant's sister. Tensions between Castile and Aragon remained acute because of the Navarre crisis. Enrique may therefore have been hoping for a coordinated attack on Castile, allowing him to reclaim the lands he considered his by right. But if so, he was soon disappointed. The royal chronicle provides a colorful account of the drama that began to unfold in October of that year. King Alfonso, we read, was in Seville, while the infante Enrique, his brother, was in Lebrija. (In fact, the king was in the north of Castile—in Burgos and Valladolid). Enrique had conspired with some noblemen "to his disservice," so the king ordered Nuño González de Lara—to whom he had delegated authority on the frontier—to capture him. Enrique narrowly escaped with his life after a skirmish in which he was injured in the face. He retreated to the coast and set sail for Valencia. Jaume I of Aragon ordered that he leave the kingdom, wishing to avoid conflict with his son-in-law. From Barcelona, Enrique crossed over the Mediterranean Sea, beginning a long exile in Tunis.

While we cannot trust these details, the chronicle reveals a real fissure at the heart of the royal family. This would not be the last time the brothers clashed. Alfonso's relationship with his siblings rarely brought him anything but trouble, and bitter experience informs some passages in his writing: "When the relatives of a king commit an offense against him, through some dislike which they entertain towards him, so that they are unwilling to serve, obey, or protect him as they ought; the king should reprove them and banish them from his presence." Enrique had indeed been banished, and by late December 1255, the king's armies had crushed a rebellion by the vassals of the lord of Haro. But the king's relationship with another brother, Fadrique—who had supported Enrique's resistance—remained extremely tense. Alfonso's junior by two years, Fadrique had long resented his brother's primacy. In what may have been an act of intellectual defiance, implicitly challenging Alfonso's self-projection as a wise king, he had previously commissioned his own translation of a work of wisdom literature, Sendebar.

Yet, on October 23, 1255, in Burgos, an auspicious event occurred. Alfonso and Queen Yolant were blessed with their first son, Fernando de la Cerda. For a medieval monarch, the birth of a male heir was a pivotal moment, and it must have instilled new confidence in the king. It is tempting to associate this event with the decision to add an epilogue to the book he himself had so valued as a young prince, the Book of the Twelve Wise Men. This epilogue, which has indeed been dated to the mid-1250s, makes explicit the turmoil that had recently enveloped the king:

"Shortly after this king Don Alfonso began to reign, great conflicts befell him with some of the infantes, his brothers, and the aristocrats of Castile and León." So the epilogue tells us, he summoned the twelve sages who had offered his father their wisdom. Two of the wise men were discovered to have passed away, and two others therefore came in their place. The sages proposed that the tomb of Fernando III be inscribed with an epitaph offered by each one so that his memory might forever be kept alive.

The *Book* thus became not only a monument to Fernando's memory but also a means for Alfonso to inscribe himself in a long line of wisdom literature associated with Christian and Muslim rulers. He would have known that it belonged to a genre crowned by John of Salisbury's *Policraticus* (1159) but owed just as much to the *Secretum secretorum*—supposedly derived from the esoteric teachings of Aristotle—which had long been circulating in the Arabic world. In the late twelfth and early thirteenth centuries, this text had been translated into Latin and most Western vernacular languages; by 1256 it had been rendered into Castilian as *Poridat de las poridades*. In turn, it served as an inspiration, a literary muse, when Alfonso turned, in the late 1250s, to the composition of his great, seven-part philosophical law code, the *Siete partidas*.

Another cornerstone of Alfonso's self-fashioning as a wise king was the new charter granted in 1254 to the University of Salamanca, one of the earliest universities in Christendom (after Oxford, Paris, Bologna, and the lesser known and relatively short-lived University of Palencia, which Alfonso VIII had patronized at the beginning of the century). Alfonso endowed Salamanca with a dozen new professorial chairs; in time, it became one of the most venerable institutions of learning in Europe. In December that year, he also created the School of Latin and Arabic Studies in Seville. If the sages of the *Book of the Twelve Wise*

Men were fictional, he did bring to his favorite city a number of "masters from the East," experts in Arabic, whom he housed in mosques near the *alcázar*. Arabic precedent may have inspired this initiative too. One pioneering study of the rise of universities in the West suggested that these new foundations shared a number of features in common with their older counterparts in al-Andalus and the Maghreb.

Modern professors might look with envy on his vision of the ideal university and the people who taught there. Men, lands, and kingdoms, he wrote, should be "protected, profited and guided by learned men and their advice." All professors, an illustrious caste, were to be exempt from taxes, and the king's special guarantee of security should cover both students and faculty coming, going, or staying throughout the kingdom. Law professors, in a more familiar pattern, resided at the very top of the hierarchy, since their subject was held to be more propitious than any other: "The science of law is, as it were, the fountain of justice, and the world is more benefited by it than by any other." They might enter the presence of "emperors, kings and princes" freely, and after teaching law for twenty years, they might be styled counts. Some passages seem to anticipate a utopian idyll of campus life. The university, Alfonso wrote, was to be set "apart from the town," with buildings near one another so that students could take more than one subject. There must be "pure air and beautiful environs, in order that the masters who teach the sciences and the pupils who learn them, may live there in health, and rest and take pleasure."

Still, there are signs that Alfonso had some inkling of the more nefarious dimensions of student life. Students in Spain appear to have had a reputation that fully matched their notoriety in the rest of medieval Europe: "It is the duty of the rector to punish and restrain the pupils from organizing factions, or fighting with the men of the towns where the schools are situated, or among themselves. . . . He should forbid them to go about at night, and order them to remain quiet in their lodgings, and exert themselves to study and learn, and live an honest and upright life." One of his songs to Holy Mary provides us with a glimpse into the kind of behavior he feared: A student in Salamanca had raped a woman and fled in fear. He was arrested and thrown into prison "where he suffered greatly from the cruel captivity."

In Toledo, Alfonso's more studious translators continued quietly burning the midnight oil, while his astronomers gazed deep into the night sky. In the latter half of the 1250s, Yehuda ben Mosé turned to the *Book of Crosses* (*Libro de las cruzes*), a translation and adaptation of an Arabic work of judicial astrology. The book takes its name from the graphic representation of the position of the Zodiac, the planets, the sun, the moon, and the constellations known as the Head and Tail of the Dragon, used for casting a horoscope. A circle is divided into six equal sectors by means of three diameters that cross in the middle. This creates six "points" on the circle, and six "angles" between the diameters, together corresponding to the twelve signs of the Zodiac—the twelve parts, or "houses," into which the celestial sphere is divided and through which the planets and constellations must move. Every house, every constellation, and every planet exerts an influence on the human world.

The Arabic original was likely written in the late eleventh century by 'Abu Marwan Ubayd Allah, who had formed part of the stellar generation of astronomers working at the court of al-Mamun, the *taifa* king of Toledo. Of Ubayd Allah, one contemporary had said, "I do not know of anyone, in the Spain of our time or even before, who can compete with him in knowing the secrets and marvels of this discipline." In the *Book of Crosses*, he is given the simplified name "Oueydalla," suggesting that he was so familiar to the men of thirteenth-century Toledo that they felt no need to identify him any further. He, in turn, had drawn on an even earlier Latin-language tradition, with its roots in Visigothic Spain. The oldest passages in the book may be those that reflect a concern with how the stars might influence weather patterns and bring rain or drought.

The *Book of Crosses*, like the *Perfect Book of the Judgment of the Stars*, reflects a range of universal human concerns, but it focuses above all on questions of interest to a king. The prologue underscores Alfonso's credentials; here is a ruler with "more wisdom, understanding and knowledge than all the princes of his time, reading various books of wise men, through the enlightenment that he had through the grace of God from whom all good things proceed." A new chapter discusses the influence of the stars over specific cities in Spain, and political threads run throughout the text. If Saturn and Jupiter conjoin in the sixth house, there will be an uprising of subjects against their lords; if they do so in the ninth house, there will be disregard for the law, and their conjunction in the eleventh augers harm to the king's favorites and those who surround him. If Saturn and Mars conjoin in the eleventh house, on the other hand, there will be discord and conflict among the king's knights, aristocrats, and lords; if they do so in the twelfth house, the king's enemies will triumph. Alfonso would have been acutely concerned, in the years after the birth of Fernando de la Cerda, about conjunctions of Saturn and the sun in the fifth house, for these signified that the heir to the throne would suffer misfortune.

The opening page of the *Book of Crosses* provides us with one further clue regarding its political importance. The prologue does not refer to Alfonso, as was usual in royal charters of this period, as king of Castile, León, Toledo, Galicia, Seville, Córdoba, and so forth—that is, as a ruler of a disparate set of realms within Iberia. Instead, he is referred to simply as "king of Spain," a title that harkened back to an earlier age when the Castilian kings had aspired to authority over the whole peninsula. Jaume I of Aragon was surely not impressed by this pretension.

But by the time the translation was completed in 1259, Alfonso was not hoping to dominate Spain alone. He also harbored high hopes of glory on the European stage. In 1254, a sophisticated Sienese nobleman had become Pope Alexander IV. The new pope held Alfonso in high regard, seeing him as a useful counterbalance to the family of the previous Holy Roman Emperor, Frederick II (r. 1220–1250). Frederick, a figure who loomed large in Alfonso's imagination, was the ruler known to some of his contemporaries as the *stupor mundi* (wonder of the world). The empire over which he had ruled was a loose patchwork of German and Italian territories. Many of the German princes were seeking greater autonomy, and seven of them—the archbishops of Mainz, Cologne, and Trier, the count palatine of the Rhine, the margrave of Brandenburg, the duke of Saxony, and the king of Bohemia—had gained the customary right to elect the emperor.

The Ghibelline towns of northern Italy that retained their allegiance to the empire were only nominally under its control. Still, the imperial title brought immense prestige. It placed the ruler in a line stretching back a millennium to Constantine and the other Christian emperors of Rome. Such a position required a suitable display of power, and on state occasions, the emperor was required to dress the part. Frederick II had worn a tunic of Sicilian silk, red shoes and stockings, red gloves studded with pearls, and a deep red mantle embroidered with gold. Sicily, in diplomacy as in styles of dress, was the key. After the extinction of the Hauteville family, the Norman dynasty that had ruled the kingdom in the twelfth century, the emperor Henry VI (r. 1189–1197) had also acquired the throne of Sicily, which thus fell into the hands of the Hohenstaufen dynasty. Frederick II had inherited both the king-dom and the empire.

For its part, the papacy, locked in ideological and military combat with the empire since the end of the eleventh century, was wracked by paranoia about the Hohenstaufens and their de-signs on Italy. Alfonso's father, Fernando III, had attempted to tread carefully among these diplomatic traps, presenting himself as mediator while attempting to claim the duchy of Swabia, which he had earmarked for his second son; Fadrique ("Freder-ick"), sent to his namesake's imperial court in 1240, had followed the emperor in his travels across Italy. But in 1245, Pope Inno-cent IV deposed the emperor, ushering in a period of open war-fare among the supporters of the papacy and the partisans of the empire. One measure of the ferocity of feeling is a rumor still cir-culating more than a century later during the Black Death (1347–1351) that Frederick II would return to life "even if he had been cut into a thousand pieces, or burnt to ashes," to restore the justice that the church had denied. "According to this claim," one friar reported, "once raised up and restored to the peak of his power, he will marry rich men to poor girls and vice versa; marry off nuns and members of secular sisterhoods; find wives for monks; restore the goods taken from wards, orphans, widows and from everyone who has been despoiled; and give justice to all."

Among the fallout from Frederick's excommunication and deposition was the departure of the infante Fadrique from the imperial court in a last-ditch attempt to salvage Castilian rela-tions with the papacy. Swallowing his scruples, Pope Innocent IV deigned to keep contact with the infante Alfonso. When Freder-ick died in 1250, a power vacuum emerged, and years of impasse followed. Innocent resolutely opposed the succession of any lead-ing member of the Hohenstaufen family—least of all Frederick

II's son Manfred, king of Sicily, a powerful player in Italian affairs. Alfonso himself represented a minor branch of the Hohenstaufen lineage, through his mother, Beatrix of Swabia, and his
path was therefore far from clear. But he sensed an opportunity,
particularly after February 1255, when Alexander IV called upon
the bishops and lords of Swabia to recognize the king of Castile
as their duke.

The pope's gesture had opened a Pandora's box. It not only
further alienated Alfonso and his brother Fadrique, with political
reverberations felt until the end of the former's reign, but also
signaled to the king that the door might now be open for him to
seek papal blessing in his claims to the imperial title. Wisely or
not, the king who had gazed at the stars would now spend the
next twenty years transfixed by the pursuit of this quarry.

4

HUNTERS

The Sun has power over the Romans and the Germans.
—YEHUDA BEN MOSÉ, BOOK OF CROSSES, 162

HIGH ABOVE THE CHOIR IN THE CATHEDRAL OF LEÓN IS A stained glass ensemble of spectacular beauty: La Cacería, or the "hunting" window. Its rich tones of blues, gold, reds, and greens, filtering the sun, fill the interior with an ocean of color. The cathedral, built in the French Gothic style, has rightly been called the greatest architectural achievement of the reign, and this window is one of its most compelling features. The window's many panels, arranged in four vertical columns, depict an almost carnivalesque scene, full of vitality and action. A group of hunters, many on horseback, some on foot, makes its way leftward across our field of vision. Our eyes are drawn quickly to the mounted noblemen. Toward the front of the party, a knight with flowing blond locks, mounted on a scarlet horse with a golden saddle, wears a green tunic and a half-circle brown cloak, tied around his neck. On his left hand he bears a large brown falcon.

Turning to it, he points upward with his right hand, sending the bird on the attack. Immediately beneath him, in the next panel down, another hunter, wearing a white tunic and red cloak, rides a horse with golden reins. At his sides two greyhounds prowl, aggressively sniffing the ground for the scent of their prey. Further back in the party, a mounted knight carries a leafy branch, perhaps to protect the most illustrious members of the group from the heat of the day. Others bear shields and standards, including those of Castile and León as well as Swabia, home of Alfonso's mother. A trumpeter blows his instrument, which he holds in his left hand while beating a drum with his right, hoping that the noise will flush out the prey. Toward the bottom of the window, four halberdiers on foot bear crossbows, lances, and swords. The whole troupe, a miniature court, progresses majestically onward. Interspersed with the hunters themselves are entertainers. One man brandishes a whip in the direction of a monkey—perhaps a Barbary macaque—riding a donkey. Another leads a second monkey, this one mounted on a camel, while a third man plays the fiddle. A diminutive young girl, no larger than his bow, dances at the fiddler's feet as she plays the castanets.

Medieval people would have marveled at what they saw in this window, which dates back to the 1260s or early 1270s. They were probably able to view the details more easily than today's visitor, because it is likely that the hunting panels were first installed much closer to eye level in a different part of the cathedral. With little difficulty, they could see the heraldic emblems at the top of the ensemble: a rampant, red-tongued lion representing the realm of León, the shield of the conjoined kingdoms of Castile and León, topped with a golden crown, and a golden imperial eagle. They may also have noticed the captions and images depicting multifarious liberal arts—grammar, arithmetic, dialectic—although the panels in question are scattered almost chaotically in the ensemble and may have been taken from a separate window when the hunting panels were moved to the higher and larger space. Without doubt, they would have noticed the most pivotal person in the scene. In the top row of stained glass panels, a crowned king rides a golden horse with silver reins and stirrups. His scarlet robe, blowing in the wind against a deep blue backdrop, wraps around a light green tunic with gold borders. In his right hand, he bears an orb, part of the regalia of the Holy Roman Emperor, the title to which Alfonso ardently aspired.

This figure is almost certainly the king, who oversaw the construction of the cathedral while his close friend Martín Fernández was bishop of León. In 1255, Alfonso granted generous financial privileges to the cathedral. He also patronized the stained glass workshop, which produced a set of windows that covers a vast expanse of the surface area of the interior. The new building was completed with remarkable speed by medieval standards—it was almost finished by 1302—and took its cues from French cathedrals such as Amiens and Reims. Adjoining panels of another stained glass window at León depict the two friends, the king and the bishop, in the company of the pope and (probably) Queen Yolant. Here Alfonso carries both the orb and the scepter, another piece of imperial regalia.

Across medieval Europe, royal courts were immersed in a hunting culture; the stained glass window in León might seem a conventional form of self-aggrandizement. Huntsmen had shadowed the traveling courts of Henry II, King John, and other Angevin kings of England, for instance, underscoring the rulers' prestige and authority and adding to their menace. But for Alfonso, the iconography had a particular and all-consuming purpose. The stained glass window in León represents an extraordinary piece of image making designed to reinforce his authority far beyond the borders of his kingdom. The construction of a French-style Gothic cathedral in León itself represented an attempt to assert Castile's European credentials, placing it firmly on the map of continental power. Its architectural echoes of Reims, where the French kings were traditionally crowned, and Saint Denis, where the patron saint of France was buried, underscored the ties between crown and church. Above all, however, Alfonso envisioned the stained glass hunting window as a means of promoting his claims to the position of Holy Roman Emperor and his worthiness as a successor to Frederick II. From 1256 onward, as he urgently sought to promote the power of the monarchy, he would throw himself headlong into the chase for this most illustrious of titles.

The depiction of the Wise King at the center of the hunting party was, it must be acknowledged, entirely in keeping with his personal passions. The *History of Spain*, the chronicle of Spain from its remotest origins composed from 1270 onward, gives us a hint of how, even as a prince, an enthusiasm for the hunt may have been high on Alfonso's agenda. Recounting the prince's 1243–1244 occupation of the kingdom of Murcia, the chronicle tells how he subjugated a number of places that resisted his authority, among them Mula, "a town that is well fortified, with a good wall, and whose castle is like a high, strong *alcázar*, with good towers, and which abounds in all the bounty of the earth and all kinds of hunting as befits a proper town."

It has long been thought that the young prince was responsible for commissioning the translation of a ninth-century Iraqi treatise on falconry, the *Book of Hunting Animals* (*Kitab al-Jawarih*), most of which comprises a highly technical manual of veterinary medicine. This Arabic treatise was deeply admired in Alfonso's age and had already been translated into Latin at the command of none other than the Holy Roman Emperor

Alfonso, heron-hunting with falcons: *Cantigas de Santa María*, no. 142, *Códice rico* (Rich Codex), Real Biblioteca del Monasterio de El Escorial, Ms. T.I.1. Reproduced courtesy of Archivo Oronoz.

Frederick II, whom the Spanish prince doubtless wished to emulate. The emperor delegated most of the laborious task of translation to his Syrian astrologer Master Theodore during the siege of the Guelph city of Faenza (in 1239), but it appears that he engaged personally in correcting the translation. The matter was of more than purely academic interest to him. Frederick seems to have lived, in large part, for hunting, to which he devoted his energies even in the midst of military and political crises. Across Apulia and Calabria, he erected hunting lodges, the grandest of which—including the octagonal Castel del Monte—resembled castles. From the Black Forest to Sicily, and while on crusade in Syria, he displayed his particular fondness for hunting with falcons, a pastime that he adopted with limitless energy. By the early 1240s, Frederick was beginning to work on his own masterpiece on hunting with birds, *De arte venandi cum avibus*, a work replete with personal observations and, in one manuscript version, lavish and highly realistic illustrations that may have been completed at his direction. "Brilliant in colouring," one modern historian observed, "the work is accurate and minute, even to details of plumage, while the representation of birds in flight has an almost photographic quality which suggests similar subjects in modern Japanese art."

The untitled Castilian translation of the *Kitab al-Jawarih*, known today as the *Libro de los animales que cazan*, had been completed by 1250. The first illuminated initial letter of the late-thirteenth-century manuscript held at the National Library in Madrid shows a figure with a crown receiving a book from the hands of a man dressed in what is conventionally described as "oriental" clothing. The opening chapter of the book underscores the linkage between hunting and military conquest. Across medieval Europe, the chase was seen as good training in horsemanship, the handling of weapons, and knowledge of landscape and strategy. As Alfonso XI of Castile and León (r. 1312–1350) was to write, "The chase is most similar to war for these reasons: war demands expense met without complaint; one must be well horsed and well armed; one must be vigorous, and do without sleep, suffer lack of good food and drink, rise early, sometimes have a poor bed, undergo heat and cold, and conceal one's fear."

After his accession to the throne in 1252, Alfonso X had been immediately concerned with protecting his hunting rights. In the Cortes he summoned that year, he decreed that no one could "remove the eggs of hawks, sparrowhawks, or falcons. They may not take or remove either hawk or sparrowhawk from the nest, and the falcons only up to the middle of April. No one may dare to remove either hawk or falcon or sparrowhawk from my kingdoms without my order. Any man who removes any of these birds from the kingdoms will be fined double the cost of the bird, plus for each bird 100 *maravedís*." More draconian punishments awaited those who damaged his hunting preserves: "I also order that no-one set fire to the forests, and furthermore that they throw anyone who does so inside, and if they cannot capture him that they seize everything that he has." Jaume I's autobiography, the *Book of Deeds*, recounts an episode traceable to July 1254 involving the Muslim leader al-Azraq (1208–1276), who controlled the south of the kingdom of Valencia and allied himself with Alfonso. "The king of Castile came to Alicante," Jaume recalls, "and he sent a message to al-Azraq to come out to him; and he met him. And the king of Castile was hunting, and al-Azraq came with ten Moorish knights, and with his personal guard who preceded him. And they told him that al-Azraq was coming and he stopped. And al-Azraq went to him and kissed his hand. And the king of Castile asked him if he knew how to hunt, and al-Azraq said to him that if he wanted, he would hunt castles of the king of Aragon."

The authorship of the *Book of Hunting Animals* remains a matter of debate. It is perfectly plausible that one of Alfonso's brothers—Fadrique, for instance—commissioned the translation. The infante Felipe, too, was perfectly capable of doing so; the sculptures of his extraordinary tomb at Villalcázar de Sirga immortalize his love of hunting with dogs and birds—a loyal dog lies at his feet and a falcon sits on his left hand. There is no doubt, however, about Alfonso's own enthusiastic commitment to the hunt.

Beyond the sport's value as a form of paramilitary training, several factors may help explain this enthusiasm. In the first

place, it was a source of pleasurable fantasy for the Castilian aristocracy and royalty. In the National Museum of Archaeology in
Madrid, visitors can still view a set of pinewood paintings, decorated with jousting and hunting scenes, as well as vignettes of
courtly life, designed for the noble Zúñiga family around 1400.
Among these panels, we find knights armed with swords, bows, or
lances in hot pursuit of their prey. The animals include wild boar,
deer, and bears (all desirable quarry for the medieval aristocracy)
and also a dragon, a lion, and a wild man whose brutish strength
serves as a foil for knightly virtues.

Alfonso was also hunting for happiness. The chase, he argued,
brought the hunter physical and psychological well-being. Hunting, he wrote, "contributes much to diminish serious thoughts
and vexations, and is more necessary for a king than for any other
man; and without considering this, it confers health, as the exer-
tion which is employed in it, when it is done in moderation,
causes a man to eat and sleep well, which is the principal thing in
life. The pleasure which is derived from it is, moreover, a great
source of joy; as, for instance, the obtaining possession of birds
and wild beasts." The Wise King's awareness of the health benefits of hunting was very much in line with the thinking of the
day. Frederick II had asserted, "The pursuit of falconry enables
nobles and rulers disturbed and worried by the cares of state to
find relief in the pleasures of the chase."

Singing the praises of exercise, Alfonso wrote that it serves "to
lengthen [a man's] life and his health, increase his understanding,
and remove from him cares and griefs, which are things that
greatly obscure the intellect: and all men of good sense should
practice this in order the better to carry their acts to completion." Cato the Wise, he added, "said that every man should, at
times, mingle joy and pleasure with his cares, for anything which
does not rest occasionally does not last long." Curiously, only at

this point does Alfonso revert to the more conventional observation that "hunting is an art, and imparts knowledge of war and conquest, with which kings should be thoroughly familiar," and he quickly returns to the chase's more interesting physiological benefits—and dangers. Hunting should not be practiced to excess, he remarks, because it might lead kings to neglect their other obligations and therefore, ironically, cause them to suffer: "The joy which they should receive from the sport will inevitably be turned into distress, for which reason serious illness will come upon them instead of health."

Hunting, in suitably "refined" forms, was also a valuable status symbol. It is true that all social classes engaged in some form of hunting in the Middle Ages; the food supply depended on it. According to John of Salisbury, the common people believed "that birds of the sky and fishes of the deep are common property" (a notion fiercely challenged by the landowning classes). But social capital was easily acquired by hunting in certain ways and for particular prey. The pursuit of certain animals was a source of cachet; the hart, the wild boar, and the bear were considered noble quarry, not least because of the dangers involved. One *cantiga* relates how a satanic servant has convinced his master to hunt on horseback in the mountains and go fishing out at sea in order that harm may come to him. The illustrations show the rider thrusting his lance at a bear precisely as the animal lunges upward. Two aggressors, almost equal in power, are aligned against each other. The very idea of a "noble quarry" implies a particular process of identification between hunter and animal inflected by social class.

Status also attached to the use of certain animals in hunting, such as the hounds depicted in León's La Cacería window of León. The social elite valued hounds highly and sometimes offered them as gifts. As today, the animals were given pet names.

One record tells of a hound called Ulgar given to the Castilian prince Alfonso Raimúndez. It was natural that friars in the thirteenth-century mendicant order of Saint Dominic referred to themselves punningly as the *domini canes* (hounds of God); many hailed from privileged social backgrounds, and class prejudice often shaped their pursuit of heresy in the countryside. By the same token, the comic illustrations in the margins of medieval manuscripts, showing hounds assailed by hares and even placed on trial and executed by them, derive their humor from the subversion of normal class relationships. Hares were common animals, an undistinguished part of the medieval diet. Hounds, in contrast, were highly prized, in a literal as well as a figurative sense: they were expensive, affordable only to the elite. The theft of hunting dogs carried a heavy penalty. Burgundian law provides a memorable example. Anyone who stole a hunting or tracking dog would "be compelled to kiss the posterior of that dog publicly in the presence of all the people."

Falconry and hawking were special markers of status. The cost of hunting birds and equipment was prohibitive, and the sophisticated methods required to train and maintain hawks and falcons put the sport beyond the resources of most medieval people. Fine distinctions were made regarding the types of bird that corresponded to each social rank. At the top of the hierarchy was the fierce gyrfalcon, the largest of the species. The most common of these was the small, dark "Norway" gyrfalcon; the other two were the grey "Iceland" and the white "Greenland" gyrfalcons, with the latter considered the best of all. When Edward I of England sent four grey gyrfalcons to Alfonso in 1282, he apologized for not being able to send any white ones. Frederick II's treatise on hunting with birds offered a definitive manual for the raising of birds of prey. Its six books—in the more complete of the two manuscript traditions—address the habits and structure of birds in general; the capture and training of birds of prey, the different kinds of lures; and the practice of hunting cranes with gyrfalcons, herons with the "sacred" falcon, and water birds with smaller types of falcon. His innumerable recommendations included the advice that a hunting hawk should be caught after first being trained by its own parents and that after its capture, it should be allowed to fly freely for some time. Then, when the time came to train the falcon, it was to be was "seeled"—its eyelids being temporarily sewn—so that it might develop more trust in its captors. From his time in Syria, Frederick had also acquired the technique of placing a hood over the bird's head.

Contact with the Arabic world was a vital stimulus to falconry as an elite sport. Three of the earliest Christian writers on the subject—Guillelmus Falconarius, Gerardus Falconarius, and a mythical King Dancus of Armenia—all seem to have been associated with the Norman court in Sicily. Adelard of Bath (b. c. 1080) had traveled in Spain, the Maghreb, and Sicily before settling in England, where he wrote a short treatise on falconry clearly deriving from Arabic tradition. Like Frederick II's own masterwork, these texts absorbed by osmosis a sense of falconry as a sign of cultural refinement, or what the medieval Arabic tradition called *adab*. In medieval Iberia, Andalusi and Castilian representations of hunting as a visual image of high status and lordship would become gradually intertwined, forming part of a common artistic language. This tradition surfaces in the fourteenth-century cycle of hunting paintings in the Hall of Justice at the palace of the Alhambra, in Granada, with their courtly and Arthurian motifs.

For Juan Gil de Zamora, Alfonso's confessor, the hawk was a royal bird (*avis regia*), endowed with a capacity for bravery even more powerful than its claws. Nature compensated for the animal's smaller size by giving it a strong and warlike spirit. Juan

Gil's case provides an indication of how deeply the craze for the chase had spread; clergymen, too, were often keen hunters, despite periodic bursts of toothless moral criticism from the church (typically focusing on the ostentatious display of wealth). Juan Gil attempted to legitimize hawking as a good Christian activity through a painfully sustained analogy between a hawk and Saint Francis—who, ironically, had preached to the birds in the belief that all creatures shared something of the divine essence. Citing the Book of Job (39:26), Juan Gil remarks that the hawk stretches its feathered wings toward the south through God's wisdom, while Francis too was transformed through divine light, extending his sentiments toward the warm love of Christ on the Cross. Just as the hawk beats his wings in order to force his children to leave the nest, so Francis had imposed a strict order on his brothers; as the hawk cures its eyes through its own bile, so the observance of the order was like a medicine for the brothers; as the hawk attacks its prey with its beak and claws, so Francis was like a bird of prey when he converted men through his preaching; and like the hawk, he showed a taste for flesh and blood, meditating constantly on the Passion of Christ. Yet, behind the laborious analogy, hawking and falconry remained a quintessentially secular, aristocratic, and royal activity.

The *Book of Hunting Animals* reflects the deep fascination with hunting with birds that prevailed at the royal court. When choosing a bird, it recommends, note that its color is pure and not mixed with any other color. The best harrier eagles are those with a yellow back; the lesser of every kind of bird is the male, and the greater is the female. The book recommends an almost regal dietary regimen for sick birds. When the bird of prey loses its appetite and does not want to eat meat, the reader is advised, take some Indian cherry plums, grind them, give them to the bird with oil on some meat hooks, and make them swallow it.

Afterward, gradually reintroduce them to the appropriate meats—beef, chicken, lamb, depending on the bird. It is best if the meat does not contain veins or nerves and is well washed, that there is no blood on it, and that it has been washed in warm water. In the event that this regimen fails after a certain number of days, the text prescribes a set of recipes involving ginger, saffron, and white sugar.

In his *Cantigas de Santa María*, Alfonso celebrates the intervention of the "Royal Virgin"—her royalty is important here—in protecting the men who assist the king in his falconry expeditions. He recounts a heron-hunting incident that nearly ends in disaster. After the falcon has completed the kill, a local man offers to jump into the fast-moving river Henares to retrieve the heron. The force of the water pulls him under two or three times before the Queen of Heaven miraculously intervenes to save him. Even more striking as an illustration of the elite nature of the sport is Mary's divine protection of the birds themselves. In one song, an Aragonese knight is brought to tears when the Virgin saves his lost hawk. Another tells of how, when a knight's hawk fails to molt, the knight becomes worried. He invests good money in the futile purchase of medicines that do no good at all. Only when he takes the hawk to the church of Saint Mary at Toro and makes a votive offering of wax in the likeness of the hawk is the bird miraculously healed.

A lyric directly involving Alfonso himself recounts an incident that probably took place in 1265. The king's brother Manuel falls ill while visiting Alfonso in Seville but is healed by the Virgin. Having recovered, he sets out with his falcons and a large group of falconers to hunt, an activity that, the song tells us, is "one of the greatest pleasures in the world." During the expedition, one of his falcons goes missing, flying over to the other side of the Guadalquivir River. Manuel chooses his most skillful experts, who soon see "a panicked bird which a soaring falcon was pursuing." This time, not even a wax votive offering does the trick—honest autobiography triumphs over pious cliché—and only Manuel's own voice calls the bird home from a field where men are plowing with their oxen. The prominence of falconry at the Castilian royal court may explain why, of all medieval English kings, Alfonso's brother-in-law Edward I was most besotted with the sport. By the age of nine, Edward had his own heron falcons, and the records of the English Exchequer bear witness to the lavish sums he spent on maintaining this passion.

Falconry was indeed the lubricant of international relations in the thirteenth century. When Henry III of England's sister Isabella—Edward's aunt—married the emperor Frederick II in 1235, the king sent gyrfalcons. He sent four more the following year (one white and three grey) and again in 1248. Edward repeatedly sent falcons to the Wise King and to another imperial ruler, the great khan, ruler of the Mongol Empire. Now, in the 1250s, falconry—captured for eternity in dazzling stained glass—evoked the necessary prestige and pedigree as Alfonso himself prepared to hunt down the title of Holy Roman Emperor.

On the surface, it seems that a delegation from the Italian city of Pisa in March 1256 encouraged Alfonso to begin his pursuit of the quarry in earnest. The ambassadors came with honey in their mouths, imploring the Wise King to assert his claims to the imperial title as heir of the dukes of Swabia and indeed suggesting that he might reunite the Holy Roman Empire with the Byzantine Empire to the east, bringing an end to centuries of division: "By succession in you the empires divided by abuse can be united, for you are descended from Manuel [I Comnenus, 1143–80] who was Emperor of the Romans; and they may be joined again in you as they were in the times of Caesar and of the most Christian Constantine" (of course, Queen Yolant, not Alfonso, was closely related to the Byzantine emperors). But it is difficult to imagine that such a bold proposal came as a bolt from the blue. One imagines that months or years of diplomatic exchanges, either directly with the Pisans or with the new pope, Alexander IV (1254–1261), had preceded this climactic moment and that Alfonso had played his part in staging the event. Soon afterward, with theatrical drama, he announced at the Cortes held in Soria that he had just been nominated as "king of the Romans," an honor that conventionally preceded papal approval of a candidate for the imperial title.

Historians have usually seen the king's chase of the imperial throne as an absurdity: a quest doomed to failure, a childish dream, or a haughty and quixotic obsession. In fact, it was in many respects a realistic goal. As the Pisans acknowledged, Alfonso was a natural heir to the imperial title by virtue of his maternal line. He was also sufficiently distant from Frederick that he was not necessarily damned by association. On a deeper level, there were close and long-standing relations between the Castilian and imperial courts, two realms engaged in frontier expansion. Certainly, Alfonso did not yet have a strong foothold in Germany, but nor had Frederick II—with his heart in the kingdom of Sicily and the hunting lodges of Apulia—ever had such a power base. And Alfonso's relationship with the papacy in the late 1250s provided him with some grounds for hope. Despite ongoing tensions relating to the marriage between his daughter Beatriz and King Afonso III of Portugal, Alfonso's relationship with Alexander was reasonably good. The pope may have seen the Castilian king as someone with whom he could do business. At the very least, Alfonso might serve as an instrument for counterbalancing Manfred, with his dangerous power base in the kingdom of Sicily and his fervent supporters in the northern port of Genoa. Alexander IV may even have orchestrated the Pisan offer as a means of dividing and ruling, a way to maintain a status quo in the face of powerful rivals for command of the Italian peninsula.

For Alfonso, the imperial title offered the prospect of a valuable weapon in advancing the Castilian military frontier south toward Granada and into North Africa. Similarly, the diplomatic campaign to achieve it would help advance the metaphorical frontiers of his cultural renaissance into Italy and Germany. The king of Castile received significant support from Pisa and other northern Italian city-states, as well as from Marseilles. But among these city-states, one in particular stands out. Some time later, in 1260, Alfonso received an illustrious emissary from Florence, a pro-papal "Guelph" city with a willingness to cross partisan lines. Alfonso represented a sympathetic imperial candidate for the Florentines, who also saw him as an antidote to Manfred. Their emissary was the brilliant humanist Brunetto Latini (c. 1220–1294), future chancellor of Florence and tutor of Dante Alighieri. As it turned out, Brunetto's mission proved fruitless: his journey also coincided with a crushing military defeat for the Florentine Guelphs, which handed the city to Manfred's supporters. Yet his journey reveals a good deal about Alfonso's projection on the European stage. By coincidence, Brunetto arrived at the Castilian court in Seville precisely at the moment that a Castilian-language account of Mohammed's nighttime journey to Jerusalem and his ascent to paradise was being translated (and amplified) from Arabic as a cornerstone of the cultural program that had already produced translations of scientific texts such as the *Book of Stones*, the *Perfect Book*, the *Book of Crosses*, and the *Picatrix*, as well as literary works such as the animal frame tales of Calila and Dimna (known in the new Castilian translation Digna).

The *Book of Mohammed's Ladder* (*Libro de la escala de Mahoma*), produced between 1260 and 1264, which may well have been an inspiration for Dante's *Divine Comedy*, has been attributed to another Jewish intellectual from Toledo: Abraham ibn Waqar, a member of the same tightly knit community as the astronomy translator Yehuda ben Mosé. Much more than a simple translation, his creation recast both Arabic and Latin material about the life of Mohammed. While perhaps intended in part as a means of reinforcing Alfonso's dominance over the newly conquered Muslim realms, it is strikingly respectful in tone, almost completely free of the aggressive denigration of Islam—and of Mohammed in particular—dominant elsewhere in thirteenth-century Christendom.

The Prophet himself narrates the story. When in his house in Mecca, lying on his bed next to his wife and meditating on the law of God, he relates, he fell asleep. Suddenly, the Angel Gabriel appeared to him, his face whiter than milk or snow, his hair redder than the reddest coral. Arise, Mohammed, the angel had said; wrap yourself in a white robe and follow me, since God wants to reveal tonight his many powers and secrets. The Prophet then recounts that he was whisked away on an animal larger than a donkey but smaller than a mule—its mane made of pearls, the crown of its head of emeralds, and its tail of rubies. Its name was Alborak, which, we read, means a male duck or goose. (In fact, it means "little lightning flash.") Mohammed is soon transported to the Temple of Jerusalem, and later across the seven skies, until he reaches the eighth and final sky, where he encounters God; there follows a long and detailed description of paradise, or rather multiple paradises.

In one climactic passage, the Angel Gabriel—who is for Mohammed what Virgil is for Dante—then reveals the sinners in hell. The parallels with Dante's description of hell are clear in this passage, at least in its broad strokes. Mohammed relates,

I saw that some sinners had their lips amputated with red-hot pincers; I asked Gabriel who they were, and he answered that they were those who make remarks that sow discord among people. Others were having their tongues torn out; these were the people who had given false witness. I also saw other sinful men who were forced to remain hung by their genitals from a fiery hook: they were the men who had committed adultery in this world. Next I saw an almost unbelievable number of women: all of them were hung from fiery timbers by their genitalia; the timbers were hanging from some fiery chains that burned in a way that cannot be described. I asked Gabriel who these women were; he answered that they were prostitutes, who had unceasingly indulged in sex and fornication.

The *Book of Mohammed's Ladder* quickly entered the bloodstream of Europe.

Despite his Italian allies, Alfonso's hunting in the diplomatic forest was beset with obstacles. While the bloc that had coalesced around Manfred, Frederick II's natural son, remained solid, the friendship of Pisa, Marseilles, and the papacy proved ephemeral. His difficulties intensified when, in late 1256, a new candidate emerged on the scene: Richard of Cornwall, the stupendously wealthy brother of King Henry III of England. As the date of the imperial election approached—it was due to take place on January 13, 1257, in Frankfurt—Alfonso, already straitjacketed by the responsibilities of governing a kingdom, found that in courting friends in Germany, he could not compete with Richard's money. The election dissolved into chaotic farce. When the appointed day arrived, Alfonso's staunchest allies, including the archbishop of Trier, barred the city gates to Richard's supporters, and the archbishop announced that the election was to be held at a later date. In response, Richard's most fervent (perhaps best paid) partisan, the bishop of Cologne, met outside the city walls with the archbishop of Mainz and Ludwig of Bavaria, electing Richard as "king of the Romans." On the new election date, the archbishop of Trier reappeared in Frankfurt, along with the representatives of Saxony, Brandenburg, and—after some vacillation—Bohemia, to elect Alfonso to the same title. Alfonso had gained a narrow majority, four out of the seven electoral votes; but this was a Pyrrhic victory. The pope responded to the contested election by maintaining strict neutrality over the coming years, acknowledging both candidates—rather strangely—as "king of the Romans" in his diplomatic correspondence.

The chase now fanned out across the continent. While his brother Manuel was dispatched to Rome to promote the king's cause, Alfonso showered the duke of Lorraine with gifts in an attempt to counterbalance his own declining influence in Germany, while the dukes of Burgundy and Lorraine and the count of Flanders became his vassals. Still further north, in 1257 and 1258, he sought an alliance with the aging king of Norway, Hákon Hákonarsson (r. 1217–1263). A desire for Norwegian wood, a valuable commodity for Alfonso's shipbuilding, not to mention the Scandinavian gyrfalcons so admired in the Mediterranean, probably enhanced diplomatic considerations.

A spectacularly garbled version of the episode appears in the fourteenth-century *Chronicle of Alfonso X*, which sets the tale fives years too early and claims that Alfonso had sought the hand of Hákon Hákonarsson's daughter, Kristín, because of Queen Yolant's supposed failure to provide him with children. More plausible is the account of a Norwegian chronicle, the *Hákonar saga Hákonarsonar*: Alfonso's messengers had come to the Norwegian court to request Kristín's marriage to one of the king's brothers. On her journey south, she passes through the crown of Aragon. Having traveled through Girona and Barcelona, she then receives an offer from Jaume I, but the Norwegians think that Jaume is too old. Kristín is instead allowed to choose between the Wise King's four younger brothers. She is tempted by "Fredrik" (Fadrique), who has the advantage of being a well-skilled hunter—a reflection of his time at the imperial court of Frederick II—but has an unattractive harelip. Instead she chooses Felipe, who is cheerful and strong enough to wrestle with bears and wild boars.

The wedding took place on March 31, 1258. This was a happy resolution for Felipe, never content with his role as archbishop-elect of Seville, if not, in the end, for Kristín, who died childless and far from home four years later. During the same year, a second son was born to Queen Yolant and King Alfonso: the infante Sancho, who was to become a painful and perennial thorn in his father's side.

The quest for empire and a public image befitting his aspirations continued, meanwhile, to stimulate the king's cultural production and his program of legal reforms. The *Chronicle of Alfonso X* is brief but emphatic. In the eighth year of his reign, it claims rather hyperbolically, Alfonso decreed that "everything" be translated from Latin into Romance—that is, into medieval Castilian Spanish. "He also ordered all the scriptures to be translated into Romance [an apparent reference to the writing of the universal history called the *General estoria*] and all the ecclesiastical material, and the art of natural science and astrology." A new law code, the *Fuero real*, taking its cues from the Code of Justinian, was to be written in the vernacular. Finally, the royal workshops began one of their most ambitious projects of all: the vast legal compendium and didactic text, aspiring to timeless truth, known as the *Siete partidas*. "If the *Partidas* had been written in Latin," one historian has written, "it would probably have been accepted as the basic code for all of Western Europe." This vision of universal, imperial authority cannot have been far from Alfonso's mind as he began production of the text.

The Wise King was deeply and personally involved in the conception of this text and the many others produced in the course of his culturally prolific reign. While we cannot envisage him as a modern author, single-handedly composing these texts, he infuses his spirit in them all and frequently fine-tunes them. In the words of the *Universal History* (*General estoria*) composed under his aegis, "The king makes a book, not because he writes it with his own hands, but because he sets forth the reasons for it, and he amends and corrects and directs them, and shows how they should be done." Among the generally anonymous lawyers, judges, and scholars active in this project was the prolific and long-lived Italian jurist Jacobo de las Leyes (d. 1294), once tutor to Prince Alfonso. Immersed in the legal learning of Bologna, Jacobo further tightened the links that bound Castile to northern Italy.

The realm of architecture mirrored Alfonso's legal, literary, and philosophical program. The principles that shaped the Cathedral of León—internationalism and a sharp accentuation of the figure of the monarch—were also at work in Burgos. The foundation stone of this royal city's cathedral had been laid in 1221 or 1222, but Alfonso oversaw a second stage of building in the early years of his reign, and the new Gothic church—soaring, elaborate, breathtaking against the Castilian skies—was consecrated in 1260. The Wise King's architects—led by Maestro Enrique (d. 1277), who later worked on the Cathedral of León—added a new upper cloister whose brilliant polychrome sculptures featured vivid depictions of members of the royal family—among them, Alfonso's parents, Fernando and Beatrix.

Image making and political theater were essential to Alfonso's self-projection on the European, Italian, and Mediterranean stage. The royal chronicler narrates one particular moment of drama, which occurred some time between 1260 and 1265: "While King Alfonso was in Seville . . . messengers came to him from the king of Egypt, Alvandexáver, and they brought King Alfonso many precious cloths of many kinds, and many very noble and rare jewels. They also brought him an elephant and an animal they called an *azorafa* [giraffe], and an ass that was striped, with one white band and the other one black. The king received these messengers very well, and did them great honor and sent them away very well paid."

If Alfonso's legal reforms evoked the image of the emperor Justinian, memories of this Egyptian episode may have been shaped by a story about Charlemagne, the original Holy Roman Emperor, whom the pope had crowned on Christmas Day in 800. According to his contemporary biographer, Charlemagne had once received from the powerful Abbasid caliph in Baghdad, Harun al-Rashid, a series of magnificent gifts; among them were many perfumes of the East and the caliph's only elephant. Alfonso must have delighted not only in the presents that the Mamluk sultan of Egypt had sent him but also in the historic parallels. The gifts may have inspired the illustrations to a *cantiga* in which we see a menagerie of exotic birds, mammals, and fishes in the presence of the Virgin. Among these creatures are a giraffe and zebra (the gifts of the Egyptians), a secretary bird, an Egyptian ibis, a flamingo, and—notably—an African elephant. A bear and wild boar (those favored wrestling companions of the newly married infante Felipe) are for once hidden in the background.

In this diplomatic context, Alfonso's self-projection as a hunter was a crucial component. No previous king had emphasized the chase in the way that the Wise King did. While his mother,

Beatrix of Swabia, may have brought something of the Germanic culture of the chase to the Castilian court, it is more certain that Alfonso saw hunting as a necessary attribute of an emperor. These thoughts surely pressed on his mind as he campaigned on the southern frontier, just as they may have preoccupied his rivals for the imperial title, among them the young duke of Swabia, Conradin. In the *Chansonnier Manesse*, an illuminated songbook produced in Zurich and dating from 1268, we find an image of Conradin, crowned and mounted on a powerful black horse, hunting in the mountains. We catch him in the act of launching a white falcon from his gloved hand. Behind him, a brown-robed falconer waits admiringly. At Conradin's feet, two black-and-white hounds look eagerly upwards. This is the kind of visual campaigning that Alfonso attempted to match in the stained glass hunting window at the Cathedral of León.

Throughout the early 1260s, in hot pursuit of the title of Holy Roman Emperor, Alfonso continued to lavish gifts on his supporters and waited in vain for the winds of papal favor to change in his favor. He simultaneously consolidated his power in Lower Andalusia and embarked on a series of military campaigns calculated to reinforce his international credentials. The peaceful annexation of Cádiz (1260–1261) and, just across the bay, the development of al-Qanatir—now rechristened El Puerto de Santa María—marked the first tentative steps toward his eventual goal: an African crusade aimed at creating a zone of Castilian influence in the Maghreb, taking advantage of the disintegration of Almohad power in the region. This policy, he hoped, might serve to unify the kingdom in a common project, bring commercial advantages through control of the strait, and protect Castile against an Islamic attack. It would also restore the full extent of the ancient Visigothic kingdom, he believed, and strengthen his claims on the empire.

The city of Jerez submitted in the late spring or early summer of 1261. A Christian garrison was then stationed in its *alcázar*, and Alfonso—confident in its future—entrusted it to his close friend Nuño González de Lara. Castilian forays against the North African coast were less successful. An inglorious pillaging expedition at the Moroccan port city of Salé in 1260 had been rebuffed by the leader of the Marinid dynasty, Abu Yusuf (r. 1259–1286), who was quickly emerging as the dominant power in northern Morocco. But within the peninsula, the Wise King was altogether more successful. A long siege of the city of Niebla, capital of a significant Muslim kingdom to the west of Seville, bore fruit when its ruler, Ibn Mahfut, surrendered in February 1262. The *Chronicle of Alfonso X* is ungenerous in its treatment of Alfonso, inserting a tale about an epidemic of insect-borne disease in the royal encampment, ended only by the intervention of two friars who arrange for anyone who brings a measure of insects to their tent to be paid two silver coins. But from a strategic point of view, the conquest of Niebla allowed the conquerors much fuller access to the Atlantic coast and enabled Alfonso to start developing the shipyards at Seville. A few years later, he designated a large part of the Doñana wetlands (to the southwest of his beloved Seville) as an exclusive hunting preserve. Filled with a fabulous array of migratory birds on their journey between Europe and Africa, including some of the flamingos that appear in the menagerie of the *Cantigas de Santa María*, Doñana presented yet another opportunity for Alfonso to don the mantle of Frederick II, an imperious and imperial hunter.

Yet the chase was soon to be interrupted by a catastrophic rebellion in the heart of the newly occupied territories of Andalusia.

5

LAUGHTER

If Saturn and the Sun are joined in the third house,
the king will move from place to place without finding
tranquility of mind.
—YEHUDA BEN MOSÉ, BOOK OF CROSSES, 19

ON THE SURFACE IT MIGHT SEEM THAT ALFONSO'S POSITION
in 1263 should have given him grounds for optimism. His
dreams of empire, both on the European continent and in North
Africa, were still alive, and his recent conquests of Cádiz, Jerez,
and Niebla boded well. But under its new Christian rulers, Andalusia was an occupied territory, a colonial society in which the
vast majority of the population remained Muslim.

In some cities, like Córdoba and Seville, the Muslim inhabitants had been expelled, and a small coterie of Christians remained among half-empty streets and malarial ponds. Some had
been living here under Almohad rule, while others were recent
settlers. But it was desperately difficult to attract colonists to the
south, and in other towns Alfonso relied on the continued

presence of the Muslim inhabitants. In Jerez, as in Murcia, municipal government and justice remained in the hands of Islamic authorities, although a lonely Castilian garrison had been stationed there. In the countryside, a dislocated population of impoverished *mudéjares* (Muslims living under nominal Christian authority) lived in resentful unease. Many, following the advice of their spiritual leaders, chose to seek safety in the Maghreb, and some became refugees across the border in the kingdom of Granada. But those who continued to live under the direct control of Christian lords faced daily humiliation.

In the constantly shifting game of diplomatic chess, Alfonso was obliged to continue collaborating with Muhammad I, or Ibn al-Ahmar, the ruler of Granada with whom his father had negotiated the surrender of Jaén in 1246. The Christians had clearly understood the terms of the treaty to mean that Muhammad had become a Castilian vassal owing military aid and advice—the chess piece that in the Middle Ages would have been known as the counselor. But either the ruler of Granada had no such understanding, as one historian has suggested, or more likely he had come to believe that the Castilians were already violating the treaty.

Early in the 1260s, Alfonso and Muhammad formulated plans for a joint military operation in North Africa, but this skin-deep and purely pragmatic alliance quickly unraveled. Alfonso later recounted the events that followed. On June 20, 1264, he wrote from Seville to the bishop of Cuenca, a close friend, "When we held our Cortes in Toledo regarding the question of the Empire, we sent a message requesting the advice of the king of Granada on this question, as a vassal and friend in whom we trusted." Muhammad, he alleged, had responded that if Alfonso was not granted the title of Holy Roman Emperor, he should instead aim to establish "an even greater and better empire"—across the Strait of Gibraltar in North Africa.

Alfonso then wrote that he had traveled to Jaén, where the king of Granada had met him—this probably occurred in May 1262. The Muslim ruler, he said, had vowed to assist in recovering Ceuta and ensuring that the Castilians had good Muslim allies in North Africa. Alfonso had answered that to do this effectively, he would need the port cities of Algeciras and Tarifa. The king of Granada had assented to his request, the Wise King wrote, and had promised to surrender these cities within thirty days. Alfonso then feigned shock that the thirty days had passed with no handover and that a second deadline had also been missed.

Modern historians have tended to see his surprise as a sign of foolish credulity, but everything rests on the context of his claims. Since 1261, Alfonso had adopted a more aggressive policy toward the newly conquered territories of southern Andalusia, seeking to underscore his own military credentials while building on his father's legacy. His development of the naval bases and settler colonies in Cádiz and Puerto de Santa María, as well as his decision to place the garrison in Jerez in 1261, his conquest of Niebla, and his expulsion of the *mudéjares* from Écija in 1263, had clearly signaled his intentions. He was now trying to drum up support for a military action against Muhammad I, calling on the bishops of the realm to preach a crusade, and wanted to paint the Muslim king as a traitor. His demand for Algeciras and Tarifa would have been unrealistic, if it had been serious; testing the limits of Muhammad's patience, it may instead have been a nonetoo-subtle reminder to the king of Granada that he was Alfonso's vassal. For his part, between 1263 and 1264 Muhammad I responded by welcoming into his realm hundreds of Moroccan *mujaheddin*, Islamic combatants seeking holy war against the infidel.

The moment of rupture was not long in coming. In early 1264, Muhammad I traveled west to renew the pact with the Castilians at Seville. Alfonso appears to have invited the king to lodge within the city walls in the palace that had once belonged to the eleventh-century Muslim kings of Seville. Accompanying the king of Granada were no fewer than five hundred horsemen and a small number of men from the powerful clan called the Banu Ashqilula. The Arabic chronicler Ibn Idhari, relying on eye-witness accounts, tells us that during the night after Muhammad's arrival, the Christians erected a wooden palisade to block the street near the palace. Afraid of falling into a trap, Muhammad fled hurriedly; Alfonso pursued him, full of innocent protesta-tions, but the damage had been done. Muhammad "swore sol-emnly that he would never again see the Christian king except to fight or combat him, and so it was." Christian claims of Muslim treachery were diametrically reversed.

In his letter to the bishop of Cuenca, Alfonso claimed that the king of Granada, "with the falseness and treachery that he has in his heart," had chosen to become a vassal of the ruler of Tunis. But Ibn Idhari's account is the more reliable of the two. It is pos-sible that Alfonso deliberately provoked Muhammad's anger to provide a pretext for military expansionism. But his difficulties in establishing control in the south, even in settling the unofficial capital city of Seville itself, together with his continuing aspira-tions to the title of Holy Roman Emperor, make it unlikely that he would have courted further danger, let alone that he was con-sciously seeking an excuse to conquer the densely populated kingdom of Granada. It is more plausible that Alfonso blundered into a trip wire and unwittingly brought upon himself a sequence of disasters that marked a turning point in his reign.

He presented what happened next as a complete and utter sur-prise. Muhammad I had talked secretly with the Moors who were living in our towns and castles, agreeing that they should all rise up on the appointed day. And when he had gathered as many troops as he could from across the sea, and had made all his preparations, and understood that we were calmed and reassured and had fewer people than those with whom we had come to this land, he let us know that he was not our vassal. Before his messengers had even left us, he attacked our lands, fought against our castles, and killed our vassals, and is now waging war as fully and aggressively as he can, with his own troops and those from across the sea.

Even if this rising—which came to be known as the Mudéjar Rebellion—did not actually shock Alfonso, the rapidity with which it spread appears to have taken him off guard. Something of this surprise element is conveyed by Jaume I of Aragon, who writes in his *Book of Deeds* that Muhammad I had conspired with "all the castles and towns where there were Moors" to rise up on the same day, capture Alfonso and Queen Yolant in the *alcázar* of Seville, and recover all the places that the Christians had conquered. Alfonso, he continues, escaped with his life but lost "three hundred cities, great towns, and castles." If such an assassination plot really existed, it is curious that Alfonso did not mention it in his own letters to the bishops. But the passage captures a moment of panic that had struck at the heart of the Castilian court.

As the towns of southern Andalusia erupted in rebellion, a simultaneous revolt was orchestrated in Murcia—the city that held such pride of place in the king's memory as his first princely conquest—and in the nearby port of Cartagena. Fearful that she and her husband were going to be dispossessed, Queen Yolant, in an act that may have been entirely of her own volition and a sign of her growing political prominence, sent an urgent message to her father, Jaume I, who consulted with his barons. The entreaty met with a generally frosty reception, but one Aragonese baron, Bernat Guillem, is said to have responded to Jaume, "When in need, a man knows his friends."

The king of Aragon vacillated, believing that his son-in-law was making diplomatic use of Yolant at this moment of crisis: "Because of the wrongs he has done me, he does not dare to ask for my help, and tries to obtain it through her." But reluctantly, he summoned assemblies in Barcelona and Zaragoza and announced that he was obliged to intervene. "I have to help him because he is one of the most powerful men in the world. And if I did not help him and he escaped from the difficulty he is now in, for all time he might hold me as his mortal enemy, since I did not help him in his greatest hour of need. And if he could seek to do me evil, he would seek to do so all the time, and he would have good motive." Besides, "if the King of Castile were to lose his land, we would be in a weak position in this our land; for it is better to defend on his land than on our own."

In August 1264, the thinly garrisoned town of Jerez was captured after what Alfonso clearly believed to be a dereliction of duty on the part of its commander—none other than his close childhood friend, Nuño González de Lara. When the Muslim people of the city launched a surprise assault on the citadel, Nuño González had found himself hopelessly outnumbered and called desperately for reinforcements. But Alfonso was deeply suspicious—buried distrust of the Lara family may well have resurfaced—and the relief force sent was not sufficient to prevent disaster. "The Moors took all the soldiers left in the castle," one *cantiga* tells us, "and destroyed the chapel of Her who is our protection, and took out the statue made in Her likeness to burn it"—although, the song adds, the statue miraculously escaped the engulfing flames.

In his sleep, the song continues, Alfonso dreams of Mary, child in her arms, running frantically from the fire. "Make haste, in God's name," she calls out in terror, "and take this child I bear in my arms so that the fire may not burn Him, and leave me behind, for if He remains alive, I can suffer no harm." Tossing and turning, he imagines himself running to take the child and mother in his arms. "Weeping and moaning," he wakes from this dream and begins to tell his wife about the vision. When Queen Yolant replies that she has had an almost identical dream, the royal couple is plunged into despair, understanding that the castle of Jerez has been lost.

The Mudéjar Rebellion was a grave threat to the stability of the kingdom. Yet, paradoxically, this decade of mounting crisis was a period of renewed cultural vitality, literary production, and aesthetic pursuits at the Castilian court. The first redaction of the *Siete partidas* was written during the revolt and completed in August 1265. The compilation of Alfonso's *History of Spain* also dates from these years, as do the earliest of the *Cantigas de Santa María*, an initial core of one hundred songs, many drawing upon international miracle collections, probably dating from 1264 to 1270. While inspired by piety, the songs are also suffused with a humane spirit and often, most surprisingly, a keen sense of humor.

Even as he was besieged by nightmares, Alfonso would have remembered the lesson he had read as a young prince in the *Book of the Twelve Wise Men*: "The king or ruler of the realm should be a good companion to his followers, and should provide them with many honors and pleasures and enjoy himself with them whenever he wishes." The mirror had shown him that a good monarch should grant his grace and favor to buffoons, musicians, and jokers.

There are many pleasures, he wrote in the *Siete partidas*, in which "a man might take comfort when oppressed with care and affliction. These include listening to songs and musical instruments, and playing chess, draughts, or other similar games," and—not to be overlooked—reading "histories, romances, and other books, which treat of those matters from which men derive joy and pleasure." "Songs," he writes, "should not be sung except for joy," just as games should not be played "except to drive away care, and to receive joy from them, and not through a desire for gain thereby" (gambling was one of his *bêtes noires*). Of course, there was a time and place for every purpose under heaven: "King Solomon said that there are appointed seasons for everything, which are proper for it and for nothing else; as for instance to sing at marriages, and to weep at funerals." But by this logic, there was certainly a time—and a need—to laugh.

Laughter and humor were not simply politically expedient; Alfonso repeatedly expressed conviction in the importance of human happiness. Ancient Greek ideas on the subject—emphasizing the virtue of entertaining oneself and others through games, stories, and other agreeable activities and finding a golden mean (*eutrapelia*) between excessive laughter and excessive work and seriousness—shaped the king's philosophy of joy, but Alfonso expanded these ideas beyond a narrow, leisured elite, applying them to all social ranks. "God desired that people might have all manner of happiness," he wrote in the prologue to his *Book of Games*, "so that they might suffer cares and troubles." Men therefore invented a variety of games: "some on horseback, like jousting and throwing javelins, fighting with a shield and lance, shooting with crossbow or bow and arrow," and others on foot, such as fencing, wrestling, running, and jumping. Such pastimes, of course, are often more than trivial pursuits; they are frequently a means of stepping out of reality into a world of greater freedom and illusion. We should not underestimate the broader value of fun and games as a cultural stimulus as well as an antidote to pain.

Counterintuitively, the comic element is central to many of the songs to Holy Mary. One song relates how "in the land of Germany" a group of young men had once come to play their favorite sport on the village green. In the manuscript illustrations, a youth with curly blond hair, wearing a pink cloak, wields what looks like a baseball bat, while another, in a blue cloak, spins a devious underarm pitch toward him; a second group of men is happily playing catch in the background. One of the young men, afraid that he will damage the ring that his betrothed had given him, casually places it on the finger of a nearby statue of the Virgin. In a moment of comic bravado, doubtless designed to make his companions laugh, he addresses the Virgin, assuring her that never in his life has he seen a lady more beautiful and that never will he love another more than her.

Mary, it seems, takes the joke rather too seriously: to the young man's disbelief, she closes her finger around the ring. The bystanders, exploiting his shock, advise him to enter a monastery forthwith, but instead he marries his earthly bride. On the wedding night, having fallen asleep, he is brusquely awakened by the jealous Virgin: "Oh, my faithless liar!" she cries. "Why did you forsake me and take a wife? You forgot the ring you gave me. Therefore you must leave your wife and go with me wherever I so will. Otherwise, from now on, you must suffer mortal anguish." The young man needs no further persuasion; he hurriedly gets up and wanders out into the wilderness, where he takes up lodging in a hermitage amid the pinewood trees.

The *cantiga* is a comedy in the classical sense—it has a happy ending—but it is also infused with an irrepressible sense of humor, gently satirizing pious cliché, that was surely enhanced in

Young men playing ball in a meadow: *Cantigas de Santa María*, no. 42, *Códice rico* (Rich Codex), Real Biblioteca del Monasterio de El Escorial, Ms. T.I.1. Reproduced courtesy of Archivo Oronoz.

performance. In other songs, demons and even the Devil himself provide an endless source of light entertainment. In one song about a priest who uses black arts to gain a maiden's heart, the artist has depicted demons with wild and comical faces. Sometimes, medieval people—like us—liked to laugh at the very things that frightened them most.

Alfonso's philosophy of humor clashed with a good deal of ancient pagan and Christian thinking. In Plato's *Republic*, describing the ideal philosopher-king, Socrates warned, "Whenever anyone gives in to violent laughter, a violent reaction pretty much always follows." The early church also absorbed the conviction that laughter was dangerous and disruptive, disturbing the rightful order of things. According to the Rule of Saint Benedict—by far the most influential set of monastic regulations in the early Middle Ages—a monk should refrain from laughing, for this was the act of a fool. In the period between the fourth and tenth centuries, the church, anxious to maintain proper spiritual decorum and silence, had stifled laughter.

The sensibilities of Alfonso's world could not have been more different. A new comic spirit had begun to emerge in twelfth-century European culture, and the party was in full swing by the 1260s. Saint Francis had advised his brothers, "Laugh in the face of those who torment you." A thirteenth-century history of the Franciscans in England tells us that at Oxford, a group of young friars had followed the saint's preaching so closely that they indulged in great outbursts of laughter, much to the chagrin of the minister general. A psalter made for the Wise King's namesake, Alphonso, the young son of his sister Leonor (Eleanor of Castile) and Edward I, featured a plate-balancing monkey in one margin. For his part, Edward II paid a court painter named James, "who danced before the King upon a table and made him laugh heartily." His cook received twenty shillings "because he rode before the King and fell oftentimes from his horse, whereat the king laughed heartily." Matilda Makejoy—an acrobatic dancer whose name Alfonso would have loved—received a large sum of money in 1296 for having performed in front of the two young royal princes.

On the other side of the channel, the crusading saint-king Louis IX of France was fully attuned to the new age, happily projecting the image of a *rex facetus*, a laughing king always at the ready to share a good joke with his courtiers. Although Saint Louis, on the advice of his friars, compromised by resolving not to laugh on Fridays, this was a culture that embraced laughter and other worldly pleasures as much as the promise of an afterlife. And in Aragon, Jaume I's *Book of Deeds* is similarly infused with a sense of fun. Some scenes in his autobiography suggest a taste for slapstick. Others revel in amusing personal reactions during tense situations, and on occasion there is even a sophisticated delight in word play.

But crudity, more than subtlety, was the hallmark of thirteenth-century humor. Many comic texts and images, carnivalesque and bawdy, were shockingly obscene. The *Dialog of Solomon and Marcolf*, for instance, presents us with a long exchange between the biblical king and a foul-mouthed "wise fool." "Learning and wisdom ought to reside in the mouth of the wise," Solomon observes piously. "A donkey ought always to be among the crops," Marcolf responds. "Where it shits, there it fertilizes. Where it pisses, it irrigates." Toward the end of the story, Marcolf triumphantly tells Solomon, "You instructed me that you would not see me any more between the eyes. But now, if you do not wish to see me between the eyes [*in mediis oculis*], you may see me between the buttocks [*in medio culo*]." The joke rests on a pun between the Latin words for eyes and ass—a pun of which we know Alfonso's courtiers were also very fond. The dialog circulated for centuries across Europe, surviving in a number of late-medieval manuscripts, but the surviving versions—vibrant, contentious, and untamed—bear the hallmarks of its thirteenth-century origins. Only very gradually would a more refined taste in humor—the comedy of smiles rather than guffaws—come to predominate. Even in late-Renaissance Italy, scatological humor remained de rigueur.

At the Wise King's court, this comic muse—crude, hard-edged, and sexually charged—was channeled into the so-called *Cantigas d'escarnho e de mal dizer*: songs of mockery and slander. These satirical and invective poems, ranging from the playful to the aggressively acerbic, were directed against other courtiers, courtesans, or whole sectors of elite society. Many involve accusations of homosexuality and/or pederasty. Others revolve around racy double entendres, or even single entendres. A good number of songs focus on a courtesan named María Pérez, known as La Balteira, who appears to have been the subject of limitless male fantasy. One of these lyrics relates how a certain Juan Rodríguez goes to take measurements at her house so that she can "take in his wood." Another relates how she has ostensibly returned from a crusade to the Holy Land with a box so heavily laden with pardons that she cannot even stand up—perhaps a suggestion of her fondness for lying down and certainly a measure of her enticingly sinful nature. Yet people keep stealing them from her, the poet asserts, so she has no pardons left: "And pardons are a most precious thing / and should be guarded most closely. / But she does not have a box with an iron latch / in which to keep them, and she cannot have one, / because, since she has lost the padlock, / the box has always been unlocked."

Beyond a simple fondness for dirty jokes, Alfonso was conscious that laughter was a good medicine. His Jewish physicians would have relayed to him the kind of medical wisdom that the twelfth-century polymath Maimonides had dispensed: "Concern and care should always be given to the movements of the psyche; these should be kept in balance in the state of health as well as in disease, and no other regimen should be given precedence in any wise. The physician should make every effort that the sick, and all the healthy, should be most cheerful of soul at all times, and that they should be relieved of the passions of the psyche that cause anxiety."

But what mattered above all to the Wise King was the ability to make people laugh *with* him. In the mid-1260s, in the face of the Mudéjar Rebellion, there was a desperate need for unity in adversity. Humor served then, as it serves now, to bring people together, diffusing tensions or creating an "in-group" of those who are in on the joke—often at the expense of others. The satirical *Cantigas d'escarnho* served this purpose well, mocking a wide variety of easy targets, among them credulous Christians who believed in supernatural auguries, lazy pilgrims who never reached their destinations, and fraudulent doctors and judges.

Both during and after the revolt, one social group was singled out for particularly sharp critique: knights and noblemen who either failed completely to appear on the battlefield or let the king down once they had arrived. Some of the satirical poets were aristocratic Portuguese exiles, dependent on Alfonso, with their own axes to grind against the Castilian nobles. The king himself wrote other poems. Nobody—not Pedro García nor Pedro d'Espanha, nor Pedro Galego (that is, neither Tom, Dick, nor Harry)—will come with me to battle, Alfonso laughingly laments in one such song; but if Pedro Galinha (Peter Chicken) won't do it, I'll find someone else! Ay, ay: Don Mendo has brought a horse but forgotten the saddle! The king, he claimed, was surrounded by cowards. Another song attributed to Alfonso, about the battle of Alcalá in 1264, describes the inglorious scene:

> *The knight*
> *When he spurs on*
> *His speedy horse*

Trembles.
The horseman
Falters.
I saw glittering horsemen
Badly frightened
And shaven knights
Scampered around us;
They had us hard-pressed
And were losing their color.
I saw spirited horsemen,
In the middle of summer
Trembling with fear
Before the Moors of Azamor,
And from them flowed a river
Greater than the Guadalquivir.

The terrified knights had peed themselves in fear, Alfonso was suggesting; the song must have elicited contemptuous guffaws. There was a difficult balance to strike. The mockery of supposed cowardice might be useful, encouraging displays of bravado, but on the other hand, the king needed to be careful not to alienate his courtiers. Individuals are therefore rarely mentioned by name. But intertwined with the king's bathroom humor and the homophobic implications of effeminacy, there was no mistaking his anger. He railed against the noblemen who wavered when he most needed them, in the battle against Muhammad I of Granada and his allies.

He who crossed the sierra
And did not want to serve the land,
Is he now, joining the fray,
Vacillating?

Since he wavers so much now,
Damn him!
He who took the money,
And did not bring the knights,
Is it to avoid the front line
That he vacillates?
Since he goes in the rear,
Damn him!
He who received great largesse
And never came campaigning,
Is it to avoid going to Granada
That he vacillates?
If he's an aristocrat or has a great host,
Damn him!
He who brought in his sack
Nothing but craft and cunning,
Is it to avoid the Vega de Granada
That he vacillates?
Since he is softer than butter,
Damn him!

The vitriol of the language probably gained a comic sheen in performance, the gestures of the performers—male and female—enhancing the accusations of buttery flaccidity. All of this served the dubious needs of male bonding at Alfonso's court. The obsessive delight in the sexuality of María Pérez and other courtesans reinforced this cohesion, and the preoccupation with sex was sometimes projected onto a battlefield setting. In another satirical song, the courtesan Dominga Eanes is locked in "combat" with a Muslim horseman. Wounding blows are struck and lances wielded in a parody of epic poetry of the Reconquest—but the subtext is sexual, and the punch line concerns venereal disease. The joke reveals real anxiety about Muslim prowess on more than one level.

The key garrison town of Jerez had probably been recaptured from the Muslim rebels by October 9, 1264. But the king's anxieties remained. Nervous about imminent invasion by the Marinid leader, Abu Yusuf, Alfonso expelled the Muslim inhabitants of Jerez soon after its surrender and received the submission of a number of rebel towns: Vejer, Medina Sidonia, Rota, and Sanlúcar de Barrameda. He then returned to Seville, demobilizing the royal army and ordering it to return for a new campaign in the spring of 1265, against Muhammad I of Granada.

In the interim, he began laying the groundwork for collaboration with dissidents within the Nasrid kingdom. The Banu Ashqilula clan—governors of Málaga and Guadix—had sent representatives with Muhammad I to negotiate with Alfonso at their ill-fated meeting in Seville but felt marginalized by the arrival of the Moroccan *mujaheddin*. For their part, the ruling Nasrid dynasty, its kingdom swollen by an influx of refugees from the towns that had submitted to Castile, was increasingly militant under siege and less and less willing to tolerate internal dissent. The schism between Muhammad I and the Banu Ashqilula was articulated in religious terms. But at its root, it was a crisis of power sharing that pushed the clan toward Alfonso. We can imagine a stream of clandestine correspondence between the Castilian court and the cities of Málaga and Guadix throughout the winter of 1264 and 1265.

During the late spring of 1265, the king launched an offensive against Muhammad I's kingdom. In June and July, he was in the military encampment on the plains of Granada, where he waited for Jaume I of Aragon, still tangled up in negotiations with his barons, to come to his aid. By the end of the year, the Aragonese had advanced into the rebel territories of Murcia—a point on which the Castilian royal chronicle is curiously silent—capturing the capital city in February 1266 and reconsecrating its main mosque as a Christian cathedral. With great reluctance, Jaume subsequently ceded Murcia to Castile, turning his sights on further expansion in the Mediterranean.

Meanwhile, at the negotiating table, Alfonso squeezed the Nasrid king for all he was worth. Some time between late August and early September, at Alcalá de Benzaide, Muhammad I agreed to pay him an annual tribute of 250,000 maravedís—a substantial increase over what had previously been due. One historian has claimed that Alfonso had made a grave error in signing the truce. While the survival of a tribute-paying Muslim king in Granada was extremely useful as a source of income, runs the argument, it presented a major impediment to an African crusade, and without such a crusade, his candidacy for the Holy Roman Emperorship might be seriously impeded. But Alfonso had little choice. Any attempt to occupy the densely populated bastion of Islamic resistance that was the kingdom of Granada would have been catastrophic.

The tension was briefly broken by some unexpected good news. One of Alfonso's great rivals for imperial power, Manfred of Hohenstaufen (son of the emperor Frederick II), had been killed in battle on January 20, 1266, defeated by King Louis IX's youngest brother, Charles of Anjou. Charles was a distant relative of Alfonso whom the pope and the Guelph party had been promoting in Italy. Having been appointed king of Sicily by papal decree in 1262, he could now be formally crowned. Alfonso may have seen Manfred's defeat as an opportunity to move into a power vacuum and a sign that an alliance with the French court might improve his fortunes.

He now began negotiations for the betrothal of his eleven-year-old son, Fernando de la Cerda (b. 1255), to King Louis IX's daughter Blanche, who had been born in Jaffa in 1253 while Louis was on crusade. The marriage must have seemed especially desirable because of the French crown's increasingly powerful influence at the papal court (half a century later, the papal court would move from Rome to Avignon, ushering in the period of "exile" that came to be known as the Babylonian Captivity). A Frenchman, Guy Foulquois, now occupied the papal throne as Clement IV (1265–1268), and Clement—like his predecessor, Urban IV (1261–1264)—enjoyed close relations with the French monarchy. In May, a Castilian diplomatic embassy was dispatched to Paris, and on September 26, in the castle of Saint Germain en Laye, the marriage agreements between the Spanish prince and the French princess were signed. The wedding, it was agreed, would take place three years later in 1269, when the infante Fernando reached marriageable age.

Wisely enough, Alfonso remained mostly in Jerez for the year between late 1267 and late 1268, focusing on the consolidation of his kingdom. There, he attempted to orchestrate the repopulation of conquered territories and to stem the spiraling inflation. The second of these problems related directly to the first: the increase in salaries needed to attract settlers was aggravating price increases, already sharp because of the influx of precious metals from the kingdom of Granada. Inflation was a political issue, since it undercut the revenues that lords received from their tenants. Financial resentment widened a breach between Alfonso and the Castilian nobility that is also reflected in the satirical *Cantigas d'escarnho*.

The lord of Lara, Nuño González, was the most active and articulate of the aristocratic party, and signs in the royal chronicle indicate that in the late 1260s his relationship with Alfonso was strained. The chronicle tells of a visit to the royal court by the young Portuguese prince Dinís, son of Alfonso's firstborn child, Beatriz, requesting that the king suspend the tribute owed by the kings of Portugal. After hearing the request, Alfonso asks for advice from his immediate entourage—his brothers Manuel, Felipe, and Fadrique and the magnates Nuño González de Lara, Lope Díaz de Haro, and Esteban Fernández de Castro. But, we read, "all of them were silent and they were a long time without saying anything. The king asked again why they did not respond to the argument that was spoken on behalf of the infante. The king became angry with all of them, but he showed more anger toward Don Nuño than any of the others who were there." The nobleman retorted, "I would never advise you that you throw away from the Crown of your kingdoms the tribute that the King of Portugal and his kingdom are obliged to give you.'"

Meanwhile, the king watched the international scene nervously. On the Italian front, the situation was extremely unstable and bewilderingly complex, thanks in part to the dramatic reappearance of his exiled brother, the infante Enrique, who since 1260 had been living at the court of the king of Tunis. The royal chronicle suggests that he had in fact become a valuable asset to the Muslim leader: "In the battles and struggles that the king of Tunis had with his Moorish neighbors, the infante Enrique served him very well, and had a great reputation for intrepid bravery and great knightly prestige in all those lands." But by the mid-1260s, the relationship had broken down. The royal chronicle points the finger at the resentment of Muslim courtiers, who, we read, conspired to trap the Castilian prince in a courtyard, where they unleashed two lions. Like a modern Jerome, unafraid, Enrique survived the lions unscathed, and the king of Tunis decided to spare his life, merely expelling him from the realm.

For the rocambolesque Enrique, who had narrowly escaped with his life when he first rebelled against Alfonso, this was merely the start of a new adventure, since he also saw rich opportunities in Italy in the aftermath of Manfred of Hohenstaufen's defeat. A source close to him suggests that he had been in contact with Charles of Anjou for a number of years. Initially he allied himself with Charles and other leaders of the pro-papal party, but their promises to reward him with the kingdom of Sardinia failed to materialize. He therefore changed course, setting himself up independently as "senator of Rome."

A tense and unstable situation descended into street fighting on the streets of Rome. Charles of Anjou ordered Enrique's assassination, and yet again, Enrique survived by the skin of his teeth—although he was excommunicated for his sins. According to our source, Enrique was then courted by the teenage head of his erstwhile enemies in the pro-imperial party: Conradin, the sixteen-year-old duke of Swabia. Conradin asked Enrique for military assistance in recovering the kingdom of Sicily for the Hohenstaufens. The Castilian prince then took command of a combined Spanish and Italian force and, on August 23, 1268, met Charles of Anjou's forces at Tagliacozzo, to the east of Rome, where his forces were crushed. Enrique then fled to the sanctuary of a Benedictine monastery but was recognized, captured, and delivered into the hands of the pro-papal party. Conradin was taken prisoner and decapitated. For his part, Enrique spent the next twenty-four years in Charles of Anjou's dungeons. Alfonso cannot have shed many tears at his brother's misfortune. But nor would he have been pleased with his rival's ascent: Charles had emerged as the pope's right-hand man in saving Rome and the church.

As the date of the royal wedding approached, the storm clouds were darkening. In November 1268, Pope Clement IV passed away, and a new phase of uncertainty enveloped Alfonso's imperial dreams. The economic crisis in Castile placed him in a weak position to buy allies or exert influence abroad, and at home the resentments of the aristocracy were mounting by the day.

Just as Alfonso cultivated relations with the rebel Banu Ashqilula clan, the Nasrid king of Granada was planting poison in the Castilian court. Near Seville, in June of that year, Muhammad I appears to have met with the lord of Lara's son and to have initiated a secret agreement of mutual support. "While the king of Granada was in his tent," reports the royal chronicle, "Nuño González, son of Don Nuño, came to talk to him and said that the king had done some wrongs and injustices to Don Nuño, his father, and to Juan Núñez, his brother, and if they should find the king of Granada willing to help and favor them, he would talk to them and make sure that they helped him." The king of Granada agreed and gave the young Lara lord some jewels and gold coins before returning to his kingdom.

A terrifying net was gradually encircling the Wise King, and in the *alcázar* of Seville, the sound of laughter was fading away.

6

FRIENDS

If there is a conjunction of Mars and the Sun in the sixth
house, the king's servants will betray him.
—YEHUDA BEN MOSÉ, BOOK OF CROSSES, 21

THE WEDDING INVITATION REACHED KING JAUME I OF
Aragon at his court in Zaragoza. The messengers would have
informed the aging conqueror that his presence was requested in
Castile. The nuptial blessing of his grandson, Fernando de la
Cerda, and Blanche, daughter of Louis IX of France, was to take
place at the end of the month. It was early November 1269.
Jaume, who had always remained close to his daughter, Queen
Yolant, accepted at once. He was shortly on his route westward
into Alfonso's realms, riding to the royal capital of Burgos. Soon
after the royal cortege had passed through Tarazona, he recalled
in his *Book of Deeds*, the two rulers met on the road: Alfonso "was
very happy to see us, and he embraced us three times, and we
cried." The public display of affection, not least the emotive
tears, might surprise us in view of recent tensions between the

two men. But such emotional displays were an important part of political culture, signaling to each party involved—and to their followers—the enduring strength of their relationship. The two rulers were not merely father- and son-in-law; they were, as Jaume's advisors had long recognized, "friends" and could rely on each other. Love and friendship between men was celebrated in the twelfth and thirteenth centuries as never before since the Greco-Roman age. One chronicler of the reign of Henry II of England (r. 1154–1189) had recounted how a French siege of an English-held town in Normandy had ended when the king of France came to love Richard the Lionheart "as his own soul," sleeping in the same bed with him and eating from the same dish. As this episode suggests, friendship was also a vital component of high-level political bonding and of kingly power.

From the Castilian court, the wedding preparations were coordinated with perfect, almost mechanical precision. As early as January 1267, the pope had granted a special dispensation from consanguinity for Fernando and Blanche. Delegates sent to and from the French court at Reims exchanged vows of commitment on behalf of the bride and groom. The betrothal had been celebrated on October 12; the wedding itself was to be held on November 30 in the newly finished Gothic cathedral of Burgos, fifty years to the day since the marriage of Fernando III and Beatrix of Swabia. The cream of the Castilian-Leonese nobility gathered for the occasion, along with many representatives from the towns. Alfonso X had called a meeting of the Cortes to coincide with the wedding, hoping to ensure a glamorous reaffirmation of young Fernando de la Cerda as the heir to his throne. Prince Edward of England, the future Edward I, was also there, taking the occasion, the fourteenth-century *Chronicle of Alfonso X* tells us, to knight many counts, dukes, and other highborn men who had come with him from England and Aquitaine. The wedding party—led by Fernando, dressed in the royal regalia emblazoned with castles and lions—would have walked through the newly designed Puerta del Sarmental, its masonry adorned with brightly colored carvings of vine leaves and grapes, symbols of fidelity and fertility. At the top of the portal, two crowns are borne aloft by angels, the upper of which is larger and perhaps represents the imperial crown that Alfonso believed destined for himself and his successors. Passing under the archway, the wedding party then headed through the breathtaking upper cloister toward the main altar. Immediately opposite the paired statues of the royal couple, just above head height on a corner column, the party would have seen a clustered sculpture group of four other crowned figures. These have variously been seen as four sons of Fernando III, presumably including Alfonso, or four sons of Alfonso X, perhaps Fernando de la Cerda himself (aged fourteen) and his brothers Sancho (eleven), Pedro (nine), and Juan (seven). All, in their newly restored colors, wear the red hose of royalty, gold-trimmed robes, and similar golden crowns. The figures appear to be stylized, rather than individualized, portraits. Yet, regardless of their identity, they strike a pose of quietly relaxed fraternal collaboration, as they turn toward each other in pairs, models of princely brotherhood.

Reality was quite different. Much to the consternation of his grandfather, King Jaume, Fernando de la Cerda appears to have knighted some of his brothers while they were gathered in Burgos but not others (among them, the highly ambitious Sancho). The Aragonese king upbraided him sternly, saying that this "would sow discord and anger amongst them, and that forever more, when they did not act well, he would reproach them, saying that he had made them knights, and the others would feel annoyance and anger." Jaume now increasingly found himself at the center of a vortex of discontent. One day, he relates in his *Book of Deeds*, while returning to his quarters in the Hospital de Burgos after visiting the sick Alfonso de Molina (Fernando III's elderly brother), he was suddenly approached by the aristocratic leader Nuño González de Lara. The two of them moved to one side, and he ordered the other members of his party to move ahead; they talked discreetly to each other as they rode onward. The lord of Lara "offered to serve us, saying that it was his intention to give more service to us than to any other man in the world, except the king of Castile, and that in certain matters he would serve us above him. Moreover, he said that if we sent him just one letter, he would come to us with one or two hundred knights. And we said that we thanked him very much for the offer he had made us, and that when we needed it, we would accept it from him." King Jaume then turned to the aristocrat, telling him directly, "Don Nuño, I know that the king of Castile does not love you, and complains of you and of other nobles of Castile. And I also know that you complain of him." Doubtless conscious of his friendship with Alfonso, he shied away from embracing the lord of Lara's offer. Promising to intervene as a peacemaker, he assured Nuño González, "You may truly believe that if he has wronged you, I will say so to him, and I will make him repair it."

In his own mind, the king of Aragon had acted effectively. "Another day," he says, he found the lord of Lara "satisfied with the king, and he said that he had endowed him with lands, and married him off, and had done him all the duties that a lord could do his vassal." But other evidence suggests that Nuño González remained far from happy—that, in fact, there had been a dramatic distancing in the close relationship that he had enjoyed with Alfonso since their childhood. Instead, the lord of Lara began to consort with other, sometimes very unexpected "friends," among them, the leader of the clan that was his principal rival for dominance at the royal court, the Haro family, with their heartland on the Rioja and in the Basque country. The *Chronicle of Alfonso* X picks up the story. While King Alfonso was in Burgos, the narrator writes, Nuño González de Lara and Lope Díaz de Haro

> made pacts of friendship and acted secretly against Alfonso. During this time, they gathered together as many friends as they could, and went to San Andres de Arroyo [a nearby Cistercian monastery], and married Lope Díaz to Juana, daughter of the infante Alfonso de Molina, who was in that monastery and was the king's first cousin. Although the king found out about it, he did not see what would follow, nor the disservice that would later come to him; nor did he want them to believe that they should be wary of him, since he needed them in the war against the Moors and also for the matter of the Empire.

As usual, the chronicler is unreliable in the details. The hasty marriage, perhaps even the abduction, of Juana—daughter of the king's uncle Alfonso de Molina (and probably under Alfonso X's tutelage)—may in fact have occurred up to two years later. But the tension between king and leading members of the aristocracy, among them his friend Nuño González, is palpable. As Jaume made his way back toward Aragon in mid-December 1269, Alfonso followed him: "He did not want to be separated from us while we were in his land." Behind the public displays of friendship between the two rulers, there must have been growing suspicion; Alfonso may have feared that Jaume might reestablish contacts with dissident noblemen in Castile. Back in Tarazona for the Christmas festivities, Jaume nevertheless hosted King Alfonso and his entourage, providing lavish meals, including plenty of partridges, for his courtiers. During the week they spent together, he offered his son-in-law a series of seven pieces of advice;

the fourth of these, informed by his own bitter experience, was that he should keep the church, the poor, and the towns on his side, since "God loves these people more than the knights, because the knights rise up more readily against lordship than the others." The storm was about to break.

To aggravate matters, injury had been added to insult. In a freakish accident, a horse had kicked Alfonso in the leg while he was in Burgos, and soon after leaving the Christmas celebrations, he began to experience serious complications. We went there immediately, Jaume writes, "and some four or five knights went with us, as well as our household, and we saw him and comforted him. And we brought one of our surgeons with us, called Master Joan, and we brought all that was needed with us. And we remained there with him for some four or five days. Then he earnestly besought us to go back, since he was cured." Yet he was not, in fact, fully healed; and in the last decade and a half of his life, Alfonso's health steadily deteriorated. Some historians have seen the horse's kick as the starting point of these physical ailments, even speculating that his illnesses help to explain the accentuation of political tensions in this period. One diagnosis is cancer: more specifically, squamous cell carcinoma of the maxillary antrum (nasal cavity). To associate this unfortunate event and the onset of cancer is risky, and to draw a connection between acute political stress fractures and the king's physical health may be to overstate the case. But it is certain that the winter of 1269, which had begun so gloriously, ended in disaster.

The wedding celebrations in Burgos had witnessed a break between two close friends, Alfonso X of Castile and the lord of Lara, and a rapprochement between former enemies, the lords of Lara and Haro, that also went under the name of "friendship." What, then, did this concept really mean in medieval Iberia? In the early twenty-first century—the new age of social media—traditional forms of friendship are under stress; the digital curtain sometimes threatens the closeness of face-to-face human interactions. Over a much longer period, however, a cultural emphasis on romantic love—particularly between men and women—has displaced the role of friendship, in our imagination, as the closest of intimate bonds. In the Middle Ages, particularly from the twelfth century onward, friendship was widely seen as the supreme personal relationship. Many of the core ideas underpinning this belief were inherited and adapted from classical antiquity. When the king of France embraced Richard the Lionheart as "his own soul," he—or perhaps the English chronicler—was summoning the ghost of Aristotle. "The Philosopher," as medieval scholars knew him, had referred to friendship of mutual and enduring attraction, deriving from harmony of tastes, as constituting "one soul in two bodies."

Ideas such as this circulated widely in Alfonso's intellectual circles. A good deal of the Philosopher's work had been translated from Arabic into Latin at the end of the previous century. In his *Nicomachean Ethics*, Aristotle had discerned three types of friendship. The first was based on utility or personal profit, the second on the joy or emotional delight it provided, and the third (the superior form) on a pure fusion between good individual souls. The person with such a friend had found an alternative self, an "alter ego." In the *Siete partidas*, Alfonso—defining friendship as a relationship that "arises when one person who loves another is beloved by him"—explicitly acknowledges the Philosopher's thinking on the issue: "As Aristotle said, no man who has any kindness in his nature desires to live in this world without friendship even though he may be supplied with all the property there is in it." Drawing upon Aristotelian thinking, he distinguishes purely utilitarian relationships from the more noble form that can exist between men and "arises solely from beneficence." Alfonso also follows the Philosopher in suggesting that there are few people with the moral caliber to enjoy pure friendship ("good men are few in number and bad ones numerous"), as well as Cicero's assertion that "nothing was so pleasant as to have, for a friend, a man to whom one could speak his mind as to himself."

True friendship, medieval Spaniards believed, was a precious rarity. A tale that first surfaced in Iberia in the collection of exemplary tales called *Disciplina clericalis*, written in the twelfth century by a Jewish author who, after converting to Christianity, assumed the name Pedro Alfonso, makes the point clearly. An Arab man, nearing death, asks his son how many friends he has acquired in the course of his lifetime. More than one hundred, the son replies. How interesting, the father comments; in my whole long life, I have gained only half a friend. Let us test your so-called friends to see how many you really have. Kill a calf and cut it into pieces, put the pieces in a sack, take it around to these friends' houses, and tell them that you have killed a man. Then we will see how many of them will support you. The son does as his father commands, but not a single one of his "friends" is willing to help. The father's half friend, though, responds quite differently. Sending his wife and family out of the house, he helps the son to bury the sack. The son returns home, lesson learned.

Transferred to the heavens, the ideal friendship remained what it was on earth: a happy coincidence of pragmatism and passion. This conviction underpins many of the songs in Alfonso's *Cantigas de Santa María*, the first of which dates from the late 1260s or early 1270s. It describes the Virgin as both daughter and friend to God and the perfect counselor and friend to humanity. More broadly, Alfonso often describes true believers as the community of God's *amigos*. In this scheme of things, the king himself is a close personal friend and lover of Mary, as well as her personal troubadour. Benefits might, of course, accrue to the true and loyal believer, as they might to any loyal friend, but this is no hollow sham of a friendship. Without passionate adherence to the Virgin and to God, the relationship is unthinkable.

The attempt to infuse Christian principles into the framework of friendship, and vice versa, went as far back as Saint Augustine of Hippo (354–430), a brilliant, tormented, and impassioned man who frenziedly wrote his way through the existential problems that troubled him. Alfonso's section on the subject admiringly cites Augustine's thinking on friendship, particularly his emphasis on selflessness. A man should make the same effort on behalf of his friends as for himself; such human bonds transcended social hierarchy. "In friendship," the king cites the saint as saying, "there is no rank higher than another, for equality should always exist between friends." Equality here is not a matter of social status but one of personal commitment.

In his *Confessions* Augustine tried to integrate his impassioned faith with the ways that the Greek and Roman thinkers he loved thought and wrote about these issues. Only God can offer us true hope and salvation, he declaimed; human friendship is illusory and proves to be a source of anxiety and pain as often as of happiness. Yet his love for his friends lived on. He refers in passing to a tale that the Wise King also tells, the story of Orestes and Pylades. These two friends, as Alfonso tells us, had recently been arrested, whereupon Orestes,

> having been condemned to death and the other acquitted, . . . was sent for to be executed, and was summoned to come forth from the place where he was kept prisoner. Pylades, knowing that his friend was to be killed, answered that he was Orestes, and the latter replied that this was not true, but that he himself

was Orestes. When the king learned of the loyalty of these two friends, and that each of them had devoted himself to death in order to save the other, he released both of them, and asked them to receive him among them as their third friend.

In his own celebration of these human relationships, Alfonso inherited a set of values that had been reinvigorated in the twelfth century, which is said to have witnessed the "rediscovery of friendship" as well as the increasing rediscovery of ancient Greek and Latin learning and the revitalization of economic life. Monastic thinkers elevated individual friendship to lofty heights, even greater than generalized "charity."

Aelred of Rievaulx (b. c. 1110) promoted friendship as a path to loving God and, in doing so, also established a model for people far beyond the monastery walls: "There was no pretense between us," he wrote of one of his own relationships, "no simulation, no dishonorable flattery, no unbecoming harshness, no evasion, no concealment, but everything open and aboveboard; for I deemed my heart in a fashion his, and he felt in a like manner towards me." The letters of one of his most famous contemporaries, the remarkable German nun and visionary Hildegard of Bingen (1098–1179), suggest that in the twelfth-century imagination, women could be bonded together with the same intensity as men.

Thirteenth-century people, in Alfonso's Castile as in early-Renaissance Italy, inhaled these ideals. In his *Livre dou tresor*, the Florentine scholar Brunetto Latini—Dante's teacher and erstwhile emissary to the Castilian court—stated that only good people might be involved in true friendship and that their relationship was pure and divine: "The one who counterfeits friendship is worse than a counterfeiter of gold or silver, since friendship is the best treasure there can be, and just as the fake coin is quickly recognized, so too is false friendship quickly discovered."

Assertions of friendship were doubtless often a practical matter, divorced from personal feelings, and might on occasion be little more than a calculated maneuver for power and influence. The expression of powerful affection was not in itself a sign of real emotional depth. In the world of the monasteries, it could serve a purely rhetorical purpose. Some letters in which churchmen express extravagant warmth were written to people the writers had never met. In the world of feudal kingship, friendship—like the family bond—was profoundly significant, since until the very late Middle Ages, political relations were always intensely personal. Lords became "friends" of their vassals in a way that reinforced their authority.

At the Castilian court, political friendship provided a sense of solidarity and cohesion, particularly in the face of external threats such as the Islamic neighbors to the south. The relationship between the roles of friend and counselor was particularly close. The *Siete partidas* state that those who formed the king's royal council "should be good friends of the king, in order to be pleased with his good fortune, and rejoice on account of it." For his part, the king "should love them well, so that they may be deeply attached to him, and may always desire to give him the best advice." In the section of the *Partidas* that deals specifically with friendship, the Wise King reads and reinterprets Aristotle in a markedly political way, emphasizing the value of this relationship for the collective well-being of his realm and underscoring the bonds of affection that exist between people from the same territory. Among the nobility, it might serve as a means of ensuring peace and social order. One kind of friendship exists, Alfonso noted, "which in former times, persons nobly born established with one another when they agreed not to dishonor or injure one another, without, in the first place, renouncing their friendship and issuing a challenge." According to customary law, Spanish noblemen were in fact required to rescind their "friendship" and wait for a period of nine days before they were allowed to kill each other. This action in turn derived from a tacit understanding that all Spanish noblemen were bound by a pact of mutual nonviolence, ensuring the peace of the realm, a practice shaped by brotherhood in arms.

Yet if, in the medieval and early-Renaissance imagination, public and private were so intertwined as to be indistinguishable, the same might well be said of practicality and affection; the two were combined in the ideal model of friendship. Not until the sixteenth century was emotional life constrained to a purely "private" sphere in which this ideal was divorced from any political benefits. For now, the two threads were woven together in Alfonso's paean in the *Siete partidas*. The Wise King recounts the simultaneously practical and emotional benefits of friendship: great tranquility and security but also, for the wealthy, the possibility of preserving and increasing riches and honors. It is easy to sense the pragmatism of many new alliances between "friends." But a relationship devoid of affection was empty and illegitimate. The emotional texture of individual friendships is often hard to trace, but those that proliferated in the political sphere—such as the ones that bound Alfonso to his father-in-law and to Nuño González de Lara—may quite frequently have combined political advantage with elements of genuine emotional intimacy.

Courtiers and king alike were awash in a sea of stories about friendship that flooded the royal court. Some of these emanated from the south. Andalusi attitudes would also have been formative for Alfonso (although their homoerotic elements were rejected with increasing firmness as a threat to masculine identity). Among the stories were the tales of Calila and Digna (translated into Castilian in 1251). This text, which ultimately has Sanskrit and Persian origins, has been described as the first literary prose narrative in the Spanish language. Its title refers to the two jackals—or perhaps, in the Spanish version, lynxes—who dominate the first set of stories in the collection. The anthropomorphized animal characters are understood throughout as representing human characteristics, and their half-comic tales convey complex, sometimes competing and contradictory, didactic lessons over which the king and his courtiers must have pored for long hours at court. Alfonso is believed to have commissioned the translation himself in the 1240s, while he was still a young prince. The translator worked using a much longer Arabic version composed in the greatest hub of Arabic learning, Baghdad, around 750, shortly after the Abbasid dynasty rose to power, that integrated Sanskrit tales like the *Panchatantra*. The urgency with which the text had been translated under the new caliph, al-Mansur, and the way in which it continued to fascinate later statesmen and rulers, including Alfonso, suggests that the tales of Calila and Digna were widely seen in both the Arabic-speaking and the Christian worlds as a "mirror for princes."

One such tale relates the capture of the Brightly Colored Dove. Once, we read, there was a hunting preserve in the land of Duzat, and in it was a large tree with densely intertwined branches. In this tree, a crow had made his nest. One day, the Crow saw a fearsomely ugly man approaching, carrying a net on his shoulders and ropes and sticks in his hands; he was looking up at the tree. The Crow, terrified, watched intently as the man set out his net and scattered grain on the ground to lure his prey. Before long, the Crow saw a flock of doves approach led by one whose name was La Colorada, the Brightly Colored. She saw the grain but not the net and unwittingly led all the other doves into the trap. When the fowl hunter approached, La Colorada turned to them. "Let no one be more concerned about her own safety than the safety of her friends," she said. "Let us work together to lift the net up off the ground." They did as she proposed, carrying the net high into the air. The hunter followed, waiting for them to fall, and the Crow, too, decided to follow. "Let us fly into the forest," said La Colorada to the other doves. "There we will find the cave of my good friend the mouse. He will gnaw through the net and free us all." When the Mouse began to gnaw through the net, she told him immediately, "Begin by freeing the other doves; it was my fault, and my fault alone, that they fell into this trap. If you free me first, you might tire of the task before you finish it, and leave the other doves still trapped." The Mouse was awed. "The other doves must love you even more for your selflessness," he told La Colorada. To the astonishment of the hunter and the Crow, he freed them all.

Collaboration between friends, then, is essential in overcoming the trials and tribulations of the world. To this, the interlocked tale of the Crow and the Mouse adds a new dimension: self-interest is self-destructive, and friendships based on self-interest are ephemeral. "I was born," says the Mouse,

in the house of a man of religion. Every day, people would bring the man a small basket of food. I would eat the leftovers from the basket, after he had gone, making use of a pile of coins in my cave to jump higher than the others could, and then share the leftovers with the other mice. But one day, when a guest in the house dug into my hole, discovered the coins, and removed them, I could no longer jump so high, and the other mice now rejected me. I realize now that their friendship had been purely pragmatic and that when people fall into misfortune, their friends and family turn their backs. Poverty is the worst of all tribulations; the man who falls into poverty loses his sense of shame and his nobility of heart. Reduced to poverty, I suffered

Story of the birds and the fowl hunter: *Calila and Dimna:* sixteenth-century Persian miniature, Golestan Palace, Tehran. Reproduced courtesy of Archivo Oronoz.

injury upon injury. I lost my sanity, my memory, and my understanding. After the guest had divided the coins with his host, the man of religion, I tried to recover some of the coins from the bag that he hung at the head of the bed where he was sleeping; but he was awoken by the noise I was making and beat me hard with a stick. I dragged myself, bruised and battered, back to my cave. Again, I tried; again, I was beaten. I came to understand how the evils that befall men in this world arise from desire and greed. There is nothing better in this world than being content with what one has. I decided to move to the countryside and became friends with La Colorada and then with the Crow. There is no pleasure in this world like the company of friends and no pain like losing them.

Among Alfonso's friends, none had been closer—since their childhood in the 1230s—than Nuño González de Lara, and none gave him more pain. The favor he had shown toward Don Nuño as a young ruler may well have been advantageous, bringing on board the leader of one of the two most powerful noble clans in Castile, but it was not inevitable. By freezing relations with the Lara family in the 1220s and banishing them from court, his father, Fernando III, had shown that he could manage without the Laras' collaboration even at moments of pressing national need. As prince and then as king, Alfonso had broken with the cultural tradition that enemies—like friends—might be hereditary, proactively adopting Don Nuño as a friend and protégé in a way that strong personal affection may well explain.

By the early 1270s, however, this friendship had broken down. At the northern Lara stronghold of Lerma, Nuño González gathered with other malcontents, among them the king's own brother Felipe—the king's relationships with his brothers had always been strained—to orchestrate a plan of resistance to Alfonso. Far away to the southeast, in Murcia, the incredulous king "begged him as a friend, and ordered him as a vassal, to quiet his heart to serve him as he was obliged to do."

Alfonso's urgent wish to leave Castile to resume his pursuit of the title of Holy Roman Emperor heightened his desperation. After a highly contentious three-year period (1268–1271) following the death of Clement IV, there had been no pope, but in late 1271 a candidate totally opposed to Alfonso's claim to the imperial title had been elected as Gregory X. Alfonso, who continued to enjoy significant support from some of the Italian city-states, was unwilling to countenance any opposition to his wish to travel to meet the new pope and to resolve the matter once and for all. The death of Richard of Cornwall in 1272 gave him temporary hope that he could secure his claims to the imperial title. In founding a new military order called Santa María de España that year, he may well have been taking direct inspiration from the German emperors' traditional patronage of the Teutonic Knights.

Yet the king could not leave while his kingdoms teetered on the brink of civil war. For their part, the rebels may well have been conscious that the king's plight offered a moment of opportunity. Their leverage increased still further when the king received news of a terrifying incursion from across the Strait of Gibraltar: a major military operation by the Banu Marin (the Marinids), successors to the former Almohad empire. Alfonso summoned his vassals to go in aid of Fernando de la Cerda, to whom he had delegated responsibility on the frontier, but they responded that they were not yet in a position to do so, instead requesting an audience with the king.

At this point, Alfonso's troubles converged. One of Nuño González's men had been intercepted with letters in Arabic, written, according to the *Chronicle of Alfonso X*, by none other than the Marinid emir Abu Yusuf. The letter to Don Nuño himself began by stating that the emir's messenger had informed him that "you have expressed grievances to Alfonso, who made illicit demands on you, created false coins, and took from you the good law code that you used in olden times, so that the worth of your possessions was transformed and things became more expensive, and that he behaved unjustly to your son, whom he exiled from the land for treason." The emir was probably referring here to the participation of Nuño's eldest son, Juan Núñez de Lara, in Louis IX's crusade against Tunis in 1270. Although not in fact in exile,

Juan Núñez was taking part as vassal of the king of Navarre, a fact that reflected the growing gulf between Alfonso and the Lara family. The emir's letter continued by offering to make Juan Núñez head of the Christian mercenaries in his service and concluded with expressions of extravagant affection: "I am letting you know this because I love you, and so that you do not go looking for anything from Alfonso. God willing, I will give you ten times the love you receive from Alfonso. Write to me, so that I may send you money, or horses, or safe passage, or whatever you wish. Let me know where you would like me to send it, and it shall reach you quickly."

Alfonso's reaction, if we can judge from the royal chronicle, was measured. While Don Nuño continued to proclaim his innocence, the king sent messengers assuring the noblemen individually that he was committed to preserving the traditional laws of the realm. This section of the chronicle, in fact, is by far the most reliable. It seems to have been written much earlier, by a contemporary who had direct access both to documents in the royal chancellery and to oral accounts from eyewitnesses. The evidence suggests that, despite the fact that this contemporary's sympathies lay above all with Queen Yolant and her son, Fernando de la Cerda, the king's behavior throughout this period was moderate and cautious. Conversely, the chronicle suggests, Nuño González and his fellow rebels behaved in an intimidating fashion. One day, we read, the king, hunting near Lerma, was surprised on the road by a large group of armed mounted men, including the lords of Lara and Haro, and sensed trouble. Immediately, he headed for his stronghold in Burgos. Rather than vilifying the noblemen as pantomime villains, as often happens in medieval chronicles, it might be safer to imagine an atmosphere in which mutual suspicion and resentment were festering. If Alfonso was nervous, so were the rebels, and if he was astounded by his friend's behavior, Nuño González was deeply disillusioned by the king.

Much like the English noblemen who had revolted against King John in 1215 and forced the signing of Magna Carta, the Castilian rebels had real, substantive grievances about the way royal government was functioning—or malfunctioning. The new laws (*Fuero real*), which the king had given to some towns from the mid-1250s, were—they said—oppressive, while the abuse of the system of wardship was depriving them of their inheritances. Taxes, they protested, should be collected less frequently; they had in fact been doubled at the Cortes of Burgos in 1269, partly in order to subsidize the push to claim the imperial title. Royal officials were doing harm across the land, and the king was infringing on traditional land rights by building new towns across the regions of León and Galicia.

The program was cohesive and not merely a litany of private complaints. Nuño González, whom the king seems to have recognized as the most intelligent of the rebels, may have emphasized common grievances and downplayed the immediate problem—Alfonso's expensive quest for the empire—in order to strengthen the resistance. Alfonso defended his policies but agreed to all the rebels' demands with astonishing alacrity. In dreaming of the Holy Roman Empire he was tireless; the pope himself, he assured the rebels, had approved his candidacy, and many other electors had sent him letters of support. His sense of urgency mounted as his ambitions melted away. When the rebels returned with an amplified set of grievances, Alfonso acceded quickly to their demands. Yet the friendship was not yet healed. Nuño González and the other aristocrats were evidently suspicious of the king's real intentions and now took the risky decision to head into exile in the kingdom of Granada. Here, the chronicler—anxious to undermine the legitimacy of the rebellion—lapses into stereotype; the noblemen, we read, left a trail of robbery and pillage as they rode south.

More interesting is the claim that one person alone is able to slow them down: Queen Yolant. The role of queens as open or secret negotiators was significant in medieval Iberia, and Yolant seems to have had considerable diplomatic skills. As daughter of Jaume I of Aragon, Yolant had particularly important connections, and she had successfully encouraged him to help put down the Mudéjar Rebellion in Murcia in 1264. After his clandestine conversations with Jaume in Burgos several years earlier, Nuño González was naturally inclined to listen to her. When the rebels' messengers arrived in Burgos, the chronicle states, "the queen kept them for two days so that they would not talk to the king, hoping to bring an agreement between the king and the aristocrats." A truce, if not a permanent agreement, was reached, allowing the rebels safe passage to the frontier.

At this point in the *Chronicle of Alfonso* X, the narrator includes an extraordinary source, a detailed account of messages sent from the king to the individual rebels. They appear to be transcriptions of letters—the contemporary who composed this section of the chronicle clearly had written evidence at hand—but they have also been read as transcriptions, perhaps elaborated after the event, of oral statements delivered to the aristocrats. They offer a rich insight into the tenor of communication between the king and the rebels. A collective message, preceding the individualized ones, accuses the aristocrats of having failed to come to the aid of Fernando de la Cerda while Alfonso was in Murcia, of having confronted him near Lerma, of having not answered his proposals properly after the meeting at the Hospital de Burgos, and in general of showing ingratitude for the king's favors in "raising you and marrying you off, and granting you inheritances."

In addressing Don Nuño, Alfonso's messengers rehearse the long trajectory of their particular friendship, expressing the king's incredulity: "You received great honor and favor from the king, more than any man of your kind ever received in Spain." When Alfonso was just a child, the letter continues, Don Nuño had been raised with him. When he was infante, he had taken him into his household and favored him against his father's wishes. After the conquest of Murcia, he had granted Don Nuño property, and later he had defended him against his enemies in the Haro family, as well as granting him the tenancy of Seville and many other sources of income. "Don Nuño," the letter protested, "you know that so large were the favors and honor that the king did for you that you came to have three hundred knights as vassals—the best in Castile, León and Galicia."

The letter appeals to shared emotional and political values. Don Nuño's attempt to reach an alliance with the king of Granada is an egregious violation of principle because Muhammad I had broken his word as a vassal of Alfonso X: "You know that the king of Granada and his Moors are enemies of God, of the faith, of the king, and of all the hidalgos of Castile and León—there is no one who does not have a dead relative—and you wish to do the king disservice precisely with the man who has lied and broken the pacts and agreements he had with him. So," the letter concluded threateningly, "you will see what is coming to you from this."

Undaunted, Nuño González and the other rebels reached an agreement with the sick and aging Muslim king. They promised to work to ensure that Alfonso adhered to the terms of the Treaty of Alcalá de Benzaide (1265), which included a promise to stop supporting the rebellious governors of Málaga and Guadix. If he did not do so, they were to provide military aid to Granada against all enemies. We grant, they added, "that we shall be friends for always to you and your sons and your grandchildren and those who may descend from you." They in turn were given assurances of military assistance if Alfonso confiscated their possessions or broke the laws of the land. Having signed the agreement, the rebels headed into the city of Granada, the last bastion of Islamic power in Spain, where they were given food and lodging. In late January 1273, the Muslim king died; the rebels then moved quickly to promote his son's claims to the throne.

Faced with this betrayal, Alfonso again delegated responsibilities to his queen. Throughout February and March 1273, Yolant was actively involved in talks with the rebels, along with her brother Sancho (archbishop of Toledo) and son Fernando de la Cerda, promising that Nuño González's possessions would be untouched if he returned to Castile.

But on the chessboard of Iberia, many players were involved. The new king of Granada, Mohammed II (r. 1273–1302), now moved another piece: he spoke to Don Nuño, encouraging him to send his son Juan Núñez to offer Alfonso some land in the kingdom of Granada. In return, he was to end his support for the rebellious Muslim governors. Alfonso, however, responded with a set of ambitious demands, sending Mohammed a letter requesting the port cities of Algeciras, Tarifa, and Málaga. This, he asserted, would cancel out payment of tribute money for ten years. Understandably refusing to countenance the offer, Mohammed rejected the Castilian king's terms. Adopting a more militant tone, Alfonso lashed out at the rebels, condemning their "pride and madness" and contrasting them with the men who had continued loyally by his side.

Somewhere among the olive fields, on the hilly road between Córdoba and Granada, two men met. At the urging of his advisers, the young prince Fernando de la Cerda had sent the master of the military order of Calatrava to talk with the rebels. On his way, the master was approached by one of the rebels, who said he "came to him as a friend, not as an emissary of the others, and he spoke to the master about their friendships." The other aristocrats and the king of Granada, he reported, were planning an attack on Castile. The master rode ahead; we may imagine him spurring his horse onward as he headed quickly to the rebel encampment from where the attack was to be launched. The king would abide by the Treaty of Alcalá de Benzaide, the master announced; one of the key demands of the king of Granada had thus been met.

A truce was signed, and war was averted. The prince wrote to his father, imagining he had done well. But the king was not pleased. Instead, he sensed the looming specter of another betrayal. It was time to write directly, and openly, to his son.

7

FATHER

If Saturn and Mars are joined in the fifth house, harm
will come to children.
—YEHUDA BEN MOSÉ, *BOOK OF CROSSES*, 19

"I SAW THE LETTER THAT YOU SENT ME," ALFONSO WROTE TO
his seventeen-year-old son, Fernando de la Cerda, in late
May or early June 1273. Even before he opened it, he continued,
he had been feeling unwell with a cold and slight fever. But he
could not believe that Fernando had credulously listened to the
masters of the military orders of Uclés and Calatrava. Beware
false advisors, he entreated him.

In Alfonso's view, the rebel nobles were behaving out of aggressive self-interest; after having been treated like kings, they
were trying to squeeze all they could from the realm—even
threatening to support Abu Yusuf, the emir of Morocco. Alfonso
VIII, the king's grandfather, had triumphed at Las Navas de Tolosa in 1212 over a greater enemy, he reminded his son, and had
lost at the battle of Alarcos in 1195 only because of the

cowardice of the Haro family. The king admonished the prince not to remove his support for the Muslim governors of Málaga and Guadix. "Don Fernando, when a man is harmed, it is no marvel, but when he does it with his own hand, this is the greatest injury of all." As for the rebels, he observed, Don Nuño González de Lara had lost everything in his madness: "People say he is the most intelligent of them all, but he did not thank God for the good He did for him, and rather than serving me loyally with all the status and honor I gave him, he managed instead to lose it all—so you can see exactly how clever he is. Besides, he comes from a lineage that has always lost everything they had. That is why they all died in misfortune."

As for the lords of Haro and Castro, he remarked, neither man was especially clever. Besides, he told his son, "you have three good men for every one of them, and better than they are, not even counting the men on the frontier." It would have been wiser to attack Granada when you had the chance, Alfonso stated, and to have launched a pincer movement. If the prince were to make a serious mistake now, it would be impossible to fix in the future.

This remarkable message from father to son found the prince at a critical moment in his political apprenticeship. Soon after his much heralded wedding to Blanche in Burgos in 1269, Fernando had begun to take on important roles in governing his father's realms. Alfonso had increasingly entrusted him with the task of representing the crown in the kingdom of León. The young prince, still only fourteen, had traveled through the city of León itself in early July 1270 and may have admired the progress on the new Gothic cathedral and its stained glass windows. By the feast day of Saint James, July 25, he had reached the pilgrimage center of Santiago de Compostela. If Fernando was seeking the saint's protection, he must also have been conscious of making the royal presence visible in a corner of Spain to which, surprisingly, his father never once traveled. The following year, while Alfonso traveled to Murcia, Fernando was busily engaged in administrative business in the northwest of Castile. His more recent role as co-negotiator with the rebel nobles alongside his mother, Queen Yolant, was a significant, and particularly delicate, extension of this apprenticeship. As his health deteriorated, Alfonso was planning for the future, intent on raising a son who could maneuver on the political chessboard.

The king's tone oscillates between firmness and sensitivity. His irritation at what he perceives as Fernando's naivety is palpable, but he is also encouraging, empowering his son, exhorting him to remain strong. Fernando had clearly shown initiative—perhaps too much for his father's peace of mind. Achieving the difficult balance between a son's nascent independence and his need to take proper advice may be a concern for many fathers of teenage boys as they move toward adulthood, but more was at stake here: the stability of the kingdom itself. Alfonso's approach, in light of the high tension that surrounded the negotiations, is a model of tact and diplomacy. The king who emerges in this message to his son is politically adept and emotionally intelligent. The evidence undercuts the image, developed in less reliable parts of the royal chronicle, of a choleric and temperamental ruler. We see a man patient in his dealings with Fernando de la Cerda and with the rebels, one more inclined to caution than to conflict.

The prince's apprenticeship quickly bore fruit. To the king's delight, Fernando de la Cerda and Yolant handled the final negotiations with the rebels in the early summer of 1273 with extraordinary success. Caught in a paralyzing impasse and still unable to begin his journey to claim the long-hunted imperial title, Alfonso had delegated responsibilities to his wife and son, sending them to Córdoba in June with a set of diplomatic guidelines. The mission was an unqualified triumph, and Fernando, soon to turn eighteen, retained his role on the frontier until early 1274. Yolant, too, was prominent in the peace talks, once again proving herself a skilled negotiator. According to the chronicle, "She resolved it better than the king had ordered." Although this passage may have been consciously written to celebrate the young prince's gradual rise to power and Yolant's role at his side, Alfonso appears to have been thrilled: "He thanked the queen as much as he possibly could, because he knew that she had worked so hard in resolving the matter. While beforehand he trusted her greatly as a wife and as someone he had raised as a daughter, he now trusted her much more because she had resolved these matters so well and so much to his service, for he was more pleased and held it as a greater honor than if he had resolved it himself."

As for the prince, Alfonso felt a glow of fatherly pride: "He also let the infante Fernando, his son, know that he was very grateful because he had known how to resolve these matters so well. While before he trusted in him as a son whom he loved deeply in his heart, he trusted in him much more because he had served him and helped him, and knew how to set straight the treaty that bad advisors had made him grant earlier."

Thirteenth-hour problems were carefully diffused. The rebel leader Nuño González de Lara agreed to return to Castile, reenter the king's service, and travel with him on his quest for the imperial title—on the condition that the king endow him with a company of 1,000 knights. Not impressed, Alfonso impatiently dismissed this extravagant request, along with other new demands from the rebel camp. But by the end of 1273, an agreement was reached. Don Nuño and the other aristocrats, alongside the king of Granada, rode out of exile to Córdoba "in honor of the queen and the prince," then on to Seville, where Alfonso X knighted Mohammed II and made him his vassal. Over the coming year, the Wise

King made exhaustive preparations for his journey northward. He summoned a meeting of the Cortes in Burgos in March 1274 to gather funds for the journey. From Seville to Asturias, supply ships laden with wheat, barley, wine, and other foods set sail for Marseilles. Other goods were sent on by land, packed onto horses and mules. In a remarkable sign of faith, Nuño González de Lara was entrusted with the military position of *adelantado de la frontera* (governor of the frontier). Arrangements were made for the infante Fernando to be entrusted with the regency in his father's absence; he accompanied Alfonso to a further meeting of the Cortes at Zamora, in June and July. But after the king left his realms at the end of the year, father and son would never see each other again.

What kind of father was Alfonso? Did he find joy in the experience of fatherhood, when the world turned against him, or did he view his children more coldly, as an instrument of political power? The popular imagination often views medieval parents—especially fathers—as distant and authoritarian figures with little emotional engagement with their children. Even some scholarly experts on the medieval family have had a pessimistic view of fathers, suggesting—wrongly—that their role as parents was limited to the reproductive act. The evidence for the Wise King's most private family emotions is often very limited, and at times we can only speculate. Yet the sources do suggest that his emotional world was richer, more complex, and more loving than the stereotype would suggest.

Alfonso's great legal-philosophical work, the *Siete partidas*, takes fathers' affection for their children for granted. One section of the work dealing at length with child care (Book 2, title 7) is embedded into a larger text that has been seen as a virtual "mirror for princes," designed to teach the ruler ideal modes of behavior. It begins by presenting the king as actively involved in raising his lawful children, the infantes, whom kings should love, we read, "because they spring from them, and are, as it were, members of their own bodies," and because they want their children to perform good deeds after their own deaths. "King Solomon said that it was a source of great praise and exceeding honor to a father to have a wise and true son." It is logical that royal children be raised with great care and understanding—after all, even animals are able to do this: "All animals which have young naturally exert themselves to rear them and provide them with what is necessary, as far as they can do so, each according to his kind."

A typical medieval father was likely to have been deeply engaged in the life of his child. In Alfonso's century, it was generally believed that men contained greater heat than women and that this heat might determine the sex of the child, the right side of the womb, like the right male testicle, was associated with conception of male children because it was held to be closer to the warm blood of the liver. Conversely, if a seed from the right part of the testicles should fall into the left-hand side of the womb, an effeminate male would be conceived. On the other hand, childbirth was usually a moment restricted to women: midwives, neighbors, or servants. In the *Cantigas de Santa María*, there are two scenes of childbirth, and in each case, we see only the mother and the midwives, who are barefoot and dressed in short, sleeveless robes. There is no sign of a husband.

However, the father soon took on an important role in raising his child. Many fathers in the upper echelons of society—Alfonso X among them—had a hand in the choice of a wet nurse. For the king himself, wet nurses should be "well-bred, healthy, handsome, belong to good families, have good habits," and (in line with his growing conviction that anger should be restrained) be able to control their temper: "Where they are not bad tempered, they can rear children more affectionately, and with greater kindness; which is something that children have much need of in order to grow rapidly; for they are frightened by derision and violence, and, for this reason, do not thrive, and contract from this source illness or death."

Like other medieval fathers, Alfonso would have been deeply invested in ensuring that his children survived the precarious first few years. Infant mortality was extremely high in this period; perhaps one-third to one-half of all children died in infancy. The Wise King had already experienced this intense personal tragedy at least once: in the Museum of Medieval Fabrics at the monastery of Las Huelgas, near Burgos, is the sleeveless robe of an unknown little child of his, worked in blue and white and lined with animal skin. One of the *Cantigas de Santa María* tells the heartbreaking tale of a mother who takes her little boy to a church dedicated to the Virgin Mary so that she might protect him from misfortune. The child, eating a piece of bread, runs up to the statue of the Christ Child with his mother and asks, "Do you want a bite?" The accompanying illustration shows him on tiptoes, reaching up to Jesus with the piece of bread in hand, while the Virgin and Child smile down indulgently. Mary then tells her son, "Tell him without hesitation not to be afraid but ask him to dine with you where there is always singing and pleasure and be rid of the cursed devil, condemned for his wickedness." The Christ Child tells the little boy, "You will eat with me tomorrow in Heaven." The little boy's mother takes him home, where—we see in the image—a loving father takes him delightedly into his arms. The child then dies the next day and enters straight into paradise.

In isolation, this tale might seem to suggest that mothers were more emotionally involved in the survival of infant children. But across Europe, miracle tales often provide evidence of the power of fathers' emotion, and in the *cantigas* there is no mistaking the trauma and anxiety of fathers when their children have accidents. A girl, we hear, lived in Elche, in the majority-Muslim southeast of the peninsula with her Christian family. "The girl went to drink from the irrigation ditch and fell in and died soon after. Her father sighed and uttered 'woe is me' / many times in grief for her." The accompanying miniature shows him lifting her limp and lifeless body out of the water, helped by some of his neighbors. In a similar disaster, a couple on their way to the Marian shrine at Salas (in Asturias) lose their child in a raging river, when their horse stumbles as it crosses the torrent. The images show the father hunched over, grief stricken, as he looks in vain for his child, the mother holding her head in her hands as she follows him. A third song identifies one traumatized father quite specifically: Diego Sánchez, a knight who lived in the city of Segovia. His son had been playing on top of a very tall building and fell head first onto the street below. The knight and his wife run desperately to pick up their child's body, assuming he is already dead, but instead they find him frolicking and laughing, excitedly telling them how the Virgin has saved him from being crushed like a lump of salt.

It is usually difficult to determine the author of individual songs. But one *cantiga* revolving around the tragic death of a small child was likely composed by Alfonso himself. "I shall tell a miracle which happened in Tudia and shall put it with the others which fill a great book," he declares at the beginning of song 347; "I made a new song about it with music of my own and no one else's." There is also a happy ending in the case of another deeply personal song in Alfonso's "great book," which tells of the nearly fatal illness of Alfonso's own father, Fernando. He "could not sleep at all nor eat the slightest thing, and many large worms came out of him, for death had already conquered his life without

Como o menino córou a o pdre e a madre como o grám S. aj.

C. leuaron o menino a aegreia de scã õ. cõ muytas candeas.

A child is miraculously unharmed after falling from a rooftop: *Cantigas de Santa María*, no. 282, *Códice de Florencia* (Florentine Codex), Biblioteca Nazionale Centrale di Firenze, Ms. B.R.20. Reproduced courtesy of Archivo Oronoz.

much struggle." He was miraculously healed after his mother took him on pilgrimage to Oña, becoming stronger and healthier than ever before.

"Is there anything more precious than a son, especially an only son, into whom we would pour, not only all our riches but also, if it were possible, our very life?" the sixteenth-century humanist Erasmus later asked. The young prince Fernando de la Cerda was not Alfonso's only son—Sancho, Pedro, Juan, and Jaime were all children or adolescents in the early 1270s—but since he was the eldest and heir to the throne, the king naturally poured his soul into raising him. It is easy to imagine him showering his son with toys like those we find in late-thirteenth-century England: metal toy soldiers or something like the little toy castle made for his English namesake, Prince Alphonso, a son of Edward I, in 1279. He surely introduced the *infante* Fernando to the intricacies of chess or the excitement of hunting. As his son grew from infancy into childhood, he would also have taken a sharp interest in the boy's education. Given the tradition of works written by fathers for their sons in medieval Europe—among them Walter of Henley's *Treatise on Husbandry* (in the thirteenth century) and Geoffrey Chaucer's *Astrolabe* (in the fourteenth)—as well as Alfonso's own intellectual sharpness, he probably gave some informal instruction to Fernando, perhaps in history, medicine, or astronomy, as well as in rulership. He would have understood this responsibility as an extension of his fatherly affection, actively helping to choose a good tutor to complement his own lessons. It is likely that Fernando's tutor was Jofré de Loaysa, once Queen Yolant's tutor, suggesting that both parents may well have made the decision.

There is no doubt that medieval fathers could be authoritarian; we should not oversentimentalize childhood in this period. In his message to Fernando in 1273, the king's tone had been kind but firm. Hierarchy within the family is as natural and unquestioned as strength of affection. In late medieval culture, this presumption shaped all written communications between fathers and sons. In the opening greetings of their own letters, sons write from a position of humble inferiority, requesting favors from their fathers. Fathers typically greet their sons more laconically, addressing their children with the same brevity they might use to address their servants. The second *partida*—the "virtual

mirror"—insists that boys should learn "to love and fear their father and mother, and their eldest brother, who are their natural
lords." Mirrors for princes had underscored the importance of
obedience, especially to fathers, for many centuries.

Discipline, too, was closely allied to fatherly love. Alfonso's
contemporaries felt that fathers needed to instill discipline in
their children from a young age to preempt the dangers of adolescence, but this was seen as effective precisely because it was born
of affection. Bartholomew the Englishman devoted a whole
chapter on fatherhood in his work *De proprietabus rerum* (c. 1245)
and underscored the importance of discipline. A father might ed-
ucate his son with words, he wrote, "but does not hesitate to correct him with beatings; he places him under the care of tutors,
and lest [the boy] become proud, he does not show the son a
cheerful countenance. . . . The more he is loved by the father, the
more diligently he is instructed by him."

Yet commentators also insisted that it was essential to avoid
cruelty. In the words of Vincent de Beauvais, children are in their
parents' charge "not like slaves, but like sons." Medieval fathers
did not have the power of life and death over their children or
other family members. Alfonso placed limits on the kinds of punishment that were legally acceptable. Fathers without the pity
and compassion that should naturally accompany parenthood,
who punished their sons with extreme cruelty, were seen as horrific aberrations to be treated accordingly. If the father's punishment of his child were to result in accidental death, he was to be
banished to "some island, or some other secure place from which
he can never escape, and is also deprived of all his property." He
might alternatively be given a life sentence to work on the buildings of the king as a penal slave, performing duties such as physical labor on his castles. If he were to use weapons or drugs to kill
his child, a more spectacular punishment awaited: he was to be

publicly whipped, placed in a leather sack with a dog, a cock, a serpent, and an ape, and tossed into the nearest sea or river.

The aberration, however, proves the rule. Duty and affection in father-child relations were envisioned as reciprocal. There was an expectation that love invested in a child would be repaid later in life. When children became older, it was hoped that they would provide for their parents. In one widely told medieval story, during a particularly cold night, a father asks his son to take a horse blanket out to his grandfather, who is sleeping in the stable. He is astonished when his son returns with only half the blanket and understandably asks what he has done. The boy replies that he is saving it for his father's old age.

It was in the end a daughter, and not a son, who would prove most loyal to Alfonso in his own old age. Of all his personal relationships, that with his first-born child, Beatriz (b. 1244)—fruit of his love affair with Mayor Guillén—is among the most compelling. Father-daughter relations, as one recent historian of the medieval family has observed, embodied the most extreme inequalities within the family, in terms of gender, age, and power, but this very inequality sometimes made for easier, freer relationships than those between father and son, which were often riddled with rivalry. The balance of power was tipped even further because she had been born out of wedlock. Beatriz is in some respects an elusive figure: the sources say little about her personality. However, it is difficult to avoid the impression that a genuine bond of affection developed between Alfonso and his eldest daughter.

Beatriz was probably raised partly at the royal court and partly in the lands belonging to the Guzmán family in northern Castile. One scholar has identified her as the young woman with hennaed hands and gold bangle bracelets who appears in one of the miniatures in Alfonso's *Book of Games*, winning at a game of chess she is playing with a blonde princess (perhaps one of her "legitimate" half sisters). In another miniature, the scholar speculates, she is learning about chess tactics from her mother, Doña Mayor. Here she is wearing a transparent dress with ruffled leggings. It is far from certain that this is indeed the king's daughter. However, we do have some indication that she grew to become a beautiful young woman—and indeed remained beautiful well into middle age. Not even Alfonso's Franciscan confessor, Juan Gil de Zamora, was able to keep his eyes off her, commenting in the 1280s, by which time she was approaching the age of forty, that she was "blessed with an elegant body."

Like her young brothers and sisters, Beatriz would indeed have been initiated into chess, the game of kings, as part of her socialization. Girls' education, like boys', is the subject of careful reflection in the *Siete partidas*. Royal daughters, Alfonso stipulated, are to be treated with great diligence by their nurses and governesses. As soon as they are old enough, they should be taught to read "so that they may read the Hours properly and know how to read the Psaltery." They should be protected from yielding to anger, "for, in addition to the evil disposition which this indicates, it is the one thing in the world which most quickly induces women to commit sin." They, like their brothers, should also be raised to be "very well-bred in eating, drinking, and talking and in behavior and dress."

As he oversaw Beatriz's education, Alfonso may have remembered the ninth-century Holy Roman Emperor whose glory he so much wished to emulate: Charlemagne. While his sons learned horsemanship, war, and hunting, Charlemagne—according to his courtier and biographer Einhard—taught his girls "to familiarize themselves with cloth-making, and to handle distaff and spindle, that they might not grow indolent through idleness, and he fostered in them every virtuous sentiment." He, too, had been emotionally invested. "When his sons and his daughter died, he was not so calm as might have been expected from his remarkably strong mind, for his affections were no less strong, and moved him to tears." Alfonso would have been no less anxious to raise well-rounded and well-behaved girls. The *Cantigas de Santa María* suggest a concern with correcting flighty misbehavior, recounting the story of a pretty girl called Musa with a fondness for dancing and having fun. The miniaturist shows her swaying voluptuously in the garden, while people gaze on admiringly from the building above. She pulls herself together only after seeing a wondrous vision of the Virgin Mary, who tells her to "leave off mirth and play, pride and arrogance," and she rids herself of her bad habits shortly before being struck down with a fatal illness.

Having been born out of wedlock, Beatriz was certainly at a disadvantage. "Legitimate" children are sacred, states the fourth *Partida*, because they are conceived without sin; God loves and assists them and endows them with strength and power. In contrast, the offspring of a premarital or extramarital relationship had more difficulty in inheriting a father's property or status. But whatever legal principles might suggest, there was more tolerance for such children across medieval Europe than we might expect. The children of stable relationships (we should discard the outdated term "illegitimate" and the pejorative word "bastard") often developed strong and lasting emotional ties with their parents, married or not. Canon law ruled that a child born out of wedlock might be legitimized when his or her parents became married. In England, where common law did not allow this, the twelfth-century writer known as Glanvill suggested that a man might nonetheless legally grant land to his natural child, while in royal circles many natural children were well favored.

Henry I, who is believed to have had some twenty children outside marriage, was able to marry his daughter Sybil to the king of
the Scots.

In 1253, with the birth of Berenguela, his first daughter within
marriage, Alfonso had sought a similarly propitious match for the
young princess Beatriz, who was not yet nine years old. Tensions
had been running high in the previous years between Castile and
the kingdom to its west, Portugal. At the heart of the conflict was
a contest for the newly conquered territories in the south, the
Algarve, compounded by conflict within the Portuguese royal
family. The previous king of Portugal, Sancho I Capelo, who had
enjoyed the active support of the *infante* Alfonso before the Castilian king's accession, had been deposed by his brother. For the
new Portuguese king, confusingly called Afonso III, the ideal resolution to this conflict lay in a marriage alliance with the Wise
King, while for Alfonso X a treaty with the Portuguese might allow him to cement his control over the Algarve. In May 1253,
the two rulers had reached an agreement whereby the king of
Castile would enjoy temporary usufruct over this territory—ending when the heir of the Portuguese king reached the age of
seven. The agreement was sealed with Beatriz's hand in marriage.
At this moment, Beatriz was about nine years old. Afonso III was
entering his early forties.

For most medieval observers, the most acute problem was the
fact that, in 1253, Afonso III was still married. His first wife,
Matilde, countess of Boulogne, spent the remaining years of her
life vigorously pursuing her rights, appealing to the papacy for
support in recovering her dowry. Well into the 1260s, Alexander
IV continued to denounce the new marriage alliance as both big-
amous and incestuous (Beatriz and Afonso were related by four
degrees of consanguinity), adding an extra level of complication
to the Wise King's hunt for the imperial title.

To modern sensibilities, the age difference between the groom and his new bride is also striking. The *infanta* may not have lived with her new partner—or had sexual intercourse with him—until 1258 (it appears that their formal marriage ceremony took place in May that year); Afonso III, a great lover of women, kept up his relationship with some of his nine known mistresses long after his betrothal. But we may imagine that relationship was in many respects unequal. Dutifully fulfilling her obligations to bear children, Beatriz gave birth at least seven times by 1269, when she was twenty-five. The reproduction process was interrupted only by the king's old age and infirmity.

Yet, according to the ethical standards of the thirteenth century, the betrothal of a young princess was ordinarily seen as a morally acceptable, even admirable move. Some of the worst fathers in the late medieval imagination were those who possessively held on to their daughters. The "good" fathers of medieval romance, in contrast, looked beyond the moment and, reflecting on the future of their lineages, considered their responsibility to secure a good match for their daughters. The Wise King must have sent Beatriz to Portugal with a heavy heart; she and her mother, Mayor Guillén de Guzmán, had remained at the Castilian court long after his marriage to Queen Yolant, right up until the birth of Berenguela. Queen Beatriz appears, in a number of ways, to have thrived at the Portuguese royal court. By 1261 at the latest—and perhaps soon after the formal marriage ceremony three years earlier—Beatriz had her own palace in Lisbon and her own household officials: there are references to her *regueifeira* (responsible for making bread for the royal table) and her *copeiro* (responsible for the wine). In his testament of 1271, Afonso III affirmed that he trusted her more than anyone else in the world.

Beatriz's role was by no means restricted purely to childbearing and the domestic sphere. In Portugal, she also intervened in political affairs on a number of occasions, although the sources are sparse. Periodically, she returned to her Castilian homeland with her own first-born daughter, Branca. It is difficult to calibrate the balance of opportunism and affection in these years, but after the death of her mother (sometime before January 1264), she inherited the lordship of Alcocer east of Madrid, and through the early 1270s she can be traced actively managing this estate.

Given her mobility and her family origins, Beatriz was a natural intermediary between the Castilian and Portuguese courts and probably played a leading role in continuing negotiations over the Algarve. She seems certain to have been involved in the decision to send her six-year-old son Dinís to Alfonso's court in the *alcázar* of Seville in 1267. When, twelve years later, her husband died and her son threw off the shackles of her regency, Beatriz began a period of voluntary exile in Castile and would remain loyally at her father's side while, one by one, other family members abandoned him.

By mid-1274, during an unusual break in the tempest unfolding around him, Alfonso had begun to feel pride in the intelligence and political skill of his eldest daughter, Beatriz, and also in his eldest son, Fernando de la Cerda. With the noble revolt finally calmed, and with Fernando as regent, he had at last felt the confidence to make one last push for the long-coveted title of Holy Roman Emperor. This campaign took place on at least two levels, one cultural and the other physical. One key dimension was the promotion of Alfonso's credentials as "emperor of culture." With an eye to a broad audience of European readers, he had the famous *Alfonsine Tables*—a set of astronomical data revising the work of al-Zarkali, an eleventh-century Muslim astronomer from Córdoba, on the basis of observations painstakingly taken in Toledo between 1263 and 1272—translated into Latin with the help of his Italian collaborators, Pietro de Reggio and Egidio de Tebaldis. Manuscripts began to circulate across the continent.

The promotion of his imperial credentials in the cultural realm, however, and the diffusion of his most sophisticated work were not enough in the hunt for the title. Despite his infirmity, Alfonso was forced to travel in person. By Christmas, he had reached his father-in-law's court in Barcelona. After the festivities, Jaume I of Aragon recalled, the king of Castile announced that "he wished to visit the pope about the wrong the said pope had done to him in the matter of the Empire." Jaume remained hostile to the idea, undoubtedly irritated by Alfonso's pretensions. At the council of Lyons, Gregory X had declared that a German prince, Rudolf of Habsburg—who had promised to lead a crusade—should succeed to the title. Jaume advised him that "he should by no means go, because it was not fitting for him to go to a land so far away and, moreover, because he would have to cross the land of the king of France, whom he feared. And he did not wish to follow the advice that we had given him, and he went to see the pope."

Jaume's words suggest an awareness of Alfonso's failing health, but the Castilian king was unmoveable in his determination. Queen Yolant accompanied him as far as Perpignan along with courtiers, including Rabbi Todros ben Joseph Halevi Abulafia, who may have been serving as her personal physician. She then remained there with the rabbi, while Alfonso continued on to Beaucaire. In Cantiga de Santa María 235, one of his most intensely autobiographical songs, the king himself took up the story. On the road to see the pope, he writes, "he fell so gravely ill that they thought he would surely die from that affliction." In Montpellier, he "became so seriously ill that all the physicians there, each and every one, firmly believed that he was surely dead." It may have been due to Alfonso's ill health that the pope traveled as far as Beaucaire, on the banks of the Rhône, to meet him. Gregory arrived on May 10, 1275. Yet the meeting, so long awaited, proved fruitless. In a sequence of several meetings, the pope constantly rebuffed Alfonso. His dream was shattered, the hunt had failed, and the king's health was destroyed.

Yet much worse was to come. The king had been convinced that now that he had made peace with Don Nuño and the other noble rebels, the Marinid emir was unlikely to attack. But on May 13, an advance contingent led by Abu Yusuf's son Abu Zayan landed at Tarifa on the southernmost tip of Spain. After resting for several days to recover from the demands of being at sea, the army then raided inland, sending back booty and slaves in chains. The Andalusis were delighted, the Moroccan chronicle *Rawd al-Qirtas* reports; they had not enjoyed a major victory since before their devastating loss at Las Navas de Tolosa (1212).

Throughout the late spring, the young crown prince Fernando de la Cerda rode urgently across the length and breadth of Castile, flitting between León, Segovia, and Atienza, in preparation for the assault to come. He was in Madrid by June 23 and in Toledo by July 10. But the document that allows us to trace his presence there proved to be his last. Quite suddenly, on July 20, 1275, he passed away from an unknown illness while staying at the new town of Villa Real (much later, in the fifteenth century, renamed Ciudad Real).

Alfonso received the unspeakable news early in his journey back to Castile, if not in Beaucaire itself. Perhaps he was able to hold back his tears, or withdrew quietly into a private space to cry, as he was later to do when he believed that his much-less-beloved son Sancho had died. Some medieval writers felt disdain for men who wept at such news. But this kind of stoicism was no longer in vogue. It would not have been strange if Alfonso had broken down. Even his battle-hardened father-in-law, the aging Jaume I, writes that he felt "great anguish" at the premature death of the young prince, heir to the Castilian throne.

Fernando's young widow, Blanche, was left alone with one small boy and another on the way. Once certain to become queen, she now had to plan for the funeral and for a precarious life of fighting fruitlessly for the rights of her children, whose claims to the throne were immediately challenged by Fernando's seventeen-year-old brother, Sancho. For his part, Sancho moved swiftly into the power vacuum. The prince quickly established an alliance with the nobleman Lope Díaz de Haro, who saw a close relationship with Sancho as a means of avoiding the dominance of his family's great rivals, the Laras.

Behind the superficial impression of brotherly rivalries and family dysfunction was a deeper pattern of long-running tensions between powerful clans that often manipulated dynastic crises to their own advantage. Lope Díaz and the young Prince Sancho headed quickly for Córdoba and the frontier, hoping to establish a reputation for incisive action in defense of the realm. After Lope Díaz had been dispatched to the fortified town of Écija and Sancho had arrived in Seville—where he began to provision the fleet for a blockade of the strait—the Marinid leader Abu Yusuf retreated to his base at the port of Algeciras.

The body of the dead *infante* Fernando was dressed in a set of rich fabrics adorned with the royal arms and buried in the convent of Las Huelgas, where the king's sister Berenguela was already refurbishing a royal pantheon. These clothes survive to this day, having been hermetically sealed inside the tomb until the mid-twentieth century. At the convent's museum of medieval fabrics, the visitor can still see the dead prince's silk surcoat, emblazoned with rampant lions and castles, colored yellow (with dyer's rocket) and terracotta red (with dyer's madder). Above this, he had worn a tunic in the same colors and materials; on his head rested a cylindrical ceremonial bonnet, the heraldic castles of Castile set in blue glass beads against a field of red coral, the lions sewn with red silk against a background of pearls. Alongside the body had been placed the young man's sword—a simple, undecorated weapon, the only nonceremonial sword that survives from this era—and a very long sword belt, which six short years earlier may well have been a wedding gift.

There was little time for mourning. The emir had now completed the preparations for his assault. It landed in wave after wave on the beaches of Andalusia, as the Marinids set up camps from Tarifa to Algeciras. Abu Yusuf himself disembarked on August 16 and then headed quickly to meet the king of Granada in Algeciras. Here, the Muslim rulers were readied to carry out holy war against the "polytheists." While the king of Granada pillaged the territories around Jaén, the Marinids ravaged the lands of the Guadalquivir basin near Córdoba, Úbeda, and Baeza.

Gleefully, the Moroccan chronicler relates how the emir's troops spread out "like a flood, or a cloud of locusts": "There was no tree they did not cut down, no village they did not destroy, no flock they did not steal, no crops they did not burn." They killed all the men they encountered and took women and children captive. The number of prisoners grew "like the flooding of the Nile." The catastrophe provides the grim setting for a *cantiga* that relates how Abu Yusuf invaded "all the land of Seville" and how the Muslims burned village upon village. Shortly before the assault, a father loses his little son "whom he loved as much as his own life." The man is then forced to abandon the boy's burial when his village (Coria del Río) is attacked. Only a mysterious "lady" who protects the boy during the attack is able to revive him. Alfonso may not have written these lines, but in the fall of that terrible year, 1275, he surely could not have heard them without relapsing into grief.

The Moroccans then received news that Nuño González de Lara, under whom the king had placed his frontier troops, was preparing a counterassault. The Muslim chronicler betrays an uncharacteristic admiration for Don Nuño: the Christians were fortunate under his command, we read, for he was a devastating plague for the Muslim realms. The army he had summoned was as thick as black night or the waves of the sea. As the two forces faced each other on the battlefield near Écija, the Christian knights advanced rapidly, confident of victory. But the emir arose, says the *Rawd al-Qirtas*, and in a rousing speech called on his men to prepare for martyrdom and to enter paradise. They embraced each other, saying their farewells, and entered the fray, their hearts beating hard, death becoming sweet to them. Chanting the name of Allah aloud, they went into battle.

As the two armies met, nothing could be seen except the arrows plummeting down upon the Christians like red sparks. Blood dripped from swords as the heads of Christians were cut off and piled up. Abu Yusuf ordered them to be counted. There were 18,000, according to the chronicle. Among them was the head of Nuño González de Lara, which was then sent as a gruesome trophy to the king of Granada. Muhammad II responded gratefully to the emir but "lamented the death of Don Nuño, since he had done much to make him king." How much greater Alfonso's mourning may have been, as he wound his way down the Mediterranean coast, we can only imagine.

In the years to come, as he entered a state of deep melancholy, the Wise King would seek healing in many forms, not least through a frenzy of creativity. In one of the panels of *Cantiga 235*, Alfonso lies on a bed surrounded by courtiers and monks, some crying and holding their robes to their eyes to stem the flood of tears. The beautiful Virgin Mary, dressed in bridal white, appears before the king, carrying the baby Jesus, as he lies in his chamber. The little boy, supported gently by his mother, crawls playfully over the prostrate king's chest, reaching up toward his face.

8

HEALERS

If Saturn and Mars are joined in the first house, men will
fall ill from melancholy and demons.

—YEHUDA BEN MOSÉ, BOOK OF CROSSES, 19

ROKEN IN SPIRIT AND BODY, ALFONSO REACHED THE FRENCH
town of Montpellier, famed as a center of medicine, in August 1275. There, in the company of Yehuda Mosca (Yehuda ben
Moshe ha-Kohen) and other Jewish court doctors, he collapsed,
becoming so seriously ill that all the physicians there believed he
was certain to die. The cumulative effect of a sequence of unbear-
able disasters and perhaps the rigors of the journey likely accelerated his cancer. He would recover, resuming his journey south to
face the Muslim invaders, but the journey brought further trage-
dies: the deaths of his nephew Alfonso Manuel and, after he
reached Perpignan, his younger daughter Leonor. Never had
there been a more acute need for a cure for melancholy, a more
urgent need for healing, a more pressing need to make sense of
the world. From suffering was born new cultural energy.

The Chronicle of Alfonso X tells us blithely that, having returned to Castile, the king was "delighted" at the way in which
his oldest surviving son, Sancho, had held down the fort. But this
account belongs to a long section of the narrative designed to
glorify the young prince. The emotional realities were quite different. Any fleeting sense of relief quickly gave way to a sense
that the rug had been pulled from under his feet, that his power
had been usurped, as in the 1240s it had been for his friend King
Sancho of Portugal: "When he entered Castile, all the people of
the lands came to meet him and told him 'A very good day to
you, lord.' However, believe you me, King don Sancho in Portugal was never betrayed so vilely. For the greater part of the nobles
conspired, as I know, to throw him out of the kingdom so that it
would belong to them, and they could divide it among
themselves."

Incapacitated by illness and grief, Alfonso now faced the
frightening specter of civil unrest as the infante assertively staked
his claim to the throne. Even the emphatically pro-Sancho narrative of the royal chronicle implies that Alfonso vacillated as to
whether to nominate the prince as his heir (a decision effectively
forced upon him). The text roundly ignores the competing claims
of Fernando's children, the infantes de la Cerda. Behind the
scenes, two aggressive camps were ruthlessly promoting their
candidate. On the one hand, the Haro family and a significant
sector of the Castilian-Leonese elite (including the infante
Fadrique, members of the Cameros family, and some bishops and
towns) supported Sancho. On the other, the Lara family vehemently supported the little infantes de la Cerda, over whom they
had been granted physical custody. The infantes also received
vocal support from their French mother's family—specifically
from the new king, Philippe III of France (r. 1270–1285)—with
whom the Laras had been cultivating close relations over the

previous few years. These conflicting claims would remain an explosive element in Spanish politics for another generation. The Wise King, debilitated and defeated, found himself caught in the crossfire. These issues may have been hammered out at a sequence of meetings about the succession in Toledo early in 1276. By the time the Cortes met in April, however, Alfonso had made up his mind: he ordered all those present to pay homage to the infante Sancho and recognize him as heir.

That summer, Jaume I of Aragon passed away as he struggled to maintain control of the city of Valencia. On June 28, already weakened by sickness, Jaume had left the town of Xàtiva, arriving the same day in nearby Alzira. Here, he writes, "our illness increased and worsened, so much so that, thanks to our Lord Jesus Christ, in our good and full memory, we confessed many times to the bishops, the Preachers, and to the Friars Minor, with great contrition for our sins and with many tears." On July 27, he died, having bequeathed his kingdom to his son, and the new king of Aragon, Pere III, successfully reclaimed Valencia.

Alfonso's own health remained precarious. In September, he headed to Navarre in an attempt to diffuse the anger of King Philippe III and fend off a possible French invasion. Ground down by stress, he fell desperately ill in the town of Vitoria and was obliged to remain there until March 1277. As he lay bedbound, he commissioned a new and lavishly illustrated edition of the *Book of Stones* (*Lapidario*). In the codex, which survives in the library of the Escorial, near Madrid, the Castilian text is interwoven with illuminated medallions in which a wise man is giving instructions for the correct extraction of the stone. His assistant is entrusted with carrying this out at a moment when the stars are aligned in such a way as to activate its properties as powerfully as possible. In the brilliant creative vision that underlies each page of the *Book of Stones*, we glimpse a sustained attempt to transcend pain and to seek healing through the power of intellect and imagination.

Retrospective diagnoses are dangerous. Some have suggested that during the mid-1270s, Alfonso was suffering from "depression," a term that did not circulate widely until the eighteenth century (although the emotion might certainly have been experienced). One recent biographer has speculated that both Alfonso and his brother Manuel may have suffered depressive episodes as early as the mid-1260s in the wake of the *mudéjar* uprising in Andalusia; others have proposed that the king suffered the depression said to be typical of cancer patients.

It is certainly not hard to find evidence of plaintive lyrics from this period that Alfonso himself may have written. In one such lyric, the author laments the loss of all joy in his life: I can no longer be happy, he says, with the song of birds, with love, work, or warfare. Dreaming of a world beyond suffering, he imagines himself freed from pain and suffering, out on the ocean, in a "fine galleon / that will take me quickly away / from the hell of these fields / where the scorpions nest. For inside, I feel their sting."

While the fields have been read as political battlegrounds and the scorpions as rebels and turncoats, there is no reason not to see the lyric as an expression of a more generalized pain. The dreams of escape, of abandoning responsibilities and care, have deep resonance:

> *I will bring a boat,*
> *And I will go to the waterfront*
> *Selling oil and flour*
> *And I will flee from the venom*
> *Of the scorpion, for I*
> *Know no other medicine.*

Once I was a sailor, writes the poet. I will return to the ocean and travel like a merchant in search of a new land where I cannot be hurt. Another poem associated with Alfonso also calls out tearfully for the helping hand of a heavenly mother: "Take some pity on me / for my eyes like rivers / run since the day I saw you; brothers and cousins and uncles, I've lost them all."

Unfortunately, we can attribute neither text definitively to the king, and it would be a mistake to assume that these lyrics are straightforwardly autobiographical. Cultural pressures led the king away from dwelling on his own sadness: in medieval times, melancholy was widely—though not universally—perceived as a vice. Yet the poignancy of the later songs to Holy Mary is unmistakable.

Often, in *cantigas* from these years, the transcendence of pain, both emotional and physical, becomes a running thread. How, he asks as he recalls his illness in Vitoria, can I but delight in praising the works of this lady, whom I have always loved, who assists me in my worries and takes away my sorrows. Have mercy, have mercy, and come to the aid of your troubadour, in such great illness and pain as your admirer now suffers; if you do so, I will be cured, if only it be your will.

Alfonso was surely experiencing an entirely normal response to personal crisis, suffering not from mental disease or from clinical depression but from grief, desperation, and a closely intertwined pattern of physical decline. All this he now alchemized into creative, artistic brilliance. Through a frenzy of creation, fed in large measure by the search to overcome his own suffering, he enhanced and deepened the Castilian Renaissance of the thirteenth century, overseeing the production of beautifully illuminated luxury editions of works such as the *Book of Stones*, the *Books of Astrological Knowledge* (*Libros de saber de astrología*) and other spectacular scientific compilations, a new universal history (the *Grande e general estoria*), and, above all, the *Cantigas de Santa María*.

The king's Franciscan confessor, Juan Gil de Zamora, writing around the year 1278, leaves no doubt as to Alfonso's artistry as a musician: "Like David," he writes, "he composed many beautiful songs in praise of the glorious Virgin, set to suitable sounds and appropriate music." It is hard to avoid the sense that Alfonso's writing was itself a therapeutic exercise, catalyzed by the experience of pain. He may have shared the sentiments of the fourteenth-century English aristocrat Henry, duke of Lancaster (c. 1310–1361), expressed in his *Book of Holy Medicine* (*Livre de seyntz medicines*) (1354): to speak of his internal, spiritual wounds, "or simply to think and write about them," gives relief from the pain. An illustrious contemporary, the Italian Renaissance humanist Francesco Petrarca (1304–1374), referred jokingly to the "disease of writing" that had begun to afflict his society. Is it incurable, he wondered, like other malignant disorders? Is it contagious? But for Petrarch, as for every prolific writer, including Alfonso, it was surely not a disease but a remedy and a cure. Musical composition, too, may also have provided the king with a source of healing. Long ago, the Greeks and Romans had given philosophical form to what, for many of us, is no more than a powerful intuition, arguing that music—like the Muses' other creations, including poetry, singing, and dancing—is essential to restoring the personal harmonies whose disruption is manifested in disease. These ideas had been transferred into the realm of actual medical practice in the ninth- and tenth-century Arabic world and then transmitted to al-Andalus.

It is difficult to determine which of the *cantigas* Alfonso wrote himself—though he clearly supervised the production as a whole—or even what it means to "compose" such a song: To write it from scratch? To adapt it from existing stories or lyrics? To set it to music? We know that the king was surrounded by songwriters from as far away as Galicia, northern Italy, Languedoc, and Aquitaine, and a number of them were likely involved in the creative process. However, we can intuit that the king's grave health problems heightened his devotion to Mary, and it is possible that he had an active hand in the majority of the songs, which have a striking stylistic cohesion. Alfonso claims explicitly, in the lyrics, to have composed both words and music for four songs.

The first of these appears to be an early piece: a delightful comic tale about a beautiful young bride who, while her husband is away on a long military campaign, becomes the object of a local knight's affections. The knight becomes mad with passion for the girl and sends a female servant as a go-between, bearing as a present a gift of some fine shoes of Cordovan leather. The bride honorably rejects them but, in the face of "a thousand arguments," finally relents and tries to put one on, whereupon she can neither get her foot into it nor take it off. It remains stuck there for a year and a month, "for the shoe clung so tightly to her foot that although two or three people tried, they could never pry it off." Only when the husband returns and magnanimously expresses his pleasure that the Virgin Mary had protected her virtue can the girl's foot be extracted.

The other three songs that Alfonso claims entirely as his own, on the other hand, seem to date from later in the king's life and are cut from a very different cloth. All three—surely responding to his bitter personal experience—relate to illness and/or emotional pain. The Virgin performed a miracle, the king writes in one case, which he shall tell us about. "I set it into melody and verse, because it delighted me so." Once there was a maiden who loved Mary so deeply, he continues, that she scorned the world, but because of her asceticism, she fell ill. The girl lay for a month in bed without being able to eat or speak. The miniatures show her wrapped in a red blanket, blonde hair falling over a richly embroidered pillow, shunning the spoon that her mother gently brings toward her mouth. Whenever people nearby spoke of the Virgin Mary, Alfonso writes, the girl placed her hand over her heart. Nothing could be done for the girl's physical health, and she passed away.

In the images, we see her father wipe his tears away with his robe, while her mother holds her hands to her head in grief. Convinced that the girl had been poisoned, they have an autopsy performed, and when her heart is cut open—the rather graphic illustration shows a large group of astonished family, friends, and physicians looking on, wide-eyed and incredulous—they find engraved upon it an image of the Virgin. "For this, they and all the people gathered there gave great praise to Holy Mary, saying, 'Blessed be you, Mother of Our Lord, for your great loyalty has no equal, nor ever will." In Alfonso's tale, there are echoes of Saint Paul's notion that the image of God's law should be interiorized, inscribed on the tablet of the human heart—which might bear witness to spiritual conscience—rather than being carved on tablets of stone (2 Corinthians, 3.2–3). Through physical pain and the curtains of individual grief, the healing light of heavenly grace has been transmitted to a whole community.

Mary's healing powers are described with an almost Gothic sense of horror in another miracle, which, Alfonso says, "I set to rhyme and music." To modern eyes and ears, the tale might appear to describe a stroke victim. Once, the king recounts, a minstrel in Lombardy foolishly mimicked the gestures of a beautiful statue of the peerless Virgin. In a culture that blurred the division between the physical statue and the saintly figure herself, this was a grave offence. Late-medieval Europe abounds in stories of holy images that come to life—such as the account of a fifteenth-century Italian child who saw the Virgin come down from a wall to clean an abandoned prison—and that have the power to carry out miraculous acts of healing. Angered by the insult to his mother, Jesus then caused the monk's mouth and chin to twist up beside his ear. His neck and arm writhed so violently that he could not remain standing and fell to the ground. Bystanders lifted up the minstrel and carried him into the church, where they prayed that day and into the next. At that point, Mary straightened his face and arm and made him well. The observers were awed, spellbound in reverence. Spiritual sickness, physical affliction, and the spectacle of healing serve again to bring light into the world.

Most moving, because of its resonance with the king's own personal experience of child mortality, is the fourth of the group of *cantigas* that Alfonso explicitly says he composed: an account of a good woman who lived by the banks of the Guadiana River in the kingdom of Seville. The woman had been unable to conceive a child, the king says, until she went on pilgrimage to the sanctuary of Saint Mary at Tudia (today, Tentudia) in the foothills of the remote Sierra Morena. She knelt before the altar, crying, and pleaded with the Virgin. Give her a son or a daughter, she promised, and she would bring the child to Mary and hold vigils there. The Virgin granted her wishes, and the woman gave birth to a baby boy—but she failed to keep her promise, reluctant to make the journey back to Tudia with the child (a difficult journey, one can imagine, across the mountains from Seville). Jesus, as in the previous *cantiga*, avenges the wrong done to his mother, and the little boy dies three years later. The desperate mother and her relatives return to the sanctuary and there recite psalms and litanies. "While they were doing this, at once, may God help me, the Queen of Virtue had pity on them and made the boy live and cry out from the coffin, so that those who were weeping began to shout with joy." The boy is fully revived, healthy and handsome, asking the people for something to eat. Private tragedy has been transformed into public happiness.

It is not that Alfonso despised medical wisdom, as his continuing reliance on Jewish doctors like Yehuda Mosca reminds us, but while faith in physicians had limited efficacy, spiritual faith was the supreme cure. Once there was a man from Aragon, we read, who experienced agonizingly painful kidney stones. The man could not eat or sleep. Nor did the doctors do him any good, despite the colorful array of green, red, and blue medicinal flasks that we see in the apothecary's shop in the accompanying illustration. (Perhaps one of them contained the pulverized stone called *marina*, to be found on the seashores of the West, which the *Book of Stones* recommended as a remedy for this medical condition: "When half a drachma's weight of it is taken in a drink, it will destroy the stone that forms in the bladder or in the kidney, so that it can be passed like fine sand.") The apothecary sits complacently, uselessly, while the poor Aragonese man dashes around desperately, open purse in hand. Only when he goes on pilgrimage to Salas is his agony relieved, thanks to Mary's incisive action. The resolution is almost comically happy: "He woke up then and found the whole kidney stone in the bed with him. It was truly as large as a chestnut, you may be sure."

A *cantiga* about a young shepherdess from Córdoba conveys a similar message about medical professionals. The Holy Queen quickly heals—runs the song's refrain—what with medicine long endures. The girl, we hear, had been suffering for several years from scrofula—a disease whose characteristic symptom is tumors in the lymph nodes. Her mother "did not hesitate to give doctors and physicians of the land whatever they asked just so that they could cure her daughter for her, begging them to examine her.

The poor woman gave them five hundred *maravedís* or more. However, no matter how much she paid them, they could not cure the girl, nor did any of the remedies they applied do any good. They took all the money she gave them, so the good woman was left in even worse distress." We may be reminded of the Doctor of Physic, described in the general prologue to Geoffrey Chaucer's *Canterbury Tales* about a century later: "He was but esy of dispence. / He kepte that he wan in pestilence, / For gold in phisik is a cordial; / Therefore he loved gold in special." Chaucer's lines bear comparison with the acerbic wit of Alfonso's satirical songs: the *Cantigas d'escarnho* present Master Nicholas, a royal physician at court, as a veritable master in separating a fool from his money. However, the English poet's wry remark about the soothing effects of gold differed in one important respect from the Spanish king's sensibility. In the *Book of Stones*, gold (described as a stone rather than a metal) is quite earnestly praised for its medicinal qualities. Men greatly appreciate gold, we read. It can be found in many parts of the world, but the best of all is to be found "in Spain, which is in the west." When it is cut and the shavings are mixed with something else and ingested, it can cure heart tremors and fear derived from melancholy. It can also cure alopecia and ringworm. Alfonso did not share Chaucer's moral relativism, the product of an uncertain age after the Black Death in which the foundations of traditional belief had been irrevocably shaken.

Nor did he share the self-serving traditions of the medieval French monarchs—the so-called *rois thaumaturges*—who claimed the ability to heal scrofula through their own quasi-divine healing touch. When a well-intentioned man introduced the sick girl's mother to the king, certain that Alfonso could help directly because "all Christians kings have this power," he waved away such claims. The Spanish king, according to the *cantiga*, answered him dismissively: "Friend, what you tell me . . . is not worth a very bad fig, however much you talk and twitter like a swallow." The culture of royalty in Castile, traditionally underpinned by military leadership, was far removed from the sacral aura of its French counterpart, and Alfonso may also have wanted to distance himself from his dangerous northern rivals. Instead, he advises, the girl should be taken to the statue of the Virgin draped in a purple robe made from Flemish cloth. Then, he directs the mother, wash the body and face of Mary and Jesus in clear water after Mass and give the girl a drink of this water from the chalice on the altar. "Have her drink it for as many days as there are letters in the name 'Maria' when it is written down, and on the fifth day the letters will be finished, and the little shepherdess will be cured at once." This is done, and the girl recovers fully within four days, "without drinking medicinal syrup nor taking a hot bath."

We can safely put to one side preconceptions about any medieval aversion to bathing. Hot baths were widely seen as a useful means of making the patient sweat, removing impurities, and improving the balance of the patient's humors. In his *Book of Holy Medicines*, Henry, duke of Lancaster, who had written of the therapeutic value of writing, perspires as he considers the Passion of Christ and hopes that he will be spiritually cured as he might be physically cured by a hot bath.

The Wise King envisioned faith not as an alternative to medicine but as a superior form of it and not as a "merely" spiritual cure but also as a holistic source of physical healing. The two realms could hardly be separated in the medieval imagination. Medieval culture, perhaps more effectively than we tend to imagine, treated "the whole person." In the fifteenth century, King Duarte of Portugal too would suggest that for the worst forms of melancholy, the advice of physicians—for instance, to have sex, abandon excessive work, and drink undiluted wine—was useless. While the conversation of good, wise friends, the reading of books of virtuous advice, and the avoidance of solitude and idleness were all helpful in mild cases, the only cure when sanity was at stake was spiritual faith. Duarte recommended pious reading as the best *meezinha* (medicine) and invoked an image of Christ as physician that was deeply ingrained in medieval culture. Long ago, Saint Augustine had affirmed in one of his sermons, "The human physician sometimes is deceived and promises health in the human body. Why is he deceived? Because he is treating what he has not made. God, however, made your body; God made your soul. He knows how to restore what He has made." Well into the Renaissance, cure of the body was intimately linked to cure of the soul, the two being complementary processes. The cutting-edge hospital wards of fifteenth-century Florence took their architectural inspiration from lofty church naves, their height providing a dramatic view of chapels and altars while at the same time responding to contemporary awareness that ventilation and the circulation of air were vital.

In Alfonso's world, Mary herself was both "hospital"—a refuge for the needy—and healing nurse. Both ideas appear in the final illustration for a *cantiga* in which the Virgin cures a woman of Saint Martial's Fire—ergot poisoning—which had eaten away the flesh of her face. In the image panel, we see a group of winged angel-nurses, supervised by Mary herself, lovingly offering spoonfuls of food to the bed-ridden sick and providing a hungry cluster of male and female patients, squatting on the floor, with both food and drink. More than an equivalent to the modern nurse, however, the Virgin was also divine surgeon. Her capacity for spectacular, sometimes magnanimous, medical intervention is a frequent motif in the *cantigas*. In one song, she heals a man who cuts out his own tongue as he leaves a gambling den after blaspheming against her when he loses a game of dice. The illustration presents the action as a direct, surgical action rather than a long-distance metaphysical miracle. In another *cantiga*, drawn from a tale circulating in France, we learn of a man who experiences such intense pain in his foot that, having prayed for a miracle alongside other sufferers in a church dedicated to the Virgin, he has his foot amputated. The corresponding illustration shows him looking away in agony as a knife slices through his right ankle and blood runs to the floor. Having become a "cripple," he nonetheless continues to pray faithfully to the Virgin for a miracle, lying before her altar. One night, while he sleeps, she "passed Her hand many times back and forth across that foot, healing the flesh with Her deft fingers." In the following image, the man sprints out of the church to spread the news, right foot first, with an Olympic athleticism that clearly astonishes the onlookers. As always, the community's role in witnessing the miracle, as well as both its spiritual health and the individual's, is vital.

Another *cantiga* recounts an incident in the town of Lugo, the Roman-walled city in the heartland of Galicia, witnessed by the local bishop and his whole congregation on the Feast of the Assumption. A woman had become horribly misshapen, we hear; both hands and arms had become twisted up near her shoulders, while her heels dug inward. Since she had no other medicine, she turned to Mary and asked to be carried to church in a small, narrow bed. On the feast day, she was immediately healed. The words of the text are viscerally powerful: "While she was being healed, each member gave a resounding crack like dry timbers in a roof when the shrunken tendon was stretched out."

Little wonder, then, that in his moment of crisis and despair, Alfonso, lying on his four-poster sickbed in Vitoria in late 1276 and early 1277, turned to Mary and to the book in which his yearnings were almost magically distilled. A servant stands behind the king, fanning him with peacock feathers, as Alfonso lies supine, crying out in pain, wrapped in a thin pink counterpane whose border is emblazoned with gold castles and rampant lions. A Jewish physician, possibly Abraham ibn Waqar, consults with another man near the foot of the bed, distant and unhelpful. Everyone believes that he will die. New doctors arrive and offer him hot cloths to purge the disease, but he refuses and waves them away. The physician has vanished; by law, he cannot administer directly to the king. Alfonso calls instead for a book, "Her Book" (the *Cantigas de Santa María*)—a handsomely bound red volume with silver clasps—to be brought, and it is. Now he rests the book upon his heart, its pages open. People fall to their knees, prostrating themselves and praising the Virgin. Others gasp in awe, and the physician too bears witness to what has occurred: a miracle. The ailing king has been restored and no longer cries out or feels any pain. He sits up in bed and puts on a bright blue robe. At the foot of the bed, the kneeling men bend over to kiss the healing book.

For it is, in some respects, the book itself that heals: it is an amulet, a talisman, with its own power to cure. So it was believed, and there is good reason to think that the use of such "textual amulets" may have been emotionally and psychologically helpful to the sick—and the healthy—in relieving pain or allowing them some sense of control over their own well-being. The medicinal use of such amuletic texts for "sacred word therapy" was widespread in medieval Europe. The Valencian-born physician Arnaldo de Vilanova (1235–1311), one of the great figures of Spanish medicine in this era, speaks of the benefits of seals with signs of the Zodiac and engraved inscriptions for curing a variety of illnesses in the head and eyes. Famous for his treatment of gallstones, Arnaldo was summoned to the Vatican to attend Pope Boniface VIII (who occupied the papal see from 1294–1303) and placed on the pope's kidneys a "golden seal" in which had been inscribed magical formulae, prayers, and biblical proverbs. For his part, Chaucer's fictional doctor is steeped in the work of "Gatesden": John of Gaddesden (c. 1280–1361), an English doctor educated at Merton College, Oxford, who explicitly recommended textual amulets for toothaches.

The early church fathers had seen such amulets as a dangerous and superstitious survival from the pre-Christian past. However, they had sanctioned their use in exorcism rituals designed to repel and cast out demons, drawing on the belief that rites and words dispensed by the clergy could win God's protection. Some medieval churchmen continued to be alarmed, arguing that faith in the healing powers of amulets was implicitly a belief in the limited power of God himself. As a pathological fear of "superstition" and demonic forces expanded in the thirteenth century, the medieval inquisition kept a close eye on such practices. But Alfonso's near-contemporary Roger Bacon (c. 1214–1294)—a man who has been described as Christian Europe's "first scientist"—differentiated between the positive goals of natural magic, aiming to protect and heal, and the negative goals of black magic or necromancy (appealing to demons, often to injure people). Bacon specifically praised the use of a textual amulet with two verses containing the names of the three wise kings—Caspar, Melchior, and Balthasar—as a cure for epilepsy. Just a few years before the moment of Alfonso's illness in Victoria, the Dominican friar Thomas Aquinas (c. 1225–1274) had wrestled with the question "Is it wrong to wear from one's neck a textual amulet based on *verba divina?*" and concluded that it was legitimate for people to wear the *Pater Noster* (Lord's Prayer) or other extracts from scripture as long as they did so in sincere Christian devotion and avoided demonic invocations, unknown names, strange words, and symbols other than the sign of the cross.

The books containing Alfonso's increasingly numerous songs to Holy Mary, then, became seen as miraculous, healing objects. The codices were cornerstones of a cultural-spiritual project whose goal was human happiness and the transcendence of pain. In the codicil to his last will and testament, the king later ordered that "all the books" of the *Cantares de los miraglos e de loor de Sancta María* be buried alongside him in Seville or wherever else his final resting place might be. The same document also indicates that a number of other material objects (both textual and artistic) had acquired special significance. If his body was buried in Seville, the king stipulated, the "retable for the relics that he ordered to be made" was also to be given to the cathedral, in honor of Saint Mary, to be carried in processions on feast days and placed on the altar; this is probably the wooden triptych, overlaid with gold and enamel, now called the *Tablas Alfonsíes*. The four books that Louis IX of France wrote, the *Historical Mirror* (*Espejo ystorial*), were also to be placed there. We can identify these as comprising the historical section of the *Great Mirror* (*Speculum maius*), a compendium of knowledge composed by the Dominican scholar Vincent de Beauvais between 1245 and 1260, which appears to have been the source of a number of *cantigas*. So, Alfonso continued, were the rich cloth that Leonor, Queen of England, his sister, had given him; the richly embroidered chasuble, dalmatic, and cape, embroidered with many stories; and the big retable with carved-ivory images depicting Saint Mary, which should be put on the altar every Saturday at Mass. Also to be placed there were two Bibles, one in three silver-plated books with large calligraphy and the other—also in three volumes—a gift from King Louis.

In reading this list, it is impossible not to sense the sacred quality that Alfonso attributes to all the books in question—and not merely the Bibles. Might the books associated with Louis IX of France—Saint Louis, the king, canonized in 1297, who perceived himself as "God's lieutenant on earth"—also have been understood as having some form of healing powers? Objects that had been touched by his sister Isabelle of France (who had also died in 1270) were understood to possess special powers. The earth around her tomb was said to have healing properties, and her pillow, goblet, and knitted nightcap were all treated as relics.

Medieval Christians, as the case of Isabelle of France's pillow suggests, envisioned a wide variety of objects as having the capacity to heal. The material world, in the medieval imagination, was organic and alive, suffused with the power of the divine. Hildegard of Bingen, a century earlier, had given particularly vivid expression to this vision of the cosmos in her descriptions of the benevolent creative energy of God, which she associates constantly with the green of nature: "I am sweet herb in all greenness," comes a voice from a storm cloud in one of her dramatic works. "My heart is full, ready to grant any kind of assistance. With my eyes I survey all needs; I unite myself to them; I lead the broken back to health; I am a healing balm for every pain." This conviction energized Hildegard's herbal healing remedies, which today continue to have many adherents. For many others, the potential powers of many objects, including water, candles, salt, and grain, could be made actively "holy" through blessing by a priest. One striking example is provided by a fifteenth-century blessing for radishes: "Oh God, who has miraculously created all from nothing, who hast commanded the earth to produce different seeds . . . and hast implanted different sorts of medicine in them, bless and sanctify this radish that it may be useful to all in soul and body."

But in addition to the part of creation we call "vegetable," the mineral was perceived to be alive. Distinctions between animate and inanimate objects, between "dead" and "alive," were far more fluid then than now. This mentality underlay the fervent devotion to the apparently inanimate relics of saints and, indeed, the purchase of the many "holy" objects available at pilgrimage centers such as Canterbury or Santiago de Compostela. Pilgrim badges, for instance, sometimes included a small mirror believed to have captured holy rays from the object to which pilgrimage was made.

The Wise King—the "last Almohad caliph"—had also inherited from al-Andalus a belief in the supernatural powers of material objects. In the city he first conquered in the 1240s, Murcia, there is widespread evidence of the use of amulets for preventative or curative purposes. These amulets were often designed to protect the owner from the genies that, it was believed, could enter the body through food or the influence of the "evil eye"—as in the medieval Christian world, belief in this influence rested on the notion that sight was made possible by the transmission of physical particles. One of the most widely used amulets was the so-called *jamsa* (five), or "hand of Fatima," based on the magical value of the number five. Traditionally, it has been claimed that it was associated with the five precepts of Islam, although scholars argue that this—like the association with the hand of Mohammed or his daughter Fatima—was merely an attempt to Islamicize a Berber belief that the Almohads brought to Spain from the Maghreb.

Other images common in al-Andalus included the "seal of Solomon" (two concentric squares forming an eight-pointed star), the key to paradise, and two birds facing each other, separated by an inverted tree, symbolizing the terrestrial world with its roots in heaven. These images appear in the plasterwork of buildings and on amulets hung from the neck. One amulet that survives from Murcia, abandoned in a well in the mid-thirteenth century, is a stylized human figure made of false agate. Now held in the collections of the Museo Arqueológico in Madrid, the amulet shows us the supernatural properties attributed to stone amulets in medieval Islamic cultures, from Syria to Spain. In al-Andalus, physicians sometimes recommended the wearing of a stone amulet as part of their prescription. Ibn Zuhr (Avenzoar), a leading physician and surgeon from Seville (d. 1161/62), is said to have prescribed the wearing of the bezoar stone to protect against poison—the self-same remedy that readers of Harry Potter will remember from the First Year Potions class offered by Severus Snape.

These ideas underpinned the *Book of Stones*, the text that had first been drafted under Alfonso's patronage while he was in his twenties and that was now produced—perhaps with some haste—in a new, luxury edition while Alfonso lay on his sickbed in Vitoria. Like the idea of material and textual amulets, the "lapidary" genre had a long and vibrant existence in Islamic and Christian cultures alike. Hildegard, for example, had produced a short *Liber lapidum*, in which—by way of example—she had recommended first focusing your attention on a piece of onyx and then placing it in your mouth as a cure for melancholy. In Alfonso's own age, the German friar and polymath Albertus Magnus (c. 1200–1280)—who was mistrusted by some of his contemporaries as a wizard, or *magus*—described the magical-medicinal power of precious stones in his *Mineralia*; in later legend, he was misremembered as the inventor of the Philosopher's Stone. Despite premises that to the modern eye might also seem supernatural and occult, Alfonso's own *Book of Stones* was intended to have authentic medical value and was fully in line with practices at the leading medical centers of the day.

Fusing astrology with geology, the book claims to be a Castilian translation of a work in turn translated long ago from

Collecting the sweet *milititaz* stone—a remedy against chest ailments—from the River of Honey, in China: *Lapidario* (*Book of Stones*) fol. 4r. Reproduced courtesy of Archivo Oronoz.

Chaldean, a language of northern Iraq, by a mysterious person called Abolays. The identity of this man is unknown, probably unknowable, and perhaps purely fictitious, although the *Book of Stones* clearly drew on a genre circulating widely in the Islamic world and specifically on a twelfth-century treatise of Muhammad ibn Mansur, which was dedicated to the sultan of Persia. It was swept into being by the tidal wave of translation from Arabic-language texts, incorporating and elaborating on ancient Greek medical knowledge, that washed over Castile and southern Italy, and beyond into the rest of western Europe, between the eleventh and thirteenth centuries. This wave, ushering in a renaissance that helped shape the culture of Florence and other Italian city-states, reenergized medical thought. In addition to being seen in a spiritual context, melancholy, for instance, might now be more clearly understood as a medical condition. The ancient Greek and Roman notion that human health relied on a balance of the "four humors"—blood, yellow bile, black bile, and phlegm—could be invoked in more elaborate and sophisticated ways to explain mental illness. Melancholy—the word derives from the Greek for "an excess of black bile"—was seen in this framework as an imbalance of humors that could be treated medically, rather than simply as a sin to be purged through confession. Understanding of this theory in medieval Spain and beyond had been heightened by the translation of works such as the *Canon of Medicine* written by Ibn Sina (Avicenna, 980–1037), a Muslim polymath who was deeply respected in medieval Christian culture.

There was no medical school in thirteenth-century Castile that matched those centers of learning that desperately attempted to identify the causes and remedies for the plague that ravaged Europe after 1347: Paris, Montpellier, and the southern Italian city of Salerno (which had first become a hub of medical knowledge as early as the ninth century). However, in late December 1254, Alfonso had set aside a building close to the *alcázar* in Seville where doctors from abroad might stay and teach; he also seems to have endowed two university chairs of medicine at Salamanca. The Wise King's interest in the healing properties of stones reflected a sustained interest in medical science and other forms of healing. The prologue to the *Book of Stones* tells us that while still a prince, Alfonso had found the book in Toledo in the house of a Jewish man who had guarded it jealously, neither wishing to use it himself nor wanting anyone else to do so. This had been in 1243, the year in which he had conquered Murcia. The prince then asked his Jewish physician, Yehuda Mosca, to translate it for him and thus make it useful for the people of the realm, a task the busy doctor completed in 1254. But if Alfonso had first encountered the *Book of Stones* in a spirit of wide-eyed intellectual enthusiasm, by his mid-fifties he brought a more bitter and painful set of life experiences to his reading.

We cannot know if the Wise King himself tried any of the astonishing range of cures that the book provides, although it has been suggested that in view of the damage cancer had caused to his eyes, he might have noted the healing effects of powdered copper: "The powders of this stone are good for reducing the fat, as well as the scabies that form in eye sockets, and for improving vision and drying up watery eyes." (On the other hand, "Whoever eats or drinks from dishes made of this copper will get many diseases, such as the one called the elephant disease and which enlarges legs, or the one called cancer"). He might also have been interested in the green variety of the stone called *tutya*, which, we read, comes from the seashore on the land of Cin and cures cancerous swellings and eye infections; it "is retentive and will make the veil disappear from the eyes. It is also good for cancerous ulcers, blisters, and ulcers in the eyes." The Spanish form of the same stone may also have been enticing: "This stone is better than any other medicine for ulcers that form on the private parts. Also, it keeps the eyes from watering and strengthens and sharpens the eyesight."

One of the book's hallmarks, however, is the enormous number of stones invoked as remedies for melancholy. We can only speculate as to whether the prominence of these cures reflects Alfonso's personal experience in the 1270s, but we can imagine him, as always, as an attentive reader of the frequently exotic remedies that he encountered in the text. One passage tells us of a remarkable cure for the symptoms of sadness:

In the mountain they called Culequin, in the land of Macedonia, there are some very large hares, and when someone kills one of them, before it reaches the age of one year, they may find in its heart a white stone, in the middle of which lies an intense red drop. Any man who wears the stone, will become so warm that he cannot be harmed by the winter's cold like someone without it, and he will also be highly attractive to women. When the stone is pulverized and mixed with wine, and is applied to tumors such as those caused by cancer or associated with melancholy, they recover very quickly.

Some of the remedies are thankfully more accessible than the heart stone of a Macedonian hare. One, as we have seen, is gold. Another is the mysterious "stone that attracts gold," which "gives great happiness to the heart, so that whoever looks at it in the morning will be happy all day, unless great efforts are made to make him sad." Black coral is prized as a potent antidepressant when "mixed into the medicines which are used to make one happy." Several varieties of jasper (yzf) are also said to bring happiness to the person who wears them, to strengthen wearers against decrepitude and the illnesses that come from melancholy, and to make their tasks easier to carry out. One of the *cantigas* tells the story of a jasper ring, set in gold, that the king has promised to give his brother Manuel. After the royal messenger loses the ring en route to Manuel's lodgings, another man finds it and promptly returns it to the grateful messenger. Had he, we might wonder, brought a double gift of happiness: a stone famed in Alfonso's court for its medicinal power against melancholy, recovered through the grace of the Queen of Heaven? The divine presence of Mary, we are reminded in another song, is present even in the mineral world, for in holy Gethsemane, precise images of the Mother of God were miraculously inscribed on the hard stone.

All things in the cosmos, then, were interrelated, in a process of divine emanation. The lowest things received their power from on high; celestial forces governed life, health, and disease on earth. These ideas might, in isolation, seem dangerously close to magic but were reconciled with Christian faith and were also expressed not only by the experts of Paris and Montpellier but by later generations of medical experts during the Italian Renaissance.

On the other hand, there was no place in Alfonso's moral universe for necromancy, the summoning of evil spirits, the power of which he accepted but harshly condemned. The *Book of Stones* contained multiple antidotes for black magic and witchcraft: for instance, the swallow stone (*piedra de la golondrina*) was potent against witchcraft when enclosed in deerskin or calfskin and suspended about the neck on a red silk thread. Similarly, it sharply distinguished between "false alchemy" and the higher art (*obra mayor*) that is beneficial and useful to humanity. The section on gold, which fills the hearts of men with joy, stipulates that those who work in this higher art must remember that alchemy entails the skill of making things better, not worse: "Hence, those who take noble metals and mix them with the common ones, understanding neither the science nor the mastery, cause damage to those which are noble and do not better those which are common. In this they commit two errors: one, they go against God's knowledge; the other, they do harm to the world."

The Wise King's commitment to human happiness on earth—one of his strongest principles and greatest contributions to later European culture—suffuses the *Book of Stones*. This commitment explains its many sexual remedies and the pervasive ideal of living a relaxed and worry-free life. In the end, the Wise King's personal pain would not be eliminated and evils continued to befall him. But as his health declined and his enemies amassed across the Strait of Gibraltar, his knowledge, creativity, and faith, one hopes, may have provided him with some means of surviving the terrors to come.

In July 1277, Abu Yusuf landed once more at Tarifa and drove north toward Seville; his forces arrived on August 2. King Alfonso came out to confront them, but the next day the Christians were routed, fleeing in the direction of the river "like donkeys, frightened by a lion," in the words of the Muslim chronicler of the *Rawd al-Qirtas*. Many were stabbed and slashed to death, and those who dived into the river were drowned. The river, we are told, ran red with blood, and the bodies floated in the water. Between September and October, the victorious Abu Yusuf went on to launch attacks throughout the Guadalquivir Valley, laying waste to the area around Córdoba. Alfonso was humiliatingly forced to sue for peace, first before the Marinids and then—at their command—before the king of Granada. While assuring the Muslim king that they sought a peace that might last for centuries, his messengers hinted at the rebellion that was about to unfold. If their king, Alfonso, did not adhere to the terms of the agreement, they stated, they would have no alternative but to launch a coup d'état. "They swore on their crosses that if Alfonso did not accept [the agreement], they would depose him, because he did not defend the crosses or guard the frontiers, or ensure the safety of the country, but rather had let his subjects become prisoners of the enemy."

Pouring salt into the wound, Alfonso faced a near-fatal illness in Valladolid and the breakdown of his marriage in early 1278. Accompanied by her daughter-in-law Blanche and the princess's two infants, Yolant left secretly for her native Aragon. The reasons remain unclear. Some have speculated that the king's physical illness itself was to blame—that the cancerous growth in his head had left him irritable and emotionally estranged from his wife, and we might imagine that a woman with Yolant's independence and intelligence would have had little tolerance for such behavior. An Aragonese chronicle pins responsibility on the king: "King Alfonso of Castile treated his wife, King Pedro's sister, wrongfully and without the marital love and honor in which she should have been held. Mistrust arose on both sides, and Pedro [Pere III] entered Castile under arms for six days. He led away with him his sister and her children." The chronicler Jofré de Loaysa, whose family was close to Yolant, indicates that "her brother the king of Aragon came for her at night, and when he had them in Aragon he separated the children from Yolant and took them to raise them in a castle in his kingdom." Regardless of where responsibility lay for the breakdown of the marriage, the temerity of Pere III's actions and the violation of Alfonso's sovereign authority, an intervention that transparently served the interests of the Aragonese, would have infuriated even the most tranquil man. The emotional toll on Alfonso must have been colossal.

Public catastrophe soon compounded private agony. In a supreme effort of will, Alfonso struggled to preempt a further wave of Muslim attacks by attempting to force the great port city of Algeciras into submission. In the summer of 1278, the king prepared a large fleet comprising eight galleys and twenty-four other ships, under the command of Pedro Martínez de Fe. By August, a naval siege was in place, and by February the following year, the encirclement was completed by land. The *Rawd al-Qirtas* reports, exaggeratedly, that 30,000 knights and three hundred foot soldiers joined the siege, adding that the city was surrounded as tightly as a bracelet surrounds a wrist; the only news of the outside world that the people could receive came with homing pigeons from over the bay, from Muslim-held Gibraltar. But relief came quickly. The Marinid emir's son, Abu Ya'qub, equipped a counterfleet directly across the strait at Ceuta and arranged support vessels in Tangier and Salé (neighboring Rabat); "the only people who remained in Ceuta," says the Muslim chronicler, "were women, the chronically sick, old people without strength, and children who had not yet reached the age of puberty." All the ships then gathered in Ceuta and set sail for Tangier on July 19, 1279, heading rapidly for the besieging Christian fleet.

On July 21, the naval battle began. Arrows fell upon the Christians "like a dense rain or a hurricane wind." Many of them flung themselves into the sea and were forced to swim as if they were frogs. Pedro Martínez was captured and held captive for two full years. As the besieging Christian armies abandoned their encampments, the people of Algeciras ransacked their tents, where, we read, they found immense quantities of money, fruit, wineskins, barley, and flour. Some elements of this account, especially the description of the Christian encampment, are dubious: the *Chronicle of Alfonso X* indicates that the impoverished besieging forces, who had not been properly paid, had begun to suffer from a terrible disease—perhaps scurvy—and that their teeth had begun to fall out. One thing is certain, however. By the summer of 1279, the Wise King's hopes had been scattered to the four winds.

9

ANGER

When Jupiter and the Sun are joined in the fifth
house, the king will change his heir, and will not give
the kingdom to the one who should govern it, but to
another.

—YEHUDA BEN MOSÉ, BOOK OF CROSSES, 20

A LITTLE MORE THAN A MILLENNIUM EARLIER, ANOTHER
deeply reflective ruler—in his military encampment—had
been contemplating the turns of fortune. Encamped near the
Danube, as he fended off the threat of the Germanic tribes beyond the frontier of the Roman Empire, Marcus Aurelius had
condensed a vast cloud of ancient wisdom into droplets of crys-
talline prose. Many of his reflections focused on how to move
beyond anger, a violent and ultimately self-destructive emotion.
"Whenever somebody wrongs you, ask yourself at once, 'What
conception of good and evil led him to commit such a wrong?'"
he proposed. "And when you have seen that, you will pity him,
and feel neither surprise nor anger." Always remember that "it is
not people's actions that trouble us," Marcus Aurelius added,

"but the opinions that we form of those actions. So eliminate your judgment that this or that is of harm to you, make up your mind to discard that opinion, and your anger will be at an end."

This vision of anger as a self-destructive vice, countered by the Christian principles of mercy, temperance, and forgiveness, became a deep vein in medieval culture. In the wall paintings of the state bedroom at Westminster Palace, at the court of Alfonso's ally and in-law Henry III of England, the personification of *Ira* (Anger) was shown being trampled underfoot by a more glamorous and imperious figure, crowned in gold and representing clemency. This figure carries a large switch of twigs in her right hand and towers over tiny, cowering Anger, who is trying to tear out her own hair. Similar attitudes prevailed in Spain. Looking up at the stained glass windows of León Cathedral, the medieval worshipper left spellbound by the "hunting" window might also have discerned richly colored images of a number of Christian vices. Among them, in the company of Avarice and Vanity, was the figure of Anger, stabbing herself in the breast.

The fourteenth-century chronicle of Alfonso's reign, on the other hand, gives us the impression that the king was ever more inclined to outbursts of anger. It tells the story of a downward spiral into increasingly irrational, arbitrary, and illegitimate violence. In the spring of 1277, the king "discovered some things about the infante Fadrique, his brother, and Simón Ruiz de los Cameros," the chronicler writes darkly. Thereupon, we are told, he immediately ordered the infante Sancho to capture and kill them. The narrative unfolds in grim, laconic detail. Sancho, according to this account, seizes Simón Ruiz in the region of La Rioja and has him burned alive in Treviño. Fadrique is captured in the royal capital, Burgos, and Alfonso himself orders his brother hanged. A separate source, another contemporary chronicle, adds the gruesome claim that after having imprisoned Fadrique in the castle in Burgos, Alfonso had him encased in a large chest full of sharp iron, in which he dies. Some have seen these events as the beginning of a new regime of terror, which became more accentuated in the next century, breaking with a past that had favored milder, less draconian punishments. But it is important, always, to approach these chronicles carefully, since they carry a heavy political agenda.

The events surrounding the executions remain extremely obscure. Every observer, including Alfonso himself, seeks to draw a veil over his real motives—although he does allude to them obliquely in the autobiographical Cantiga 235, recalling venomously, "The son of God wished that he take vengeance on those who were his enemies and hence his also. Just as a candle burns, / so burned the flesh of those who did not want a woman. Others went to the devil, and if God wills it, so will anyone else who commits such a deed. As for what evil befalls them, I care little." The manuscript illustration in the Florentine Codex of the *Cantigas de Santa María* shows a crowd of spectators in the main square in Treviño, as the body of Simón Ruiz is consumed by raging fire. Among them are five members of the municipal militia, daggers sheathed. One bystander holds a robe up to his eyes, either to wipe away his tears or to shield himself from the sickening scene. The killing of the king's own brother, on the other hand, is too shocking to be depicted. In the corresponding image panel, the artists have left the space beneath arches and towers completely empty. Their visual silence speaks to their horror.

It is possible that the two condemned men had embraced heresy, particularly if the obscure reference to "his enemies" refers to the enemies of Christ. The song also implies their homosexuality, but it is unlikely that this was sufficient motive to warrant two high-profile executions. A conspiracy against Alfonso is more

The burning of Simón Ruiz, with blank panel for the scene corresponding to the infante Fadrique's execution, during the king's illness: *Cantigas de Santa María*, no. 235, *Códice de Florencia* (Florentine Codex), Biblioteca Nazionale Centrale di Firenze, Ms. B.R.20. Reproduced courtesy of Archivo Oronoz.

probable, given the endemic tension between crown and nobility in this period. The same song describes a noble plot to "throw him out of the kingdom so that it would belong to them," although this line is not directly associated with the killings. Some historians speculate that Alfonso's deteriorating health had got the better of his judgment. This also seems to be what the infante Sancho thought—or at least what he said. The king later charged that Sancho had claimed his father was "demented and leprous, and that he is a liar and a perjurer in many things, and that he killed people without reason, as he killed Don Fadrique and Don Simón." Yet the same line implies that Alfonso himself considered these claims to be utterly false and that he had legitimate reasons for executing the two men.

Having reached a peace agreement with Abu Yusuf, he turned his sights once more to the kingdom of Granada, the chronicle recounts. In February or March 1280, he gathered in Badajoz with other members of his family—his brother Manuel and his sons Pedro, Juan, and Jaime—to prepare an assault. His grandson King Dinís, however, refused to join them, fearful that Alfonso would force him into the custody of his mother, Beatriz, and instead sought safety in Lisbon. In the ensuing military action, Sancho is cast, rather unpersuasively, as the heroic figure. Leading an army into the Vega (lowlands) of Granada, he sends the master of the military order of Uclés, Gonzalo Ruiz de Girón, into action; the master is ambushed and mortally wounded along with many of his comrades on June 23. A significant part of the royal army is about to defect from the campaign, but Sancho prevents this, instead launching a pillaging raid into the Vega de Granada before returning to Córdoba, where his father is appropriately pleased with his handling of events.

Alfonso then embarked—the narrator suggests—on a murderous course of violence. In September 1280, allegedly angered by the inability of his Jewish tax collectors to supply money that could have prevented failure in the doomed siege of Algeciras, he ordered his Jewish financier Isaac ibn Zadoq (known to the Spanish as Zag de la Maleha) and others to be imprisoned. This is presented as a capricious act of revenge on Prince Sancho, who is said to have spent valuable resources ensuring the return of his mother, Queen Yolant, to Castile in the summer of 1279. Soon after, Alfonso has his financier executed on the east bank of the Guadalquivir, a stone's throw away from the Jewish quarter. This was undoubtedly a moment of crisis for the Jews of Castile, and it would be a mistake to downplay the king's actions. The Jewish polemicist Ibn Sahula chose this moment to condemn those of his coreligionists who had made the mistake of becoming enmeshed in the royal court, betraying the interests of their fellow Jews.

However, we need to remain careful about the agenda of the Castilian chronicle, which is resolutely pro-Sancho. Again and again, it contrasts Alfonso's supposed ineffectuality as ruler with his son's incisive military action. In the autumn of 1280, secret negotiations with the French in Gascony (neutral territory, held by Edward I of England) to discuss the claims to the throne of Alfonso de la Cerda go badly; when Alfonso offers to give the child—now a French protégé—the old kingdom of Jaén, in exchange for becoming Sancho's vassal, both sides are disappointed, and Philippe III returns to France. When Alfonso mobilizes his forces for a renewed assault on the Vega de Granada in June 1281, Sancho again leads the charge, occupying a hill overlooking the city. A Muslim force counterattacks, but the prince repels them bravely. Alfonso, meanwhile, attempts to enlist a shadowy group of bandits who have been preying on people in the mountains. He offers to pardon them if they join the attack, but the plan spectacularly backfires when the bandits attempt extortion,

saying that unless the king meets their demands, they will commit great violence across the land—whereupon Alfonso has them
summarily killed. From the pages of the text, a tyrant emerges—
almost a Spanish Nero. When—at the Cortes he summons in
Seville in November 1281—Alfonso proposes minting two new
types of coin to raise funds for the military campaign against the
Marinid invaders, the assembly responds, "more with fear than
with affection, that he should do whatever he considers good."

By his own admission, Alfonso clearly inspired some measure
of fear. A *cantiga* set against the backdrop of the meeting of the
Cortes in Seville recounts how—after high nervous tension in
the king's kitchens—Holy Mary had miraculously supplied
enough fish to feed the many people who had come to attend the
assembly from across the realm and whom the king had invited to
dine with him. All the way from Toledo to Santiago to La Rioja,
the song says, there was no one who failed to come to the assembly "for fear of incurring his disfavor." Forty years earlier, in the
Book of the Twelve Wise Men, the young prince had read that a
king "should be more feared by the great than by the small, and
should rule over them with greater authority." Referring to one of
Aesop's fables, the book had advised, "All should fear his wrath
and be afraid of erring and angering him with their bad deeds and
failings, so that the same not happen as when Jupiter threw the
log among the frogs, who were at first afraid and they climbed on
top of the log." Across Europe, royal anger was in fact considered
necessary within limits. Indeed, it was dangerously "soft" for a
king not to show his wrath.

The chronicler of Alfonso's reign, however, does not present
the king's rage as a righteous and necessary means of maintaining
honor or authority. Instead, he portrays it as an emotion that
fractures the realm. Shortly after the Cortes of Seville (November 1281), Alfonso renewed negotiations with the French,

seeking a treaty to settle the claims of Fernando de la Cerda's children. Sancho told his father that he refused to have anything to do with such a treaty. "King Alfonso became enraged at this reply, and told him that since he did not wish it, he would not hold back from doing it either for him or for the homage that the people of the land had done him, and that he made him and would unmake him."

Swallowed into a vortex of verbal violence, Sancho retorted, "My lord, you did not make me; God did so, and did much to make me, for he killed my brother [Fernando de la Cerda] who was older than I, and who was your heir to these kingdoms if he lived longer than you. God killed him simply so that I should inherit after you die. You may well be sorry for this word that you said to me, and the time will come when you will wish that you had not said it." Father and son, says the chronicle, left bitterly angry with each other. The relationship broke down, destabilizing the kingdom. When the royal council reconvened, many felt aggrieved by the king's decision to demand new coins for the military campaign—but they did not dare tell him. Instead, they turned to Sancho, seeing him—if we can believe the chronicle—as a means of righting his father's wrongs. In December, ensconced in Córdoba, Sancho's brothers Pedro and Juan agreed to join him in rebellion against their father. Thus began a conflict that brought Alfonso to his knees.

You will regret your anger, Sancho had warned his father. The words, if indeed spoken, must have resounded in the king's imagination, taking him back forty years to the *Book of the Twelve Wise Men*. "If the lord or prince does not temper his anger with moderation," Alfonso had read as a young prince, "he may easily do something to the great harm of his people, of which he may repent and may perhaps be unable to remedy." Certainly, the king was unable to remedy the disaster that now unfolded across Castile. Sancho appears—from a narrative deeply sympathetic to his cause—to have gathered widespread military support. The infante Juan, his younger brother, rallied the towns of León to Sancho's side and seized the *alcázar* of Zamora after threatening to kill the newborn child of the lady of the castle (a detail that reveals more about the violence of the coup than it perhaps intends). Sancho himself strengthened his power base in Andalusia, quickly gaining the support of the towns of Andújar and Úbeda and taking command of the towering castle of Jaén. The masters of the military orders of Santiago and Calatrava also joined his camp. In a series of letters, he informed city councils and churchmen across the realm that he was speaking out against the king on their behalf, asking that Alfonso cease his executions and no longer impose unjust taxes or deprive them of their legal rights.

Sancho then summoned an assembly in Valladolid in April 1282. Here, the chronicle states, it was agreed that he should now be called "King Sancho" and that power should be invested in him. The infante Manuel, Alfonso's brother, read a sentence condemning Alfonso for his supposed abuse of power. The sentence, which survives in a document in the archives of Burgos Cathedral, invokes the killing of Fadrique and Simón Ruiz de los Cameros, the alleged disinheritance of hidalgos, and the familiar claim that Alfonso had imposed unjust taxes. For Alfonso, the involvement of his dearly beloved brother Manuel must have been especially painful. In a frontispiece illustration showing the king and his family, in the so-called primitive version of the *History of Spain (Estoria de Espanna)*, probably dating from the spring of 1274, his children are painted to his left and his brothers to his right. One of these brothers, a figure wearing a cylindrical skullcap, seems to have been deliberately damaged with a wet cloth, and this figure is most likely Manuel. It may well have been the king himself who, in 1282, erased the image of his brother in a gesture of despair.

In his last will and testament, issued in November, Alfonso lamented the many fronts on which he had been betrayed and let down. Sancho, he explained, had spread lies among Alfonso's other sons in order to turn them cruelly against him, even though he had raised them, married them off, and advanced their interests. His natural vassals had abandoned him. King Dinís of Portugal, son of his daughter Beatriz, had proven naively sympathetic to his enemies, he states, while the king of Aragon, his brother-in-law and long-standing friend, was more interested in going to crusade to conquer Africa and did not heed his calls. For his part, Edward I of England, married to Alfonso's half sister Leonor, ("Eleanor of Castile"), was preoccupied with wars in his own land—a hurtful blow, since the personal relationship between Edward and Alfonso had been particularly warm.

Isolated and cornered, Alfonso now made a dramatic decision to appeal for assistance from his archnemesis, Abu Yusuf, emir of the Marinids. The turnaround was remarkable, even for a period in Spanish history in which religious and geographical borders were extremely porous. Soon after the siege of Algeciras, the emir's son Abu Ya'qub had returned confidently from al-Andalus with several captive Christian noblemen, including Alfonso's admiral, in an effort to conclude a peace agreement with the Castilians. At this point, the emir himself (for whom peace does not appear to have been a high priority) lost his temper. In the Moroccan *Rawd al-Qirtas*, his rage clearly signals his righteous commitment to jihad. Angrily, he swore that he did not wish to see the Christians unless it was in their own country—that is, on the battlefield—and immediately began preparations for another phase of holy war. However, his plans were frustrated. The Marinids had become distracted by tensions in the Maghreb. A newly agreed pact between the rulers of Tlemcen, in modern Algeria, and Muhammad II of Granada prevented the emir from renewing his assault on al-Andalus.

In this context, Alfonso made his appeal. While "King Sancho" was summoning his assembly in Valladolid in April 1282, Abu Yusuf received a number of Castilian emissaries at his palace in Marrakech. According to the Moroccan chronicle, the king's envoys transmitted Alfonso's desperate request for military support in the face of Sancho's rebellion. The message expressed indignation at the rebels' claims that Alfonso was mentally imbalanced. "O victorious king," he reportedly declaimed, "the Christians have violated their oath of fidelity and have rebelled against me, together with my son. They say, 'He is an old man who has lost his judgment and whose reason is disturbed.' Help me against them and I will go with you to meet them.'" The claim was a powerful one, loaded with political intent: Alfonso, his enemies were suggesting, was no longer fit to rule. Commentators had long suggested that kings might become so consumed by anger that they lost their reason and became insane. Instead of righteous anger, they behaved with *furore*, a raving and bestial emotion. Alfonso, on the surface, seems to have fallen into this emotional trap.

The emir immediately accepted the invitation to intervene in the peninsula, doubtless sensing an opportunity for new profits as well as holy war. Alfonso, for his part, was reluctant to reach this Faustian bargain. In one early version of the *Chronicle of Alfonso X*, seemingly more sympathetic to its protagonist than others, the narrator recounts how—in the church of Santa María in Seville (that is, the former great mosque)—the old king addressed a congregation directly: "You see, my friends, to what situation I have been brought, that by necessity I must be the friend of my enemies. God knows this is no pleasure for me. Know that I have placed my love with King Abu Yusuf, and with him I am going to see where God considers it good for us to end."

The emir arrived in Algeciras in the late summer of 1282. His messengers found Alfonso approaching near Zahara, and—according to this same early version of the chronicle—he ordered a great and noble pavilion erected, with two divans embroidered with gold and silk. He sent two of his men to kiss Alfonso's foot, "as is the custom of the Moors," while the Castilian king sat mounted on his horse. Approaching the entrance to the pavilion, the king embraced the emir, who told his followers, "Great is the nobility of this King Alfonso." The king may have gained some breathing space. In his testament, he defended his alliance with Abu Yusuf, suggesting that "many good things" had arisen from it. The Castilians had been able to emerge from the shadow of their enemies and to make those enemies more cautious about attempting to attack, he stated; on a personal level, during the four months that he stayed with the emir he had recovered his health to such an extent that he was able to ride and walk again.

Sancho's star, meanwhile, began to wane. Facing danger on multiple flanks, the prince rode first to Badajoz, where at the end of August 1282 the people had recognized Alfonso as the legitimate king, and then back to Córdoba to fend off the combined force of the king's military contingents and those of Abu Yusuf. The emir waged war against the city for three weeks in September, although he was unable to capture it. He then sowed destruction far to the north, through the region of Toledo and as far as Madrid. "This was an expedition such as there had not been in the previous centuries," the *Rawd al-Qirtas* noted proudly. In November, the emir then returned to his base at Algeciras, remaining there until the end of March. Alfonso's own forces, under the command of Fernán Pérez Ponce, led a new attack on the city of Córdoba. To the surprise and shock of the royal troops, a series of municipal militias led a countercharge from within the city, and battle was joined. Alfonso's troops at length emerged as victors. The chronicle tells us that Ferrán Muñoz, the rebel leader in Córdoba, was decapitated and that his head was taken to Alfonso X in Seville, who ordered it hung by iron hooks from a scaffold. Sancho, for his part, appears to have been furious that his forces had left the city to engage in battle against his father's men. If Ferrán Muñoz were still alive, the early version of the chronicle reports, Sancho would have ordered him burned at the stake or boiled alive in a cauldron.

The rebellion started to unravel; across the kingdom, Sancho faced defections. His youngest brother, Jaime, and a number of leading noblemen all deserted his cause, and another brother, Pedro, was on the point of doing so when he died. A papal bull issued on August 9, 1283, requesting that Edward I of England intervene to stop the conflict, deplored the "roaring of the storm" in which brother was pitted against brother and the son took up arms against his father, while subjects rose against the lord, all violating their duty of fidelity. Pope Martin IV, "a Frenchman," as the chronicle drily observes, ordered that any-one who did not support Alfonso be excommunicated. From Toro in the north to Mérida in the south, there were major ris-ings against the prince within Sancho's territory. The coup d'état could not be completed; the old king had kept his throne by the skin of his teeth.

Had Alfonso really lost his judgment, as Sancho claimed? Had he become maddened by fury? In the first century AD— about a hundred years before the reign of Marcus Aurelius—the Stoic philosopher Seneca had left a vivid description of "the people whom anger seizes." Such people groan and bellow, he had written. "Their speech is inarticulate and halting, they repeatedly clap their hands together and stamp the ground [and] they have the repellent and terrifying features of people who are deformed and bloated—it would be hard to say whether the vice is more abhorrent or disfiguring." If the Wise King had become deformed in this way, misshapen by anger, it would have been a profoundly ironic—if all-too-human—betrayal of principle: for Seneca was one of his favorite authors.

It is likely Alfonso had a copy of Seneca's works in his private library. He saw him quite rightly as a fountain of practical, real-life wisdom and identified closely with the Roman philosopher. The king emphasized the dangers of emotional "inflammation of the blood" and the way in which rage, anger, and hatred torment the hearts of men: "On account of the great desire they have of carrying out their wishes against those whom they dislike, they live in constant vexation and anxiety, waiting for the proper time to do them injury, and by thinking on this, they injure themselves, before they can do so to others."

Alfonso's concern with restraining anger was not merely ethical but also psychological and medical. The king should be patient in his anger, he had stipulated, because "rage obstructs the heart of man in such a way that it does not permit him to distinguish the truth." It also "causes him to tremble, and lose his judgment, and change his color, and alter his behavior, and makes him grow old before his time, and die before his days are accomplished." Anger can causes health problems "as from it arises sadness, and protracted thoughts, which are two things that greatly injure the health and understanding of [a] man, and shorten his life." Some of the passages on anger in the great law code are specific to kingship: the ruler should avoid hatred toward those who do not deserve it, because this will show him to be too proud, or toward the good, because that will reveal him to be envious. The *Siete partidas* stipulate that a ruler might lose the love of his people "when he conducted himself so harshly towards them that they were compelled to entertain great fear of him" and that "a contract or agreement which a man makes through fear shall not be valid. For through such fear not only weak men, but also those who are strong, are induced to promise or perform certain things." But many of the king's reflections, with their roots in ancient Stoic wisdom, seem to anticipate modern thinking about stress, tension, and spiritual equilibrium.

The songs to Holy Mary similarly suggest that Alfonso was keenly aware of how dangerous and socially disruptive anger could become. One tells of a gambler who, losing at a game of dice being played near a church in Catalonia, stands up abruptly and seizes a crossbow and quiver full of arrows. "When he loaded the crossbow," he says, "For once, I shall strike God or His Mother right through with an arrow." Having said this, he shoots the arrow up into the sky. "It took forever / To come back. Meanwhile, just like before, he began to play dice with another / companion of his. Then the arrow came down and struck the gaming board all covered with blood." The shock is enough to persuade the gambler to repent his sins and enter a religious order.

The Wise King was steeped in ideals of emotional restraint that had become dominant at a number of European courts. These ideals gained fresh momentum in the thirteenth century under the influence of the Dominicans and Franciscans. In the final years of his life, Alfonso must have heard them whispered in his ear over and over again. Immediately before the break between the king and his son, his prolific Franciscan confessor Juan Gil de Zamora had been busy writing a historically minded "mirror for princes" for the infante Sancho. This book (*De preconiis hispaniae*) provides a history and geography of Spain from its origins, through the eighth-century Muslim occupation and the Reconquest. As a historian, Juan Gil was rather unreliable—he evidently thought that both Aristotle and the Prophet Muhammad were Spanish—but his concern with conveying, through historical example, ethical ideals to which a ruler should aspire makes his work compelling. One such ideal was patience, the archenemy of anger. Patience, Juan Gil tells us—just as he must have told Alfonso and prince Sancho—is the ability to endure insults and verbal accusations and the capacity to tolerate physical suffering. It is also the ability to forgive insults. Remember the case of the first-century emperor Vespasian, he suggests. When an indignant herdsman cried out at the covetous emperor, "The fox can change its fur but not its nature, and the emperor cannot change his greed!" Vespasian responded philosophically, "We should laugh at these sayings, but we should correct ourselves."

It would be understandable if Alfonso found it difficult to respond so magnanimously in the face of an armed rebellion spearheaded by his eldest surviving son. But words were an instrument of war. If Sancho really claimed that his father was insane, his judgment clouded, and his reason gone, this may well have served as a means of justifying his bid for power. If his father had lost control of his emotions, the infante was suggesting, he deserved to lose control of his kingdom. The same can be said for words written two generations later; they, too, were grinding an ideological axe. The many incidents in the mid-fourteenth-century *Chronicle of Alfonso X* that suggest the emergence of a tyrant all come from a section described as a masterpiece of pro-Sancho propaganda, designed to undercut the claims to the throne by Fernando de la Cerda's eldest son, Alfonso de la Cerda.

This section begins precisely at the moment after Fernando de la Cerda's death, when Sancho first stakes his own claim that he should inherit the kingdom after his father dies. It aims to legitimize Sancho's eventual succession and therefore the lineage of kings that followed (it probably dates to Sancho's own reign from

1284 to 1295). Simultaneously, it is designed to show Alfonso in as negative a light as possible and to strengthen the image of his later namesake, Alfonso XI, as the unrivalled paragon of Castilian kingship.

The evidence of the most—perhaps the only—reliable passages in the chronicle, on the other hand, suggests that the king had frequently behaved with restraint in the political realm, even at moments of high political tension, such as the rebellion of Nuño González de Lara and the other nobles in 1272. Although Alfonso's marriage may well have been in trouble in his later years, there is no firm evidence supporting the notion of a psychological meltdown, an extraordinary degree of fury, or—least of all—a spiraling descent into a regime of terror. Sancho's own role in the capture and execution of Simón Ruiz de los Cameros is conveniently downplayed. The description of Alfonso in this final section of the chronicle is useful, in the end, mostly as a reminder of how the restraint of anger was seen as an essential quality of leadership.

It was in the midst of the civil war that Alfonso issued his last will and testament (November 8, 1282). After an initial expression of faith, Alfonso asked Saint Clement ("on whose day we were born"), Saint Alfonso ("whose name we share"), and Saint James ("who is our lord, defender, and father") to intercede with Mary and her son, protecting the loyal vassals and sons who had stood up against the great treacheries being committed against him and against God. The king also commended to Jesus his lands and kingdoms and all he had granted to him and "those heirs who henceforth may rightfully possess it."

If the vagueness about who should be the rightful heir is pointed, it is soon dispelled. After the death of his eldest son Fernando, the king declares, he had initially granted the succession to his son Sancho, drawing upon "old law and the law of Reason, according to the law of Spain," because "he was closer in the direct line of succession than our grandchildren, the sons of Don Fernando." He had trusted Sancho because he was now his eldest son, and "because of the great and true love that we had for him." "Although we had done some wrongs to him, as fathers do to sons," Alfonso admitted, "so great was the good that we did and were doing for him that we believed that all that had been forgotten and that he should love us more than anything else." But the more we tried to advance his interests, the king says, the more he tried to damage our own; the more we tried to honor him, the more he dishonored his father; the more we invested him with power, the more he disempowered us; the more we tried to ennoble him, the more he tried to bring us down. He is therefore disinherited and cursed by God and Saint Mary.

The decision to disinherit Sancho must have been a bitter one for Alfonso, the last straw for his physical health. But the rhetoric of the document has little in common with the picture of mental imbalance that we find in the royal chronicle (which, revealingly, does not mention it). Instead, it lays out the strategy of a king who had been cornered on the political chessboard and provides an articulate defense of his alliance with Abu Yusuf, who—despite the difference in religious laws and the fact that the Moroccans were always hostile to Spain—had promised to help Alfonso out of respect for the honor of his "house"; he had first sent his sons and relatives and then arrived in person. Alfonso declares that he had never wanted to disinherit Sancho or any of his other sons but that he had had no option. He would now seek a permanent alliance with the crown of France, for while "the Spanish are brave, intrepid warriors . . . the French are rich, peaceful, well-regarded, and orderly." If they joined together, not only would the whole of Spain be won, the king confidently prophesied; so would all the other lands that belonged to the enemies of the Catholic Church. Lordship over the realm would pass, after his death, to the king's grandchildren, the sons of Don Fernando. The elder son (Alfonso de la Cerda) was therefore heir, Alfonso stated, and might make suitable arrangements for his younger brother, Fernando. If both young brothers were to die childless, the king of France himself was to succeed to the throne.

On the same day, the king issued a second, accompanying document: a legal sentence condemning Sancho's rebellion. The prince, he states, had caused "grave and multiple injuries" to his father and to the realm while in Córdoba with the masters of the military orders of Calatrava and Uclés, the prior of the Knights Hospitaler, and the comendador of the Knights Templar. Further, Sancho had signed a peace treaty with the king of Granada, who was the king's vassal and had been paying tributes to him. When Alfonso had summoned his son to Seville, Sancho had indicated his intention to travel to Castile and León, ostensibly to calm unrest there, promising that he would then "return to us with good news," but instead he stirred rebellion there, saying that the king had broken the traditional laws, liberties, and customs, and sworn oaths of mutual support with the rebels.

The language then intensifies dramatically. Sancho, his father declares, "vomited out many unjust things against us," including his claim that "the king is demented and leprous . . . and that he killed people without reason as he killed Don Fadrique and Don Simón." The prince had usurped royal authority in the cities and castles, appropriated royal treasures and money in Toledo and elsewhere, and disinherited many members of the royal family and royal vassals. Alfonso had sent messengers to him, calling on him "through our paternal love" to meet him at Toledo or Villa Real, but Sancho had responded by violently detaining the emissaries. "Blinded by ambition," the prince had summoned the

April assembly in Valladolid and bribed many of those present through promises, money, and grants, while intimidating others. He had ensured that Alfonso was sentenced not by a judge but by his sworn enemies. Sancho had gathered militias from across Castile in order to be able to capture his father before leading them out toward Seville with this aim; he should therefore be considered a parricide. Unable to carry out his goal, he had attacked Badajoz and, failing to take it, had devastated the region and killed many people. He had then returned to Córdoba and fortified it against the king. "We therefore curse him, as a man deserving paternal malediction, condemned by God, and one who should be despised by all men, living henceforth as a victim of this divine and human curse, and we disinherit him as a rebel against us, as being disobedient, unrepentant, ungrateful."

The rhetoric is virulent; we might well imagine that the king was psychologically shattered, as well as broken in body. But the document is not a transparent window onto Alfonso's real emotional state. It was instead part of a public performance of anger. The sentence was read in the palace of Seville "in the presence of a great many clergymen, soldiers, and citizens, and an immense multitude of the people." All royal charters were ceremonially read aloud, forming part of a ritual event that impressed the onlooker with an image of royal majesty; people generally heard rather than read them. The sentence was political theater.

For now, the king remained steadfast in his decision to disinherit the prince, although—under tremendous pressure—he vacillated about who should take his place. The results were dizzyingly complicated. Evidently deciding that it was not practical for Fernando de la Cerda's little children to inherit in this moment of crisis, the king suddenly announced in a codicil to his testament, issued on January 10, 1284, that that his son Juan should now succeed to the thrones of Castile and León. His

youngest child, sixteen-year-old Jaime, was to receive the kingdom of Murcia, while Beatriz was to receive some lands in Seville
and Badajoz. But under no circumstances was Sancho to succeed
him: "Everyone knows that Don Sancho, who committed such a
great act of treachery against us, will soon do his worst to [Prince
Juan] and to the other children of ours who remained with us."
Juan was also entrusted with the responsibility of maintaining a
close alliance with the king of France and with the church,
"which were and are always the same thing, because the house of
France always served the church." If he failed to do this, "may he
face the wrath of God and the curse of our ancestors, and may he
be considered a traitor" (a preemptive threat of anger with its
own long tradition in royal charters).

Yet there was one final twist in the tale. In the spring of 1284,
the royal chronicle recounts, Sancho fell seriously ill while staying
in Salamanca. Believing that his son was about to die, the king
was struck with grief and wept profusely. He denied that this sadness was born of love: "I am not crying for the infante Sancho, but
for myself, a miserable old man, for now that he is dead, I shall
never recover my lands, for so great is the fear that the townsmen
and aristocrats and military orders have for me because of the error
they have done to me, that they will not wish to give them to me.
I would sooner recover them from the infante Sancho, if he were
alive, for he is just one man, than I will from all of them." The
chronicler suggests that the king was disguising his true affection
for Sancho at this moment of his son's near-fatal illness.

On March 23, 1284, Alfonso appears to have written to the
pope, begging him to absolve his "dearly beloved" son. Prince
Sancho, he said, had been led to stray from the path of devotion
to his father as a result of his youth and the false claims of some
of his rivals. But now, enlightened by the truth, Sancho was con-
trite in heart, tearfully seeking his father's mercy. Alfonso, who

(the letter continues) was more inclined to be merciful than vengeful, stated that the role of the father was to bring errant children back to the path of truth. And if he, "forced by necessity and tempted by wrath," had ever said, decreed, or ratified anything against Sancho, "we revoke and declare it of no weight." The letter survives in a "certificate of authenticity" issued in Zamora. Some historians have suspected it to be a forgery, but there is no definitive proof of this, and the letter is, in the end, more flattering to Alfonso than to his son.

If Sancho's rebellion had really tempted Alfonso to wrath, we could hardly blame him. But as he lay dying, the Wise King may have done what many never achieve: let go of his anger.

Epilogue

As Ptolemy said in the Almagest, the man who has given
life to science and knowledge never dies, and the man
who has devoted himself to understanding is never poor.
—Yehuda ben Mosé, Book of Crosses, 1

On April 4, 1284, having received communion, the
sixty-two-year-old king passed away. His eldest son was not
by his side but far to the north, in Ávila, where he was proclaimed
Sancho IV the following day, with the support of a powerful sector of Castilian and Leonese society. The new king would rule for
eleven years; his close diplomatic relationship with Pere III of
Aragon meant that the young pretenders, the infantes de la
Cerda, were kept safely out of the picture, detained in Xàtiva.
The French too would acknowledge Sancho as ruler. Only in Seville did he encounter resistance to his authority. There, in line
with the Wise King's last will and testament, the infante Juan
declared himself the new sovereign. But in the face of Sancho's

approaching armies, marching south into Andalusia, this resistance quickly dissolved.

In the codicil to his testament, Alfonso had said nothing of his estranged wife, Yolant, whose political wisdom and diplomatic skill—in the years before her flight to her native Aragon—had done so much to ensure that the Wise King remained on the throne. Yolant had remained in his realms after her return from Aragon in 1279. Two years before her husband's death, she had founded and endowed a Clarissan convent in Allariz, in Galicia. She devoted her patronage primarily to this institution, and she would be buried there in the winter of 1300–1301, possibly after returning from a pilgrimage to Rome. In contrast, the king had been generous to his daughter Queen Beatriz of Portugal, who was to receive the town of Niebla for the duration of her lifetime, and to her daughter Blanca, who was to receive 100,000 *maravedís* for her marriage dowry. After her father's death, Beatriz withdrew from managing the lordship that he had granted her in Alcocer, leaving these business matters to Branca. She lived until 1303 and was buried in the monastery of Alcobaça in central Portugal.

As for himself, Alfonso had asked in the codicil that his body be buried in one of the two parts of his realm that had remained loyal to him throughout his reign: either in the Cathedral of Seville or in the Church of Santa María la Real in Murcia, the city that he had so triumphantly captured as a young prince. This was "the first place that God wished us to gain in His service and in the honor of King Fernando, our father." If interred in Seville, he should be buried next to his father and mother, his head placed next to their feet.

Alfonso's desire to be reunited with his parents was fulfilled, although it was accompanied by another, seemingly more peculiar, request. His heart was to be carried to the Holy Land and buried on Mount Calvary, "where some of our grandfathers lie," while the rest of his internal organs were to be entombed in Santa María la Real, the former mosque that would be consecrated as a cathedral seven years later. The command was less morbid than it might appear. In medieval society, the division of a body after death was a widely accepted means of ensuring that a number of different churches and monasteries might pray for the soul of the deceased, and of bringing luster to different parts of a realm, just as the partition of saints' relics diffused their holy presence across Christendom. In the end, the king's heart and internal organs alike were buried in Santa María la Real, where they remain to this day.

His reign had ended in turmoil; the king had been cornered, if never checkmated. But despite a massive uprising among the Muslim population of Andalusia and Murcia, two prolonged phases of rebellion from within the royal court, and existential threats to his kingdom from the Marinid Empire, he had managed to retain, consolidate, and slightly expand his father's conquests. Beneath the immediate civil conflicts, and to a certain degree provoking them, there was also a deeper political change. Alfonso's legal and administrative reforms, aimed at rationalizing and centralizing government in his realm, had marked a first step away from an older feudal order in which kings had effectively shared power with the aristocracy as the first among equals. His vision of monarchy was not absolutist; he did not think of himself as above the law, and never doubted that the king and his people had mutual obligations. The king may have misjudged his friends and his own capacity to enact his political vision. He may never quite have shaken off the impetuous side to his character, which he had first shown in his decision—as a young prince—to launch an incursion into Portugal, and it proved impossible to subjugate the Castilian aristocracy as he surely wished. Still, his conception of an ideal, unified state belonged, for better and for worse, to a pattern that would come to dominate early modern Europe.

While retaining his mother's passionate faith, Alfonso had also advanced the pursuit of beauty, knowledge, science, and human happiness. Inspired by contact with Andalusi learning and by the personal experience of grief and suffering, he had accelerated the revitalization of European culture. This process, galvanized by economic development, relative political stability, and cultural exchange, had originated in the eleventh- and twelfth-century Mediterranean and now reached an apex in the thirteenth. Alfonso was at once the inheritor of this medieval rebirth and its most influential and imaginative figure.

The Castilian Renaissance did not "lead" to the Italian Renaissance. The process was not linear but rather assumed a diversity of cultural forms across the Mediterranean, as well as in northern European centers of wealth and commerce such as the Low Countries. The Andalusi and Spanish phases of this rebirth, long eclipsed in our historical memory by colonial, ethnic, and religious prejudices and by the self-promoting amnesia of later Renaissance humanists, accompanied and sometimes predated the Italian phase, but this does not establish a causal connection.

The cultural tides that lapped the shores of the two peninsulas ebbed constantly back and forth. The twelfth-century Italian scholar Gerard of Cremona had traveled to Toledo, translating the work of al-Zarkali and other members of the Andalusi intelligentsia for a broader European audience; new generations of Italians would arrive at the court of the Wise King, drawn to this beacon of learning. Meanwhile, Italy served as an important transmitter of Arabic astronomical studies such as al-Sufi's *Book of the Fixed Stars*. Italian scholars also helped to diffuse the work of Cicero and Seneca—authors who deeply shaped Alfonso's thinking—as well as new religious movements such as the Franciscans, beloved by the kings of Castile. Vernacular literature flourished in thirteenth-century Spain and Italy alike. Later Italian humanism would wash over Iberia, strengthened by the political links that bound the crown of Aragon to Naples and southern Italy. If the cultural hybridity of the Castilian Renaissance was to be echoed in fifteenth- and sixteenth-century Venice, the reasons lay not in al-Andalus but above all in the intimate relations between the Serene Republic and the highly cultured sultans of Ottoman Turkey. The waves rose and fell, encompassing the whole breadth of the Mediterranean and crossing the borders of religious identity.

Even if we cannot quite imagine Alfonso as the king who saved civilization—a claim made for too many rulers and peoples—it is important to acknowledge the many points of connection between Castile and the northern Italian regions conventionally seen as the epicenter of the Renaissance, as well as the southern regions once ruled by Frederick II. To the network of commercial connections that linked Seville with Genoa, Pisa, and other Italian port cities and that had facilitated the dissemination of Andalusi culture, philosophy, and material goods over the previous two hundred years, the quest for the empire added a significant new dimension. This quest had been no quixotic adventure. It had followed long-standing diplomatic strategy at the Castilian court, and had Alfonso not faced sustained rebellion and the constant threat of invasion from North Africa, it is not impossible that he might have succeeded.

As Holy Roman Emperor, Alfonso would have had an even more powerful platform for his cultural program in Italy and Germany. Some have speculated that the Florentine Codex of the *Cantigas de Santa María* found its way to Italy as a result of his journey to Beaucaire—that it had been intended as a diplomatic gift to Pope Gregory X. In fact, the codex landed in the hands of the Medici family only in the eighteenth century. Nonetheless, the support of the Pisans in 1256 and Brunetto Latini's embassy on behalf of the Florentine republic four years later had tightened the bonds between the two peninsulas and disseminated Alfonso's personal fame: there was no one under the moon, Brunetto proclaimed, who matched the nobility of the great king of Spain, now king of the Romans, awaiting—God willing—the imperial crown.

The *Cantigas de Santa María* reveal the closeness of the links. More than twenty have an Italian setting. At the Benedictine abbey of Sagra di San Michele near Turin, Mary restores a wine-stained chasuble to purest white, in Pisa she narrowly saves a handsome and wealthy priest from breaking his vow of chastity on his wedding night after his relatives have persuaded him to marry, and in Siena she miraculously makes a white marble sculpture of the devil turn black. This last piece of news must have reached Alfonso's court very recently; the sculpture—part of a new pulpit designed by Nicola and Giovanni Pisano—had been built between 1266 and 1268. Much further to the south, a miracle tale transmitted by word of mouth tells how the Virgin had succeeded in extinguishing a major eruption of Mount Etna in Sicily.

Two songs provide accounts of another recent incident said to have occurred in the Cathedral of Foggia in Apulia, where a Byzantine icon of Mary was venerated. A "crazed" German woman, possibly a camp follower, was gambling in the cathedral. As she started to lose, she hurled a stone at the icon, but a stone angel intervened. "The angel forever after held its hand outstretched, which it had thrust in front of the statue to protect it." Because of the song's reference to the presence of Conrad IV, the occasion of the miracle has been dated quite precisely to Candlemas

(February 2) or Annunciation (March 25), 1252, just a few months before Alfonso X's accession to the throne.

Some of Alfonso's texts enjoyed widespread circulation in Italy and beyond in the centuries to come. Ironically, the *Cantigas de Santa María*—so intimately linked to the king himself—would not be among them. His wish that the manuscripts be deposited in the Cathedral of Seville was respected, and for centuries they were metaphorically buried along with him. The satirical *Cantigas d'escarnho e de mal dizer*, on the other hand, seem to have appealed to the biting Renaissance sense of humor. The early fifteenth-century Italian humanist Angelo Colocci, secretary of Pope Leo X, would keep a copy in his personal library for his own enjoyment.

The *Alfonsine Tables* were similarly admired. Pietro de Reggio, who had also participated in a Latin translation of the *Perfect Book of the Judgment of the Stars*, may have taken a copy of the *Tables* with him when he traveled with a Castilian embassy to Paris in 1280. There, a group of important astronomers adapted the *Tables* for the Paris meridian, and their text became the cornerstone of all astronomical tables in the late Middle Ages and Renaissance. One copy, dating to 1492, is still to be found in the Biblioteca Nazionale Centrale in Florence and was signed and annotated by none other than Galileo Galilei. Copernicus's copy (from the same year) is currently located in the library of the University of Uppsala. After the invention of the printing press, the text was widely published, beginning with an edition printed in Venice in 1483. In almost all the printed editions, Alfonso is referred to as "king of the Romans and Castile," reflecting his pursuit of the empire. As for the science of astrology—applied astronomy—which he had patronized and helped to pioneer, and which became more important than ever as a component of medical knowledge, the fourteenth and fifteenth centuries would mark an apex. The Renaissance humanist, physician, and philosopher Marsilio Ficino would compose a particularly influential work on astrological medicine titled *Three Books on Life* (1489).

The *Book of Mohammed's Ladder*, too, appears to have enjoyed an illustrious afterlife in Italy. Bonaventura of Siena, one of a number of writers and notaries from northern Italian towns at Alfonso's court—probably Ghibelline exiles—produced a Latin version soon after its completion. A century ago, a Spanish priest named Miguel Asín Palacios provocatively proposed that the work had helped shape Dante Alighieri's *Divine Comedy*: a point of view, once scorned, that some recent scholars have embraced. In the *Inferno*, Dante did not mask his admiration for the Muslim philosopher Averroes (Ibn Rushd). As his protagonist makes his way toward hell in the company of his spiritual guide, Virgil, he spies—on the enamel-green lawn that lies within the towering castle of pagan genius—"Averroes, who wrote the weighty glosses," alongside such pre-Christian intellectual giants as Aristotle, Socrates, Plato, Cicero, and Seneca, as well as the Persian polymath Avicenna.

Alfonso's realms, far from being at the periphery of Christian Europe, were inextricably intertwined with its development. The king would have known this, and would have drawn strength from it in his quest for the title of Holy Roman Emperor. Dante, too, would envision a Christian emperor who could restore peace and order to war-torn Italy, hounding down the bestial forces of darkness in his path. In the opening scenes of the *Inferno*, in the wild and menacing wood, we read, "He shall not feed on lands or lucre / But on wisdom, love, and power . . . / He shall hunt the beast through every town / till he has sent her back to Hell."

Alfonso was not to be the emperor of whom Dante dreamed. Still, within the later Spanish Empire, the *Siete partidas*—his legal and philosophical masterpiece—would be applied for centuries, becoming the law of the land in many parts of the Americas. In the Louisiana Territory, ruled by the Spanish monarchy between 1762 and 1800, sections of the *Partidas* remained applicable after the Louisiana Purchase—although anything that related to the authority of a king was studiously avoided. In 1820, the state legislature ordered that a new translation of excerpts from the *Partidas* be sent to the judges of the Louisiana state courts, to the executive branches of other US states, and to the president. One historian has suggested that the great law code was his "greatest gift to posterity."

Ultimately, his importance stretches beyond Italy, the borders of empire, and the realm of law. His commitment to the pursuit of happiness in this world, as well as the next, would become a hallmark of modernity. His contemporary Saint Thomas Aquinas (1225–1274) also helped articulate the theological possibility of earthly felicity by diminishing an earlier emphasis on original sin. Building on the legacy of the twelfth-century Renaissance, the Italian humanists Pico della Mirandola and Lorenzo Valla would respectively seek to establish the dignity of man and to embrace worldly pleasures; for his part, Benedetto Morandi would ask how someone who could not find a way to be happy in this life could do so in the afterlife. But before Thomas Jefferson, whose marble relief portrait hangs alongside Alfonso's in the US House of Representatives, few disciples of happiness shared the combination of political, cultural, and intellectual power that Alfonso X had enjoyed.

The explosion of creative energy and scientific inquiry that characterized Alfonso's reign had been inspired by a deeply humane quest both for his personal contentment and for that of his subjects. His commitment went far beyond boisterous camaraderie and underlay his whole intellectual enterprise. He attempted to transcend physical and emotional pain through the power of intellect and imagination, embracing a spirit of joie de vivre that has little in common with stereotypical notions of medieval grimness and austerity. In songs and games, as well as in reading, men might find joy, he had written. He relished laughter for its own sake, not just as a political tool, and in his private life he sought contentment in flesh-and-blood human relationships. His longterm premarital liaison with Mayor Guillén de Guzmán preceded an unusually monogamous marriage with Queen Yolant. Contrary to the caricature of the medieval father as a cruel and distant authoritarian, he was fully aware of the joys that fatherhood can bring and until the end of his life remained close to his firstborn child. His friendships with other men were also intensely meaningful for him. He might have agreed with the Mouse in the tales of Calila and Digna: "There is no pleasure in this world like the company of friends," said the Mouse, "and no pain like losing them."

For the Wise King, happiness was to be sought on earth as it was hoped for in heaven. In his view, the alignment of the stars affected all material life on our planet: it could activate the secret properties of stones, many of which had healing powers that could cure human illnesses, including depression. These ideas were articulated and beautifully illustrated in the luxury edition of the *Book of Stones* that he commissioned in the mid-1270s. He had conceived his songs to Holy Mary, too, as a contribution to human happiness and a source of healing. The idea that medieval people universally subscribed to a cult of pain, suffering, and martyrdom—as denizens of a dark and miserable era—is, in other words, quite wrong. This was rarely a pleasure-hating world. Men and women of the thirteenth century were more and more inclined to embrace both laughter and joy, for their intrinsic value as well as for their political use. The humane spirit of Alfonso's reign infused his cultural projects with life and beauty. Through these projects, he bequeathed his impassioned search for felicity to later generations of readers, viewers, and listeners—including us.

Tragedy had repeatedly scarred the king's life. Some later historians were to point the finger of blame at Alfonso himself, seeing his problems as a parable illustrating the dangers of intellectual enthusiasm. For the Jesuit historian Juan de Mariana, writing at the end of the sixteenth century, he had been a ruler with his head in the clouds, a bumbling, professorial king, unwilling or unable to cope with the rocky terrain of reality: "While he contemplated the heavens, and gazed at the stars," Mariana wrote, "he fell on the earth." Mariana's words echoed an ancient joke about absent-minded philosophers, dating back to *Aesop's Fables* and beyond. Socrates himself, claiming that philosophers were hopelessly abstracted from the real world, had made an example of Thales of Miletus: "I will illustrate my meaning by the jest of the witty maidservant, who saw Thales tumbling into a well, and said of him, that he was so eager to know what was going on in heaven, he could not see what was before his feet."

But Alfonso would have laughed off this joke. He was far more grounded than the Jesuit historian wished his readers to believe, and his sense of humor had been positively earthy. The catastrophes that befell him had to do with forces that were largely beyond his control: the difficulty of finding people to settle the newly conquered and precarious territories of Andalusia, the problems caused by spiraling inflation, a growing fissure between the interests of the crown and those of the aristocracy, and the emergence of the Marinid dynasty in North Africa. His correspondence with his eldest son suggests that he was an astute political operator, keenly conscious of the movements of the different players on the chessboard. He understood the tension between his dreams and his realities—this was precisely the force that drove his fearsome creativity. The vitality of the reign generated art of the highest order—the *Cantigas de Santa María*, the cathedrals of León and Burgos, and the *Book of Games*. It catalyzed a cornucopia of scientific knowledge and deep insights into the human condition.

Alfonso's life presents us with the compelling paradox of an intelligent and thoughtful man, reflecting deeply on many of the central issues of human existence, whose day-to-day life was nonetheless plagued by troubles, grief, and frustration. After the mid-1260s, he had been restricted to a defensive and reactive political position; his middle and later years had unfolded beneath a gathering storm of setbacks, culminating in a civil war that threatened to engulf him entirely. If—in the *Book of the Twelve Wise Men* or in the palace of Seville—Alfonso found the keys to happiness, it is true that he sometimes mislaid them. His reign was characterized by the *chiaroscuro*—the dramatic contradictions between darkness and light, beauty and violence, hope and despair—that later lay at the heart of the Italian Renaissance.

Yet wisdom, in the end, may be measured not simply in a tally of failure and success but in the strength of the human spirit in the face of changing fortunes. Just as the extraordinary inventiveness of the Italian artists of the fifteenth and sixteenth centuries can only be understood as a response to tensions and contradictions at the heart of their society and in their own turbulent personal lives, Alfonso's response to a mounting sequence of troubles and catastrophes was the production of some of the most sophisticated and beautiful works to have graced the Middle Ages. His efforts to wrestle with these crises—both inward and external—sometimes got the better of him. In the last dozen years of life, he often stumbled and fell, losing his battles with personal demons and political enemies. But his struggles, both as a ruler and as a human being, were distilled—in the texts he wrote and commissioned, in art, and in architecture—into something sublime, a distant reflection of our own aspirations: a medieval mirror for modern readers.

ACKNOWLEDGMENTS

This book was inspired, in part, by a lively conversation in the Monroe Lecture Center at Hofstra University. Without the friendships, collegiality, and intellectual dialogue I have enjoyed in the Department of History and the Hofstra University Honors College, I might never have returned to Alfonso the Wise: a figure who flitted back and forth across the pages of my first book. My warm thanks, therefore, to Stanislao Pugliese, whose award-winning biography of Ignazio Silone is a model of scholarship and who helped start the ball rolling; to Susan Yohn, who arranged for a teaching schedule that allowed me enough time to write; and to Warren Frisina and Neil Donahue, for their skillful steering of our team-taught course Culture and Expression, as well as to our friend, former colleague, and fellow writer Donna Freitas. I am equally indebted to my students, including those who, in the spring semesters of 2012 and 2015, explored the reign of the Wise King, offering an endless array of excellent questions and providing thoughtful feedback on the penultimate draft.

Research for this book was facilitated by a series of grants from the Hofstra College of Liberal Arts and Sciences, and by Jay Barksdale, who offered me the chance to work in the tranquility of the Allen Room at the New York Public Library. To have many months of access to the resources of a world-class research library was an extraordinary privilege, and I am thankful to all the NYPL staff. Two teaching fellowships from the National Endowment from the Humanities—the first for a project on the Berbers in medieval Iberia and the Maghreb, the second an Enduring Questions grant to develop a new course on the history of friendship—further paved the way. I am also grateful for the financial support of the Ministerio de Educación, Cultura, and Deportes (Spain), and its Programa Hispanex de Ayudas para la Cooperación Cultural con Universidades Extranjeras.

As every scholar of Alfonso X knows, the Wise King's cultural production was an intensely collaborative process. Writing his biography has been anything but solitary. I have been fortunate to be able to count on a network of marvelous friends, whose energy, expertise and eagle-eyed reading have enormously enhanced this book. Simon Barton, Matthew and Melanie Deans, Jerrilynn Dodds, Kirstin Downey, Rachelle Friedman, Antonella Liuzzo Scorpo, Rachel Moss, Leyla Rouhi, Janina Safran, Miriam Shadis, Michael Solomon, and Aengus Ward all read chapters, in some cases the entire manuscript, and their astute observations have been invaluable. Jesús Rodríguez Velasco performed double-duty as reader and photographer, as well as generously sharing his digitized manuscript and pointing me in the direction of a highly creative web designer, Miguel Ripoll.

Rarely did a day pass, in writing *The Wise King*, in which I did not need to call on the wisdom of others. An exhaustive list of debts incurred would take this manuscript beyond my word limit, but I owe special thanks to Kim Bergqivist; Janna Bianchini; Maria João Branco; Brian Catlos; Jean Dangler; Julio Escalona; Juan Escourido; Mário Farelo; Luly Feliciano; Ryan Giles; Jonathan Lyon; Denis Menjot; Alicia Miguélez; Joseph O'Callaghan; Steven Parkinson; Lucy Pick; Simone Pinet; Robey Patrick; José Manuel Rodriguez Montañés; Mike Ryan; Connie Scarborough; Belén Vicens; Ellie Woodacre; and Juan Zozaya Stabel-Hansen, whose remarkable knowledge of medieval Castilian archaeology is matched only by his kindness. Ala Alryyes, too, has reminded me that, in the words of the Mouse in *Calila et Digna*, "there is no pleasure in this world like the company of friends." Jason Sagebiel and Aleksandra Kocheva have shed new light on Alfonso's emphasis on the therapeutic value of music.

Throughout the process, Deirdre Mullane has offered a thousand insights into the publishing world and the task of writing for a new audience: I look forward to continuing our collaboration. At Basic Books, Alex Littlefield offered a series of sensitive critiques, and Dan Gerstle has masterfully shepherded the project to completion; I also remain thankful to Liz Dana, Clay Farr, Nicole Jarvis, Jen Kelland, Collin Tracy, Liz Tztetzo, and Cindy Young.

Had it not been for Queen Yolant, Alfonso might never have kept his throne; had it not been for Benita, I might never have kept on track in the quixotic task of writing about a man so seemingly far removed from us. Above all, then, I am grateful to her for her emotional and intellectual support; to our own Beatriz, as loyal and beautiful as the Wise King's favorite daughter; and to Breogán, whose limitless capacity for joy Alfonso would have embraced.

NOTES

NOTES TO PROLOGUE

xvii **the Book of the Twelve Wise Men:** John K. Walsh, ed., *El libro de los doze sabios: O tractado de la nobleza y lealtad [ca. 1237]: Estudio y edición*, Anejos del boletín de la Real Academia Española 29 (Madrid, 1975).

xviii **The union ushered in a period:** John Carmi Parsons, *Eleanor of Castile: Queen and Society in Thirteenth-Century England* (New York: St. Martins Press, 1995); Sara Cockerill, *Eleanor of Castile: The Shadow Queen* (Stroud, UK: Amberley Publishing, 2014); Theresa Earenfight, *Queenship in Medieval Europe* (New York: Palgrave Macmillan, 2013), 145–147.

xix **his wife Marguerite of Provence:** On Marguerite and her three sisters, all married to kings, see Earenfight, *Queenship*, 123–125.

xix **Here, in another part of the Mediterranean world:** David Abulafia, *Frederick II: A Medieval Emperor* (Oxford: Oxford University Press, 1988).

xix **"the first ruler of the modern type who sat upon a throne":** Jacob Burckhardt, *The Civilization of the Renaissance in Italy*, trans. S. G. C. Middlemore (New York: Penguin, 1990), 20.

xx **The most influential of these codes:** See Robert I. Burns, SJ, ed., *Las siete partidas*, trans. Samuel Parsons Scott, 5 vols. (Philadelphia: University of Pennsylvania Press, 2001). The comparison with Justinian and Napoleon is made by Robert I. Burns, SJ, "Jews and Moors in the *Siete partidas* of Alfonso X the Learned: A Background Perspective," in *Medieval Spain: Culture, Conflict and Coexistence; Studies in Honour of Angus MacKay*, ed. Roger Collins and Anthony Goodman (New York: Palgrave Macmillan, 2002), 46–62, at 46. The relief portrait is accessible online at "Alfonso X," Architect of the Capitol, http://www.aoc.gov/capitol-hill/relief-portrait-plaques -lawgivers/alfonso-x (accessed March 16, 2015).

xx **A stereotype of Spain as a fanatically religious and intolerant culture:** Richard L. Kagan, "Prescott's Paradigm: American

Historical Scholarship and the Decline of Spain," *American Historical Review* 101, no. 2 (1996): 423–446. The TV series *Toledo, cruce de destinos* aired in 2012 on Antena 3 (Spain).

xxi **Lovers of early music:** The principal edition of the *Cantigas* is Alfonso X, o Sábio, *Cantigas de Santa María*, ed. Walter Mettman, 4 vols. (Coimbra: Universidade de Coimbra, 1959–1972). Here, however, I will provide page references to Kathleen Kulp-Hill, trans., *Songs of Holy Mary of Alfonso X, the Wise: A Translation of the Cantigas de Santa María* (Tempe: Arizona Center for Medieval and Renaissance Studies, 2000), which contains all the *cantigas* and provides English-language translations, which I have occasionally modified in part. When possible I have also cited the selected translations in Stephen Parkinson, ed., *Alfonso X the Learned, Cantigas de Santa María: An Anthology*, MHRA Critical Texts 40 (Cambridge, UK: Modern Humanities Research Association, 2015). The *cantigas* cited here are nos. 54, 100, and 112, in Kulp-Hill, *Songs of Holy Mary*, 70, 125, 138.

xxii **Adopting a role as personal troubadour:** Amy G. Remensnyder, *La Conquistadora: The Virgin Mary at War and Peace in the Old and New Worlds* (Oxford: Oxford University Press, 2014), 50–57.

xxii **"Towards 1250 . . . Heaven, moved to pity by the noble spirits":** James B. Ross and Mary M. McLaughlin, eds., *The Portable Renaissance Reader* (New York: Penguin, 1977), 140–145, at 144.

xxii **In reality, the Italian Renaissance was just one spectacular stage:** This argument was made a century ago: "It was in the first three centuries of the present millennium that the rebirth of Europe took place. The term 'Renaissance' applied to the Italian and Italianate culture of the fifteenth and sixteenth centuries is a misnomer stamped upon current notions by the traditions of that culture itself." Robert Briffault, *Rational Evolution (The Making of Humanity)* (New York: Macmillan, 1930), 176.

xxv **arena of hybridity and overlapping influences:** María Rosa Menocal, *The Ornament of the World: How Muslims, Jews, and Christians Created a Culture of Tolerance in Medieval Spain* (Boston: Little, Brown, 2002); Cynthia Robinson and Leyla Rouhi, eds., *Under the Influence: Questioning the Comparative in Medieval Castile* (Leiden: Brill, 2005); Jerrilyn D. Dodds, Maria Rosa Menocal, and Abigail Krasner Balbale, *The Arts of Intimacy: Christians, Jews, and Muslims in the Making of Castilian Culture* (New Haven, CT: Yale University Press, 2008).

xxv **This was the phenomenon that some modern scholars have termed** *convivencia*: Américo Castro coined the term in *España en su historia* (Buenos Aires: Losada, 1948). Maya Soifer, "Beyond *Convivencia*: Critical Reflections on the Historiography of Interfaith

Relations in Christian Spain," *Journal of Medieval Iberian Studies* 1, no. 1 (2009): 19–35, offers an astute appraisal of historical scholarship in the Castro tradition.

xxv **In Christian kingdoms across the peninsula, delicately carved works of ivory:** Mariam Rosser-Owen, "Islamic Objects in Christian Contexts: Relic Translation and Modes of Transfer in Medieval Iberia," *Art in Translation* 7, no. 1 (2015): 39–64.

xxvi **the "Scientist Pope" Gerbert of Aurillac:** Nancy Marie Brown, *The Abacus and the Cross: The Story of the Pope Who Brought the Light of Science to the Dark Ages* (New York: Basic Books, 2010), is an accessible biography.

xxvi **a desire to conquer and dominate al-Andalus:** Hence the value of postcolonial theory: see Nadia Altschul, "The Future of Postcolonial Approaches to Medieval Iberian Studies," *Journal of Medieval Iberian Studies* 1, no. 1 (2009): 5–17; David Wacks, "Reconquest Colonialism and Andalusi Narrative Practice in the *Conde Lucanor*," *diacritics* 36, no. 3–4 (fall-winter 2006): 87–103.

xxviii **sometimes call bluntly for the complete elimination of Islam:** *Cantigas de Santa María* [hereafter CSM] 360, 401: Kulp-Hill, *Songs of Holy Mary*, 439, 482.

xxviii **Mary herself, the subject of Alfonso's undying devotion:** Remensnyder, *La Conquistadora*, 47–57.

xxviii **Italian city-states would later become interlinked with Ottoman Turkey:** Jerry Brotton, *The Renaissance Bazaar: From the Silk Road to Michelangelo* (Oxford: Oxford University Press, 2002), 1.

xxviii **Even his devotional songs, the *Cantigas de Santa María*:** Manuel Pedro Ferreira, "Andalusian Music and the Cantigas de Santa María," in *Cobras e Son: Papers from a Colloquium on the Text, Music, and Manuscripts of the 'Cantigas de Santa María,'* ed. Stephen Parkinson (Oxford: Legenda, 2000), 7–19; Manuel Pedro Ferreira, "Rondeau and Virelai: The Music of Andalus and the Cantigas de Santa Maria," *Plainsong and Medieval Music* 13, no. 2 (2004): 127–140.

NOTES TO CHAPTER ONE

1 **"adept at all the arts a good knight should possess":** Alfonso el Sabio, *Setenario*, ed. Kenneth H. Vanderford (Buenos Aires: Instituto de Filología, Universidad de Buenos Aires, 1945), 13 (my translation).

1 **would eventually be acknowledged as a saint of the Catholic Church:** Fernando was formally canonized in 1671, but an informal cult was already well developed in the late thirteenth century: see Cynthia Chamberlin, "'Unless the Pen Writes as It Should': The

Proto-Cult of Saint Fernando III in Seville in the Thirteenth and Fourteenth Centuries," in *Sevilla 1248: Congreso internacional conmemorativo del 750 aniversario de la conquista de la ciudad de Sevilla por Fernando III, rey de Castilla y León*, ed. Manuel González Jiménez (Madrid: Fundación Ramón Areces, 2000), 389–417.

2   **All the world's a chessboard:** Olivia Remie Constable, "Chess and Courtly Culture in Medieval Castile: The *Libro de ajedrez* of Alfonso X, el Sabio," *Speculum* 82, no. 2 (April 2007): 301–347, esp. 313–315, 341–347; cf. Albrecht Classen, "Chess in Medieval German Literature: A Mirror of Social, Historical, and Cultural, Religious, Ethical and Moral Conditions," in *Chess in the Middle Ages and Early Modern Age: A Fundamental Thought Paradigm of the Premodern World*, ed. Daniel O'Sullivan (Berlin: De Gruyter, 2012), 17–44, at 27.

2   **the pieces might even revolt:** A pattern of defections to the neighboring kingdom of León may have shaped the portrayal of the famous epic hero El Cid: Simon Barton, "Reinventing the Hero: The Poetic Portrayal of Rodrigo Díaz, the Cid, in Its Political Context," in *Textos épicos castellanos: Problemas de edición y crítica*, ed. David G. Pattison (London: Queen Mary and Westfield College, 2000), 65–78.

2   **the most powerful aristocratic family in the land:** Simon R. Doubleday, *The Lara Family: Crown and Nobility in Medieval Spain* (Cambridge, MA: Harvard University Press, 2001), ch. 3.

2   **Berenguela—aged thirty-seven—had inherited the throne:** Berenguela has been the subject of three excellent recent biographies: Miriam Shadis, *Berenguela of Castile (1180–1246) and Political Women in the High Middle Ages* (New York: Palgrave, 2009); H. Salvador Martínez, *Berenguela la Grande y su época (1180–1246)* (Madrid: Polífemo, 2012); and Janna Bianchini, *The Queen's Hand: Power and Authority in the Reign of Berenguela of Castile* (Philadelphia: University of Pennsylvania Press, 2012), which points out that she did not—as traditionally stated—relinquish authority to her son (141–142).

3   **Beatrix of Swabia:** Her elder sister had also been named Beatrix but had died young, in 1212; having originally been given the name Elisabeth/Isabella, she appears to have taken the name Beatrix— which was also her mother's name—on her sister's death (Jonathan Lyon, personal communication to author). In general, I have retained the names of foreign-born queens in their original language as a marker of each's distinct identity and as one sign of the international diversity of royal courts.

3 **The queen mother, Berenguela, had chosen her son's bride carefully:** Shadis, *Berenguela of Castile*, 107–110.

3 **Beautiful and refined:** H. Salvador Martínez, *Alfonso X, the Learned: A Biography*, trans. Odile Cisneros (Leiden: Brill, 2010), 35–40.

3 **a solemn occasion:** Thomas N. Bisson, *The Crisis of the Twelfth Century: Power, Lordship, and the Origins of European Government* (Princeton, NJ: Princeton University Press, 2009), 541.

4 **a pair of polychrome statues:** Francisco Javier Hernández, "Two Weddings and a Funeral: Alfonso X's Monuments in Burgos," *Hispanic Research Journal* 13, no. 5 (October 2012): 417–420.

4 **the Christians crushed an Almoravid army:** Amy G. Remensnyder, *La Conquistadora: The Virgin Mary at War and Peace in the Old and New Worlds* (Oxford: Oxford University Press, 2014), 27, places this incident in cultural context.

4 **These "Mozarabs":** Richard Hitchcock, "Christian-Muslim Understanding(s) in Medieval Spain," *Hispanic Research Journal* 9, no. 4 (September 2008): 314–325, at 322.

6 **a cultural flourishing:** Jerrilyn D. Dodds, Maria Rosa Menocal, and Abigail Krasner Balbale, *The Arts of Intimacy: Christians, Jews, and Muslims in the Making of Castilian Culture* (New Haven, CT: Yale University Press, 2008), ch. 2.

6 **entrusted very early to a wet nurse:** Manuel González Jiménez, "Alfonso X, Infante," *Acta historica et archaeologica mediaevalia, homenatge al Dr. Manuel Riu* 22 (2001): 292; Nicholas Orme, *Medieval Children* (New Haven: Yale University Press, 2001), 58.

6 **Wet nurses often used to hug and kiss the babies:** R. C. Finucane, *The Rescue of the Innocents: Endangered Children in Medieval Miracles* (New York: Saint Martin's Press, 1997), 40–41.

7 **the Dominican friar Vincent de Beauvais:** Irina Nanu and Miguel Vicente Pedraz, "Una aproximación al *Regimen puerorum* en el *Speculum doctrinale* de Vicente de Beauvais y su posible relación con la *Segunda partida* de Alfonso X el Sabio," Universitat de València, Parnaseo, http://parnaseo.uv.es/Memorabilia/Memorabilia9/Irina/index.html (accessed June 5, 2015).

7 **"The sages . . . declared that boys learning":** Robert I. Burns, SJ, ed., *Las siete partidas*, trans. Samuel Parsons Scott, 5 vols. (Philadelphia: University of Pennsylvania Press, 2001), law 2.7.4, 2:302.

7 **good manners:** Stephen Jaeger, *The Origins of Courtliness: Civilizing Trends and the Formation of Courtly Ideals, 939–1210* (Philadelphia:

University of Pennsylvania Press, 1985), 12; Shadis, *Berenguela of Castile*, 46–47.

8   **"closely wrapped in a beautiful and well-made mantle of silk cloth":** Cited in Shadis, *Berenguela of Castile*, 47.

8   **In elite circles across Europe:** Orme, *Medieval Children*, 278–281; Philip David Grace, "Providers and Educators: The Theory and Practice of Fatherhood in Late Medieval Basel, 1475–1529" (PhD diss., University of Minnesota, 2010), 145n123.

8   **They should take care not to put "a second morsel":** Burns, *Las siete partidas*, law 2.7.5, 2:302–303.

8   **Nor should they drink as soon as they wake up:** Burns, *Las siete partidas*, law 2.7.6, 2:303–304.

9   **"not uttered loudly, or in a very low voice":** Burns, *Las siete partidas*, law 2.7.7, 2:304.

9   **"walk in a graceful manner, not holding themselves too straight":** Burns, *Las siete partidas*, law 2.7.8, 2:305.

9   **"Although I was a little boy":** CSM 256: Kathleen Kulp-Hill, trans., *Songs of Holy Mary of Alfonso X, the Wise: A Translation of the Cantigas de Santa María* (Tempe: Arizona Center for Medieval and Renaissance Studies, 2000), 312.

9   **Though the queen was saved:** Joseph O'Callaghan, *Alfonso X and the Cantigas de Santa María: A Poetic Biography* (Leiden: Brill, 1998), 48–50.

10 **Hearing her cry, Beatrix flung open the chapel doors:** CSM 122: Kulp-Hill, *Songs of Holy Mary*, 150.

10 **Two years later, Fernando remarried:** Shadis, *Berenguela of Castile*, 107–110.

10 **The new couple would have five more children:** Martínez, *Alfonso X*, 40.

10 **This may partly have been a response to the loss:** On Mary as unfailing mother, see Remensnyder, *La Conquistadora*, 99–105.

11 **he proved to be "sharp-witted":** Fidel Fita, "Biografías de San Fernando y de Alfonso el Sabio por Gil de Zamora," *Boletín de la Real Academia de la Historia* 5 (1885): 308–328, at 319.

11 **In addition to Latin and the spoken language of the region:** Martínez, *Alfonso X*, 73–75.

11 **The *Book of the Twelve Wise Men*:** John K. Walsh, ed., *El libro de los doze sabios: O tractado de la nobleza y lealtad [ca. 1237]: Estudio y edición*, Anejos del boletín de la Real Academia Española 29 (Madrid, 1975), 23–33.

11 **"The shouts and the cries of the Moors":** Ramón Menéndez Pidal, ed., *Primera crónica general de España*, 2 vols. (Madrid: Gredos, 1955) [hereafter *PCG*], 2:726, ch. 1043.

12 **illustration from the *Book of Games*:** Sonja Musser, "Los libros de acedrex dados e tablas: Historical, Artistic and Metaphysical Dimensions of Alfonso X's *Book of Games*" (PhD diss., University of Arizona, 2007), 727–728, suggests that the blond youth playing chess with an older man on folios 10v and 23r may be the infante Alfonso.

12 **Seville, in particular, enjoyed fame as a center for chess:** Constable, "Chess and Courtly Culture," 301–306; Marilyn Yalom, *Birth of the Chess Queen: A History* (New York: Harper Perennial, 2005).

12 **may not have seen spiritual meaning:** Dario del Puppo, "The Limits of Allegory in Jacobus de Cessolis's *De ludo scaccorum*," in *Chess in the Middle Ages and Early Modern Age: A Fundamental Thought Paradigm of the Premodern World*, ed. Daniel O'Sullivan (Berlin: De Gruyter, 2012), 221–240.

12 **"Four Seasons Chess":** Musser, *Los libros de acedrex dados e tablas*, 576–581.

14 **Pilgrimage to Santiago—by sea as well as by land:** For a fictional evocation of such links in the twelfth century, see Lucy Pick, *Pilgrimage* (Brooklyn: Ciudono Press, 2014). See also Ana Echevarría Arsuaga, "The Shrine as Mediator: England, Castile, and the Pilgrimage to Compostela," in *England and Iberia in the Middle Ages, 12–15th Century: Cultural, Literary, and Political Exchanges*, ed. María Bullón-Fernández (New York: Palgrave, 2007), 47–65.

14 **two powerful neighbors:** Denis Menjot, "Les royaumes chrétiens péninsulaires dans l'Europe à l'aube du XIIIe siècle," in *Las Navas de Tolosa, 1212–2012: Miradas cruzadas*, ed. Patrice Cressier and Vicente Salvatierra (Jaén: Universidad de Jaén, 2014), 197–210. On the betrothal of Berenguela, see Martínez, *Alfonso X*, 20–23.

15 **locked in a series of fierce conflicts:** CSM 229: Kulp-Hill, *Songs of Holy Mary*, 275; O'Callaghan, *Alfonso X and the Cantigas de Santa María*, 37–38.

15 **The systematic and violent exploitation of the European peasantry:** Thomas N. Bisson, *Tormented Voices: Power, Crisis, and Humanity in Rural Catalonia, 1140–1200* (Cambridge, MA: Harvard University Press, 1998).

15 **The turbulent consolidation of feudal kingdoms:** Bisson, *The Crisis of the Twelfth Century*.

16 **participated in crusades in the Eastern Mediteranean:** Simon Barton, "From Tyrants to Soldiers of Christ: The Nobility of Twelfth-Century León-Castile and the Struggle Against Islam," *Nottingham Medieval Studies* 44 (2000): 28–48.

16 **luxury goods trade:** María Judith Feliciano, "Medieval Textiles in Iberia: Studies for a New Approach," in *Envisioning Islamic Art and*

Architecture: Essays in Honor of Renata Holod, ed. David Roxburgh (Leiden: Brill, 2014), 46–65; Benjamin Liu, "'Un Pueblo Laborioso': Mudéjar Work in the *Cantigas*," *Medieval Encounters* 12, no. 3 (2006): 462–474, at 470.

16   **The city had a *funduq*:** Olivia R. Constable, *Housing the Stranger in the Mediterranean World: Lodging, Trade, and Travel in Late Antiquity and the Middle Ages* (Cambridge: Cambridge University Press, 2003), 110.

16   **Málaga, Valencia, and Denia were also flourishing:** Olivia R. Constable, *Trade and Traders in Muslim Spain: The Commercial Realignment of the Iberian Peninsula, 900–1500* (Cambridge: Cambridge University Press, 1994), 18–23.

17   **One highly controversial study:** Margarita Torres Sevilla and José Miguel Ortega del Río, *Los reyes de Grial* (Madrid: Reino de Cordelia, 2014). The authenticity of the documents that Gustavo Turienzo encountered in Cairo continues to be hotly debated.

17   **Textiles, leather, paper, and spices:** Constable, *Trade and Traders*, 44–48; Teófilo Ruiz, *From Heaven to Earth: The Reordering of Castilian Society, 1150–1350* (Princeton, NJ: Princeton University Press, 2004), 23–24.

17   **"In all their behavior nothing can be noted":** Guibert de Nogent, "Own Life," Fordham University, Medieval Sourcebook, http://www.fordham.edu/halsall/source/nogent-auto.asp (accessed October 4, 2014).

17   **pair of leather shoes:** J. Yarza Luaces, ed., *Vestiduras ricas: El monasterio de las Huelgas y su época, 1170–1340* (Madrid: Patrimonio Nacional, 2005), 182.

18   **Around 1100, Ibn Tumart, son of a mountain chief:** One English-language introduction is Roger Le Tourneau, *The Almohad Movement in North Africa in the Twelfth and Thirteenth Centuries* (Princeton, NJ: Princeton University Press, 1969); more recently, see Allen Fromherz, *The Almohads: The Rise of an Islamic Empire* (London: I. B. Tauris, 2010).

19   **"Kill them wherever you may find them":** E. Levi-Provençal, ed. and trans., *Documents inédits d'histoire almohade* (Paris: P. Geuthner, 1928), 2–3 (my translation).

19   **The Almohads pursued a spirit of jihad:** Abigail Krasner Balbale, "Jihād as a Means of Political Legitimation in Thirteenth-Century Sharq al-Andalus," in *The Articulation of Power in Medieval Iberia and the Maghrib*, ed. Amira K. Bennison (Oxford: Oxford University Press, 2014), 87–105.

20   **To begin with, the Almohads were:** Amira K. Bennison and María Ángeles Gallego, "Religious Minorities Under the Almohads: An

Introduction," *Journal of Medieval Iberian Studies* [hereafter *JMIS*] 2, no. 2 (2010): 143–154.

20 **between supposed enemies:** Allen Fromherz, "North Africa and the Twelfth-Century Renaissance: Christian Europe and the Almohad Islamic Empire," in *Islam and Christian-Muslim Relations* 20, no. 1 (2009): 43–59; Eva Lapiedra Gutiérrez, "Christian Participation in Almohad Armies and Personal Guards," *JMIS* 2, no. 2 (2010): 235–250; David Abulafia, "Christian Merchants in the Almohad Cities," *JMIS* 2, no. 2 (2010): 251–257.

20 **The central mosque in Marrakech was called the Kutubiyya:** Fromherz, "North Africa and the Twelfth-Century Renaissance."

20 **Mainomides lived under the Almohads:** I have relied in this passage on Sarah Stroumsa, *Maimonides in His World: Portrait of a Mediterranean Thinker* (Princeton, NJ: Princeton University Press, 2009), esp. 6–12, 18–23, and 53–83; quotation on 7.

20 **Another of the brightest jewels:** Lenn Evan Goodman, ed., *Ibn Tufayl's Hayy Ibn Yaqẓān: A Philosophical Tale* (Chicago: University of Chicago Press, 2009); Lawrence I. Conrad, ed., *The World of Ibn Tufayl: Interdisciplinary Perspectives on Ḥayy Ibn Yaqẓān* (Leiden: E. J. Brill, 1996).

21 **"a Renaissance man before civilization knew the term":** Chris Lowney, *A Vanished World: Medieval Spain's Golden Age of Enlightenment* (New York: The Free Press, 2005), 168.

21 **Although exiled to Lucena as the result of a conspiracy:** Delfina Serrano Ruano, "Explicit Cruelty, Implicit Compassion: Judaism, Forced Conversions and the Genealogy of the Banū Rushd," *JMIS* 2, no. 2 (2010): 217–233; Fromherz, "North Africa and the Twelfth-Century Renaissance."

21 **His writings embody a deep reflection on ancient Greek rationalism:** S. D. Goitein, "Between Hellenism and Renaissance—Islam, the Intermediate Civilization," *Islamic Studies* 2 (1963): 217–233.

22 **This unlikely alliance of the warring northern kingdoms:** Lucy K. Pick, *Conflict and Coexistence: Archbishop Rodrigo and the Muslims and Jews of Medieval Spain* (Ann Arbor: University of Michigan Press, 2004), 21–70.

22 **As the Christian troops rode into battle against the Almohad caliph:** Remensnyder, *La Conquistadora*, 32.

22 **huge psychological blow:** Martín Alvira Cabrer, "Las Navas de Tolosa: The Beginning of the End of the 'Reconquista'? The Battle and Its Consequences According to the Christian Sources of the Thirteenth Century," *JMIS* 4, no. 1 (2012): 45–51.

22   **Thousands of Muslim men and women were killed:** Miriam Shadis, "Women and Las Navas de Tolosa," *JMIS* 4, no. 1 (2012): 71–76.

22   **hurling of the Almohad governor:** Dan Manuel Serradilla Avery, "Seville: Between the Atlantic and the Mediterranean, 1248–1492" (MPhil thesis, University of St. Andrews, 2007), 20, points out that this was a peculiarly literal overthrow of power.

23   **conquered the hearts and minds of the conquerors:** Juan Carlos Ruiz Souza, "Castile and al-Andalus After 1212: Assimilation and Integration of Andalusi Architecture," *JMIS* 4, no. 1 (2012): 125–134; Juan Zozaya Stabel-Hansen, "Deus ex machina? Economic and Technological Progress in Castile at the time of Rodrigo Jiménez de Rada," *JMIS* 4, no. 1 (2012): 119–123.

23   **The archbishop of Toledo became a great patron of this translation movement:** Pick, *Conflict and Coexistence*, 71–126.

24   **These robes, divested of any specifically Islamic significance:** María Judith Feliciano, "Muslim Shrouds for Christian Kings? A Reassessment of Andalusi Textiles in Thirteenth-Century Castilian Life and Ritual," in *Under the Influence: Questioning the Comparative in Medieval Castile*, ed. Cynthia Robinson and Leyla Rouhi (Leiden: Brill, 2005), 101–131; cf. Jerry Brotton, *The Renaissance Bazaar: From the Silk Road to Michelangelo* (Oxford: Oxford University Press, 2002), 137.

24   **more mercurial than the ponderous form of chess:** Musser, *Los libros de acedrex dados e tablas*, 90.

24   **The form of the game that most closely captured the Castilian political scene:** For a full description and analysis of the game, see Musser, *Los libros de acedrex dados e tablas*, 498–523.

24   **"who is like the head and lord of his whole army":** Alfonso X el Sabio, *Libro de los juegos: Acedrex, dados e tablas; Ordenamiento de las tafurerías*, ed. Raúl Orellana Calderón (Madrid: Biblioteca Castro, 2009), 317. I have slightly adapted here the excellent translations by Sonja Musser Golladay, accessible online at "The Annotated Grant Acedrex," The Chess Variant Pages, http://www.chessvariants.org /historic.dir/lj/grand-acedrex.html (accessed June 5, 2015).

25   **"He was an expert in all types of hunting":** Alfonso, *Setenario*, 13 (my translation).

25   **Alfonso always venerated his father:** Alfonso, *Setenario*, 8–9.

25   **"a bird that has authority over all the other birds":** Alfonso, *Libro de los juegos*, 317.

26   **her "weapon of choice":** Bianchini, *The Queen's Hand*, 260.

26   **"with breasts full of virtues she gave him her milk":** Shadis, *Berenguela of Castile*, 145.

26 **If there were few medieval queens like her:** Bianchini, *The Queen's Hand*, 261.

27 **It was she who had orchestrated Fernando's accession:** Shadis, *Berenguela of Castile*, 145–147; see also Theresa Earenfight, *Queenship in Medieval Europe* (New York: Palgrave Macmillan, 2013), 165–166.

27 **Not content with having organized the pivotal battle of Las Navas de Tolosa:** Pick, *Conflict and Coexistence*, 73.

27 **The crocodile . . . "is so powerful":** Alfonso, *Libro de los juegos*, 318.

27 **Acknowledging his political maturity, King Fernando now granted:** González Jiménez, "Alfonso X, Infante," 294–295.

28 **he also became lord of Ribadavia:** Henrique Monteagudo, *A nobreza miñota e a lírica trobadoresca na Galicia da primeira metade do século XIII: a personalidade histórica do trobador Johan Soayrez Somesso. Os trobadores Afonso Soarez Sarraça e Estevan Fayan*. Noia: Editorial Toxosoutos, 2014, 123–124; António Resende de Oliveira, "D. Afonso X, infante e trovador. I. Coordenadas de uma ligação a Galiza," *Revista de Literatura Medieval XXII* (2010) 257–270.

28 **"jumps a great distance sideways or forwards":** Alfonso, *Libro de los juegos*, 319.

NOTES TO CHAPTER TWO

30 **The Hungarian queen was an astute political player:** Theresa Earenfight, *Queenship in Medieval Europe* (New York: Palgrave Macmillan, 2013), 175–176.

30 **strategic advantages to both sides:** Damian Smith and Helena Buffery, eds., *The Book of Deeds of James I of Aragon: A Translation of the Medieval Catalan Llibre dels fets* (Burlington, VT: Ashgate, 2003), ch. 278, p. 228; Richard Kinkade, "Violante of Aragon (1236?–1300?): An Historical Overview," *Exemplaria hispánica 2* (1992–1993): 1–37.

31 **Archeological evidence suggests that urban centers in the region:** Jorge A. Eiroa Rodríguez, "Historians, Historiography and Archaeologically Imperceptible Change" *JMIS* 4, no. 1 (2012): 21–25.

32 **The messenger himself was hanged from a tree:** Smith and Buffery, *Book of Deeds*, chs. 339–340, pp. 260–261.

32 **"since it was of our conquest and he had our daughter as his wife":** Smith and Buffery, *Book of Deeds*, chs. 341–342, pp. 261–262.

33   **"We departed . . . as good friends":** Smith and Buffery, *Book of Deeds*, chs. 343–349, pp. 262–266.

33   **a treasury of culture and knowledge:** Francisco Márquez Villanueva, *El concepto cultural alfonsí* (Barcelona: Ediciones Bellaterra, 2004), 169–178.

33   **Completed eleven years later, this translation:** See Chapter 8.

33   **"The stone's color is like that of an egg yolk":** Ingrid Bahler and Katherine Gyékényesi Gatto, eds. and trans., *The Lapidary of King Alfonso X the Learned* (New Orleans, LA: University Press of the South, 2000), 71.

34   **"This stone is highly valued in the land":** Bahler and Gyékényesi Gatto, *Lapidary*, 52–53.

34   **intimately involved with the noblewoman Mayor Guillén de Guzmán:** Pablo Martín Prieto, "Las Guzmán alfonsinas. Una dinastía femenina en la Castilla de los siglos XIII y XIV," *Mirabilia* 17, no. 2 (2013): 250–272, at 253–254.

34   **"The Holy Church forbids Christians to keep concubines":** Robert I. Burns, SJ, ed., *Las siete partidas*, trans. Samuel Parsons Scott, 5 vols. (Philadelphia: University of Pennsylvania Press, 2001), law 4.14, 4:950. See also Eukene Lacarra Lanz, "Changing Boundaries of Licit and Illicit Unions: Concubinage and Prostitution," in *Marriage and Sexuality in Medieval and Early Modern Iberia*, ed. Eukene Lacarra Lanz (New York: Routledge, 2002), 158–196.

35   **a natural and medically advisable expression:** Contemporary medical wisdom, both Arabic and Christian, deemed that regular sex was necessary in order to maintain men's bodily equilibrium; for a later medieval expression of this tradition, see Michael Solomon, *The Mirror of Coitus: A Translation and Edition of the Fifteenth-Century Speculum al foderi* (Madison: Hispanic Seminary of Medieval Studies, 1990).

35   **Equally, there was a surprising tolerance:** Rachel E. Moss, *Fatherhood and Its Representations in Middle English Texts* (Cambridge, UK: D. S. Brewer, 2013), 48–56, 60–71, 184–187.

35   **In mid-1244, Alfonso led a successful military campaign:** Manuel González Jiménez, "Alfonso X, Infante," *Acta historica et archaeologica mediaevalia, homenatge al Dr. Manuel Riu* 22 (2001): 292–309, at 298–299.

35   **The prince formally granted the town of Elx:** Julio González, *Reinado y diplomas de Fernando III, 1 estudio* (Córdoba: Publicaciones del Monte de Piedad y Caja de Ahorros de Córdoba, 1980), 103.

35   **one of the most affectionate of all his personal relationships:** See Chapter 7. Alfonso later had at least three other children

outside marriage: Urraca Alfonso, Martin Alfonso, and Alfonso Fernández.

35 **"The people see the chaste Prince or ruler as a mirror":** John K. Walsh, ed., *El libro de los doze sabios: O tractado de la nobleza y lealtad [ca. 1237]: Estudio y edición*, Anejos del boletín de la Real Academia Española 29 (Madrid, 1975), 79.

35 **they will "degrade the nobleness of his line":** Burns, *Las siete partidas*, law 2.5.3, 2:287.

36 **"impels man to lasciviousness on improper occasions":** Burns, *Las siete partidas*, law 2.7.6, 2:304.

36 **Alfonso's *Cantigas de Santa María*, which were composed from the 1260s:** Amy G. Remensnyder, *La Conquistadora: The Virgin Mary at War and Peace in the Old and New Worlds* (Oxford: Oxford University Press, 2014), 105–110; Joseph Snow, "Alfonso as Troubadour: The Fact and the Fiction," in *Emperor of Culture: Alfonso X the Learned of Castile and His Thirteenth-Century Renaissance*, ed. Robert I. Burns, SJ (Philadelphia: University of Pennsylvania Press, 1990), 124–140.

36 **"marriage was instituted in paradise":** Cited by Philip Grace, "Aspects of Fatherhood in Thirteenth-Century Encyclopedias," *Journal of Family History* 31, no. 3 (2006): 211–236, at 218–220. I have modified the punctuation of his translation from Bartholomaeus Anglicus, eliminating, for instance, the ellipses.

37 **"never recovered the missing part with which he had sinned":** CSM 26: Kathleen Kulp-Hill, trans., *Songs of Holy Mary of Alfonso X, the Wise: A Translation of the Cantigas de Santa María* (Tempe: Arizona Center for Medieval and Renaissance Studies, 2000), 36–37; Stephen Parkinson, ed., *Alfonso X the Learned, Cantigas de Santa María: An Anthology*, MHRA Critical Texts 40 (Cambridge, UK: Modern Humanities Research Association, 2015), 42–45. Other *cantigas* also emphasize the need to control one's lust: among them, CSM 137 ("The lustful knight who was made impotent"), CSM 151 ("The priest who renounced his mistress"), and CSM 336 ("The lustful knight who was freed from desire").

37 **After she awakes from her swoon:** CSM 7: Kulp-Hill, *Songs of Holy Mary*, 12–13; Parkinson, *Cantigas de Santa María*, 32–33.

37 **The boat is overturned:** CSM 111: Kulp-Hill, *Songs of Holy Mary*, 137.

37 **"maintained that an infallible way":** Rosemary Horrox, ed., *The Black Death* (New York: Manchester University Press, 1994), 29.

38 **His tales of lascivious men and women:** On this basis, Alexander Lee, *The Ugly Renaissance: Sex, Greed, Violence and Depravity in an Age of Beauty* (New York: Doubleday, 2013), 127–131, presents the plague as a turning point, paving the way for "the triumph of pleasure."

Page 254 notes chapter two

38   **Al-Andalus may not have been a paradise:** Ibtissam Bouachrine, "In the Absence of Men: Representing Andalusi Women's Sexuality in the Context of Military Conflict," *JMIS* 4, no. 1 (2012): 77–81; Manuela Marin, "Marriage and Sexuality in al-Andalus," in Lacarra Lanz, *Marriage and Sexuality*, 5.

38   **"Hardly had I beheld that leg":** Olivia Remie Constable, ed., *Medieval Iberia: Readings from Christian, Jewish, and Muslim Sources* (Philadelphia: University of Pennsylvania Press, 1997), 236.

38   **The two recline beneath pink-purple silk sheets:** CSM 115, 135: Kulp-Hill, *Songs of Holy Mary*, 141–143, 167–168.

40   **Later, more puritanical censors appear to have attempted:** Fol. 48r. See Ana Domínguez Rodriguez, "Retratos de Alfonso X en el *Libro de los juegos de ajedrez, dados y tablas*," *Alcanate: Revista de estudios alfonsíes* 7 (2010–2011): 147–161, at 156–158.

40   **These women are probably courtesans or concubines:** Cynthia Robinson, "Preliminary Considerations on the Illustrations of Qissat Bayad wa Riyad (Vat. Arab. Ris. 368): Checkmate with Alfonso X?," in *Al-Andalus und Europa zwischen Orient und Okzident*, ed. Martina Müller-Wiener (Petersberg: M. Imhof, 2004), 285–413, at 291; cf. Sonja Musser, "Los libros de acedrex dados e tablas: Historical, Artistic and Metaphysical Dimensions of Alfonso X's" *Book of Games*" (PhD diss., University of Arizona, 2007), 743.

40   **In the imagination of its conquerors:** On the relationship between political power and sexual possession, see Simon Barton, *Conquerors, Brides, and Concubines: Interfaith Relations and Social Power in Medieval Iberia* (Philadelphia: University of Pennsylvania Press, 2015).

40   **an elegy to the city:** Al-Shaqundi, *Risala fi-fadl al-Andalus*, trans. Emilio García Gómez, *Revista de Occidente* 11, no. 120 (1933): 347, excerpted in Claudio Sánchez Albornoz, *La España musulmana*, 2 vols. (Buenos Aires: El Ateneo, 1946), 2:248–250. My translation is from the Spanish.

41   **away from al-Andalus and toward the Maghreb:** Camilo Gómez Rivas, "Las Navas de Tolosa, the Urban Transformation of the Maghrib, and the Territorial Decline of al-Andalus," *JMIS* 4, no. 1 (2012): 27–32.

41   **Al-Shaqundi was in this sense articulating a distinctively "Spanish" sensibility:** Emilio García Gómez, "Elogio de al-Andalus por al-Saqundi," *Revista de Occidente* 11, (no. 120 1933): 341–350.

42   **"Orders had been given to the governors of Granada and Guadix":** Ibn Sahib al-Sala, *Al-mann bil-imama*, ed. Ambrosio Huici Miranda, Textos medievales 24 (Valencia: Anubar, 1969), 189–190. My translation is from the Spanish.

42   **The caliph gave the supreme order to begin construction:** Ibn Sahib al-Sala, *Al-mann bil-imama*, 196–197.

42   **"rises up in the air and into the sky":** Ibn Sahib al-Sala, *Al-mann bil-imama*, 200–201.

43   **In 1198, the four golden balls known as a *yamur*:** For the chronology of rebuilding, see Enrique Luís Domínguez Berenjeno, "La remodelación urbana de Ishbilia a través de la historiografía almohade," *Anales de arqueología cordobesa* 12 (2001): 177–194.

43   **"With such mastery was it made":** Ramón Menéndez Pidal, ed., *Primera crónica general de España*, 2 vols. (Madrid: Gredos, 1955) [hereafter *PCG*], 2:768–769, ch. 1128.

44   **Prince Alfonso was more impetuous:** González, *Fernando III*, 1:104; González Jiménez, "Alfonso X, Infante," 303.

45   **Gil de Zamora . . . picks up the tale:** Fidel Fita, "Biografías de San Fernando y de Alfonso el Sabio por Gil de Zamora," *Boletín de la Real Academia de la Historia* 5 (1885): 320.

46   **negotiated the surrender of the city:** Barbara Boloix, "La inestable frontera castellano-nazarí en el siglo XIII: Del vasallaje a la insurrección (1246–1266)," in *Encrucijada de culturas: Alfonso X y su tiempo; Homenaje a Francisco Márquez Villanueva*, ed. Emilio González Ferrín (Seville: Fundación Tres Culturas, 2014), 197–247, esp. 201–221.

46   **"It had streets and squares for every craft":** *PCG*, 2:768.

47   **In the following weeks, the parties seem to have agreed:** Manuel González Jiménez, *Documentación e itinerario de Alfonso X el Sabio* (Sevilla: Universidad de Sevilla, 2012), doc. 30, 99; González Jiménez, "Alfonso X, Infante," 305–306.

47   **After one month's grace period:** Manuel González Jiménez, Mercedes Borrero Fernández, and Isabel Montes Romero-Camacho, *Sevilla en tiempos de Alfonso X* (Sevilla: Ayuntamiento de Sevilla, 1987), 7–11.

47   **"organized his city very well and nobly":** *PCG*, 2:769–770.

48   **Enrique was infuriated by Alfonso's proposal to their father:** González Jiménez, "Alfonso X, Infante," 306.

48   **The same week, two papal bulls:** González, *Fernando III*, 1:105.

48   **"I am going to Valladolid to receive the blessings":** Manuel González Jiménez, ed., *Diplomatario andaluz de Alfonso X* (Seville: El Monte, Caja de Huelva y Sevilla, 1991), doc. 3, 5–6, dated January 8, 1249. This date is modified in González Jiménez, *Documentación e itinerario*, doc. 34, 99.

49   **Yolant, elegantly seated upon her throne:** Domínguez Rodriguez, "Retratos," 147–151. Sonja Musser Golladay believes there are further portraits on folios 16r, 18r, 47v, 49r, 54v, and 56r of the *Book*

of Games, attributing to the queen a "distinctive wide, square nose and penetrating gaze" (Musser, *Los libros de acedrex dados e tablas*, 79), but these identifications are highly speculative.

49   **It is impossible to go further:** Joseph O'Callaghan, *Alfonso X and the Cantigas de Santa María: A Poetic Biography* (Leiden: Brill, 1998), 19–21.

49   **the ideal wife "should come of a good family":** Burns, *Las siete partidas*, law 2.6.1–2, 2:298–299.

49   **The *Partidas* also express a view of the queen consort:** Earenfight, *Queenship*, 167.

50   **Alfonso married off his first-born child, Beatriz:** Martín Prieto, "Las Guzmán alfonsinas," 254.

50   **the aesthetic style of Almohad Seville:** Robinson, "Preliminary Considerations."

50   **adopted a style of leadership:** Maribel Fierro, "Alfonso X 'the Wise': The Last Almohad Caliph?," *Medieval Encounters* 15 (2009): 175–198.

50   **On the last night of May in 1252:** Manuel González Jiménez, ed., *Crónica de Alfonso X: según el ms. II/2777 de la Biblioteca del Palacio real (Madrid)* (Murcia: Real Academia Alfonso X el Sabio, 1998) [hereafter CAX], 4n1. On Santa Clara, see Pablo Oliva Muñoz and Miguel Ángel Tabales Rodríguez, "De palacio a monasterio: Génesis y transformación del Real Monasterio de Santa Clara de Sevilla," *Arqueología de la Arquitectura* 8 (2011): 141–162.

50   **"My son," he is said to have declared:** PCG, 772.

51   **Yet the deathbed scene:** Cynthia Chamberlin, "'Unless the Pen Writes as It Should': The Proto-Cult of Saint Fernando III in Seville in the Thirteenth and Fourteenth Centuries," in *Sevilla 1248: Congreso internacional conmemorativo del 750 aniversario de la conquista de la ciudad de Sevilla por Fernando III, rey de Castilla y León*, ed. Manuel González Jiménez (Madrid: Fundación Ramón Areces, 2000), 403–404.

52   **Alfonso would in fact build on these legacies:** Márquez Villanueva, *El concepto cultural alfonsí*, 41–48; David Rojinsky, *Companion to Empire: A Genealogy of the Written Word in Spain and New Spain, c. 550–1550* (Amsterdam: Rodopi, 2010), ch. 2: "The Vernacular Letter of the Law in the Siete Partidas."

52   **It has been said that Alfonso so deeply valued the minaret:** Antonio Ballesteros-Beretta, *Alfonso X el Sabio* (Barcelona: Salvat, 1963), 312; Rafael Cómez Ramos, *Arquitectura alfonsí* (Sevilla: Seix Barral, 1974), 22–23.

52   **"privileged and enriched the church of Seville above all others":** Fita, "Biografías," 321.

Notes to Chapter Three

Notes to Chapter Three

53 **But as he rode out into the streets of Seville:** Joseph F. O'Callaghan, *The Learned King: The Reign of Alfonso X of Castile* (Philadelphia: University of Pennsylvania Press, 1993), 6–7; H. Salvador Martínez, *Alfonso X, the Learned: A Biography*, trans. Odile Cisneros (Leiden: Brill, 2010), 99–103.

54 **"Our king, Don Alfonso," they wrote:** José Chabás Bergón and Bernard R. Goldstein, *Las tablas alfonsíes de Toledo* (Toledo Diputacias alfonsíes de Toledod R2008), 36–37, cited in Laura Fernández Fernández, "El ms. 8322 de la Bibliothèque de l'Arsenal y su relación con las tablas alfonsíes. Hipótesis de trabajo," *Alcanate: Revista de estudios alfonsíes* 7 (2010–2011): 235–267, at 253.

54 **As teacher to his people:** Francisco Márquez Villanueva, *El concepto cultural alfonsí* (Barcelona: Ediciones Bellaterra, 2004), 25–40.

55 **"It was always a custom, in Spain":** Robert I. Burns, SJ, ed., *Las siete partidas*, trans. Samuel Parsons Scott, 5 vols. (Philadelphia: University of Pennsylvania Press, 2001), law 2.9.27, 2:328.

55 **"Wisdom is the love of all loves":** John K. Walsh, ed., *El libro de los doze sabios: O tractado de la nobleza y lealtad [ca. 1237]: Estudio y edición*, Anejos del boletín de la Real Academia Española 29 (Madrid, 1975), 78–79.

55 **In learning, as in all things:** Burns, *Las siete partidas*, law 2.5.4, 2:288.

55 **"He who places his secret in the power of another becomes his slave":** Burns, *Las siete partidas*, law 2.5.16, 2:294.

55 **"the remarkable events that transpire":** Burns, *Las siete partidas*, law 2.5.16, 2:294.

56 **He soon became personally involved in the writing:** Márquez Villanueva, *El concepto cultural alfonsí*, 141–159.

56 **This model had passed down to the Spanish-Muslim rulers of al-Andalus:** Márquez Villanueva, *El concepto cultural alfonsí*, 79–87.

56 **Ibrahim ibn Said produced two brass celestial globes:** Jerrilyn D. Dodds, Maria Rosa Menocal, and Abigail Krasner Balbale, *The Arts of Intimacy: Christians, Jews, and Muslims in the Making of Castilian Culture* (New Haven, CT: Yale University Press, 2008), 57–58.

57 **Columbus reached America, it has been said:** Emilio González Ferrín, "Al-Andalus: The First Enlightenment," *Critical Muslim* 6 (April 2013): 8.

57 **The Umayyad emirs of al-Andalus had employed:** Julio Samsó, "The Early Development of Astrology in al-Andalus," *Journal for the History of Arabic Science* 3 (1979): 228–243. Reprinted in Julio Samsó, *Islamic Astronomy and Medieval Spain* (Brookfield, VT: Variorum, 1994), ch. 4, at 228–229.

57 "divination accomplished by the aid of astronomy": Burns, *Las siete partidas*, law 7.23.1–2, 5:1431–1432.

58 "the last Almohad caliph": Maribel Fierro, "Alfonso X 'the Wise': The Last Almohad Caliph?," *Medieval Encounters* 15 (2009): 175–198.

58 These newcomers included a small number of Jewish court officials: Yitzhak F. Baer, "From the Age of the Reconquest to the Fourteenth Century," in *A History of the Jews in Christian Spain* (Philadelphia: Jewish Publication Society of America, 1978), 1:112–113.

58 Most were small-scale artisans and tradesmen: Manuel González Jiménez, Mercedes Borrero Fernández, and Isabel Montes Romero-Camacho, *Sevilla en tiempos de Alfonso X* (Sevilla: Ayuntamiento de Sevilla, 1987), 59–88.

58 The city remained woefully underpopulated: Isabel Montes Romero-Camacho, "Las minorías étnico-religiosas en la Sevilla del siglo XIV: Mudéjares y judíos," in *Sevilla, Siglo XIV*, ed. Rafael Valencia and Mercedes Borrero Fernández (Sevilla: Fundación José Manuel Lara, 2006), 135–155, at 142–154.

58 "The noble city of Seville has been depopulated and ruined": Manuel González Jiménez, ed., *Diplomatario andaluz de Alfonso X* (Seville: El Monte, Caja de Huelva y Sevilla, 1991), doc. 270, 298–299; Heather Ecker, "How to Administer a Conquered City in al-Andalus: Mosques, Parish Churches, and Parishes," in *Under the Influence: Questioning the Comparative in Medieval Castile*, ed. Cynthia Robinson and Leyla Rouhi (Leiden: Brill, 2005), 45–65, esp. 51–65.

58 Within the *alcázar,* he began to construct: Miguel Ángel Tabales Rodríguez, *El alcázar de Sevilla: Reflexiones sobre su origen y transformación durante la Edad Media* (Sevilla: Junta de Andalucía, 2010), 271–282.

58 But beyond the palace walls: Alfredo J. Morales, "'Quien no vio a Sevilla, no vio maravilla': Notas sobre la ciudad del trescientos," in Valencia and Borrero Fernández, *Sevilla, Siglo XIV*, 69–85, at 69–70.

59 This motivated the first preemptive strike: Manuel González Jiménez, ed., *Crónica de Alfonso X. según el ms. II/2777 de la Biblioteca del Palacio real (Madrid)* (Murcia: Real Academia Alfonso X el Sabio, 1998) [hereafter CAX], ch. 2, p. 9.

59 the development of new royal shipyards: Rafael Cómez Ramos, *Arquitectura alfonsí* (Sevilla: Seix Barral, 1974), 26.

59 As harvests failed, there was a shortage of bread: Antonio Ballesteros-Beretta, *Alfonso X el Sabio* (Barcelona: Salvat, 1963), 84–86.

59 **He seems to have contemplated a marriage:** John Carmi Parsons, *Eleanor of Castile: Queen and Society in Thirteenth-Century England* (New York: St. Martins Press, 1995), 13.

60 **Even the archbishop and his masons:** Juan Carlos Ruiz Souza, "Toledo entre Europa y al-Andalus en el siglo XIII. Revolución, tradición y asimilación de las formas artísticas en la Corona de Castilla," *JMIS* 1, no. 2 (2009): 233–271.

60 **In the tower of the Church of San Román:** Dodds, Menocal, and Balbale, *Arts of Intimacy*, 167.

60 **It was probably here, two years into the reign:** O'Callaghan, *Learned King*, 7.

61 **Some fifty years later, Matthew Paris:** Peter Linehan, *Spain, 1157–1300: A Partible Inheritance* (Oxford: Blackwell, 2008), 2.

61 **"The English . . . have a liking for no other nation":** Jennifer Goodman Wollock, "Medieval England and Iberia: A Chivalric Relationship," in *England and Iberia in the Middle Ages, 12–15th Century: Cultural, Literary and Political Exchanges*, ed. María Bullón-Fernández (New York: Palgrave, 2007), 11–28, at 16.

61 **A spectacular copy of the marriage agreement:** National Archives (Kew), E 30/1108.

62 **At precisely 6:28 a.m.:** Aly Aben Ragel, *El libro conplido en los iudizios de las estrellas, Partes 6 a 8: Traducción hecha en la corte de Alfonso el Sabio*, ed. Gerold Hilty (Zaragoza: Instituto de Estudios Islámicos y del Oriente Próximo, 2005), introduction, xvii–xxvi.

62 **the "heart of European Jewry":** Robert I. Burns, SJ, "Jews and Moors in the *Siete partidas* of Alfonso X the Learned: A Background Perspective," in *Medieval Spain: Culture, Conflict and Coexistence; Studies in Honour of Angus MacKay*, ed. Roger Collins and Anthony Goodman (New York: Palgrave Macmillan, 2002), 53.

62 **In practice, he allowed for ample Jewish self-government:** Baer, *History of the Jews*, 115–118.

62 **As a minority that did not represent a military threat:** Jonathan Ray, "Between the Straits: The Thirteenth Century as a Turning Point for Iberian Jewry," *JMIS* 4, no. 1 (2012): 101–105, at 102.

63 **"When I went to the king to enter his service":** Todros ben Judah Abulafia, "Two Poems in Honor of Alfonso X el Sabio," trans. Raymond Scheindlin, in Olivia Remie Constable, ed., *Medieval Iberia: Readings from Christian, Jewish, and Muslim Sources* (Philadelphia: University of Pennsylvania Press, 2012), 391.

63 **Only now, in the thirteenth century:** Márquez Villanueva, *El concepto cultural alfonsí*, 71–77.

64 **Al-Sufi's work became a powerful influence:** Paul Kunitzsch, "The Astronomer Abu 'L-Husayn al-Sufi and His Book on the Constellations," in *The Arabs and the Stars: Texts and Traditions on*

the Fixed Stars, and Their Influence in Medieval Europe (Northampton, UK: Variorum Reprints, 1989), ch. 11, 56–81. On MS 1036 and the northern Italian origins, see M. T. Gousset, "Le *Liber de locis stellarum fixarum* d'Al-Sûfi, ms. 1036 de la Bibliothèque de l'Arsenal à Paris: Une reattribution," *Arte medievale* 2 (1984): 93–106.

64   **the model of archbishop Rodrigo Jiménez de Ruda:** Lucy K. Pick, *Conflict and Coexistence: Archbishop Rodrigo and the Muslims and Jews of Medieval Spain* (Ann Arbor: University of Michigan Press, 2004), 127–181, 206–207.

64   **This was a society in which religious minorities:** Burns, *Las siete partidas*, laws 7.24–25, 5:1433–1442.

64   **anti-Semitic stereotypes:** Amy G. Remensnyder, *La Conquistadora: The Virgin Mary at War and Peace in the Old and New Worlds* (Oxford: Oxford University Press, 2014), 134–139.

66   **The Wise King employed many Jews:** Baer, *History of the Jews*, 120–126.

66   **Both in Toledo and across Castile, Jewish thinkers:** Márquez Villanueva, *El concepto cultural alfonsí*, 101–111.

66   **For Ibn Sahula, the Spanish Muslim courts:** Alexandra Cuffel, "Ibn Sahula's Meshal ha-Qadmoni as Restorative Polemic," *JMIS* 3, no. 2 (2011): 165–186.

66   **The translation begins:** Aly Aben Ragel, *El libro conplido en los iudizios de las estrellas*, ed. Gerold Hilty (Madrid: Real Academia Española, 1954), introduction, 9–17.

67   **Its geographical scope remains largely rooted:** Aly Aben Ragel, *El libro conplido, Partes 6 a 8*, Part VIII, ch. 34, 304–305.

67   **We can imagine Alfonso poring over the sections:** Aly Aben Ragel, *El libro conplido, Partes 6 a 8*, Part VIII, chs. 15–17, 256–268.

68   **Alfonso perhaps gazed at the night sky:** Aly Aben Ragel, *El libro conplido, Partes 6 a 8*, Part VIII, ch. 25, 281–284.

68   **one of the most widely respected astrological treatises:** Aly Aben Ragel, *El libro conplido, Partes 6 a 8*, introduction, xxxiii–xxxix.

68   **"shadowy land of magic":** Michael A. Ryan, *A Kingdom of Stargazers: Astrology and Authority in the Late Medieval Crown of Aragon* (Ithaca NY: Cornell University Press, 2011), 80–86, 94–101.

69   **There, in the monastery church, Edward:** Ballesteros-Beretta, *Alfonso X el Sabio*, 99–102.

70   **While some of her English subjects mistrusted:** Theresa Earenfight, *Queenship in Medieval Europe* (New York: Palgrave Macmillan, 2013), 145–147.

70   **"agreed with all the *ricos omes* (aristocrats)":** González Jiménez, *Diplomatario andaluz*, doc. 3, 5–6.

71 Her closeness to Enrique gave rise to rumors: Ballesteros-Beretta, *Alfonso X el Sabio*, 104–111; Parsons, *Eleanor of Castile*, 16.

72 Jaume I of Aragon ordered that he leave the kingdom: CAX, ch. 8, pp. 22–23.

72 "When the relatives of a king commit an offense against him": Burns, *Las siete partidas*, law 2.8.2, 2:309.

72 In what may have been an act of intellectual defiance: Robey Clark Patrick, "*Sendebar*: A Literary Rebellion," *La corónica: A Journal of Medieval Hispanic Languages, Literatures, and Cultures* 43, no. 1 (2014): 39–68.

73 so the epilogue tells us: Walsh, *El libro de los doze sabios*, 117–118. For the dating of this passage, see 22–33.

73 a genre crowned by John of Salisbury's *Policraticus*: Adeline Rucquoi and Hugo O. Bizarri, "Los espejos de príncipes en Castilla: Entre Oriente y Occidente," *Cuadernos de historia de España* 79, no. 1 (2005), http://www.scielo.org.ar/scielo.php?script=sci_arttext&pid=S0325-11952005000100001.

74 he did bring to his favorite city: Márquez Villanueva, *El concepto cultural alfonsí*, 161–167.

74 One pioneering study of the rise of universities in the West: George Makdisi, *The Rise of Colleges: Institutions of Learning in Islam and the West* (Edinburgh: Edinburgh University Press, 1981).

74 All professors, an illustrious caste: Burns, *Las siete partidas*, law 2.31.2, 2:527.

74 They might enter the presence: Burns, *Las siete partidas*, law 2.31.7, 2:530.

74 The university . . . was to be set "apart from the town": Burns, *Las siete partidas*, law 2.31.2, 2:527.

74 "It is the duty of the rector to punish and restrain the pupils": Burns, *Las siete partidas*, law 2.31.6, 2:529.

75 "where he suffered greatly from the cruel captivity": CSM 291: Kathleen Kulp-Hill, trans., *Songs of Holy Mary of Alfonso X, the Wise: A Translation of the Cantigas de Santa María* (Tempe: Arizona Center for Medieval and Renaissance Studies, 2000), 351.

75 Yehuda ben Mosé turned to the *Book of Crosses*: José A. Sánchez Pérez, "El libro de las cruces," *Isis* 14, no. 1 (1930): 77–132, at 78–79, 87–89.

75 The Arabic original was likely written: José M. Millás Vallicrosa, "Sobre el autor del *Libro de las cruces*," *Al-Andalus* 5, no. 1 (1940): 230–234; Margarita Castells, "Un nuevo dato sobre *El libro de las cruces* en al-Ziy al-mustalah (obra astronómica egipcia del siglo XIII)," *Al Qantara* 13, no. 2 (1992): 367–376, proposes some alternate possibilities without definitively rejecting Millás's hypothesis.

75 **"I do not know of anyone, in the Spain of our time or even before":** His full name was Abu Marwan Ubayd Allah b. Jalaf al-Istiyi: see Millás Villacrosa, "Sobre el autor," 230–234.

76 **The oldest passages in the book:** Julio Samsó, *Alfonso X y los orígenes de la astrología hispánica (Discurso de recepción leido el día 2 de abril de 1981 en la Real Academia del Buenas Letras de Barcelona)* (Barcelona: Real Academia de Buenas Letras de Barcelona, 1981), 21–31.

76 **"more wisdom, understanding and knowledge":** Alfonso el Sabio, *Libro de las cruzes*, ed. Lloyd Kasten and Lawrence Kiddle (Madrid: Consejo Superior de Investigaciones Científicas, 1961), 1.

77 **Instead, he is referred to simply as "king of Spain":** Alfonso, *Libro de las cruzes*, 1.

77 **Frederick II had worn a tunic of Sicilian silk:** Abulafia, *Frederick II*, 11.

78 **Frederick II had inherited both the kingdom:** Carlos Estepa Díez, "Alfonso X y el 'fecho del imperio,'" *Revista de Occidente* 43 (1984): 43–54.

78 **"even if he had been cut into a thousand pieces":** Rosemary Horrox, ed., *The Black Death* (New York: Manchester University Press, 1994), 155.

NOTES TO CHAPTER FOUR

81 **a stained glass window of spectacular beauty:** José Fernández Arenas and Cayo Jesús Fernández Espino, *Las vidrieras de la Catedral de León* (León: Ediciones Leonesas, 1982), 79–80. I owe sincere thanks to José Manuel Rodríguez Montañés for clarifying the composition of the Cacería window to me.

83 **This figure is almost certainly the king:** Victor Nieto Alcaide, "La vidriera español," *Cuadernos de arte español* 98 (Madrid: Historia 16, 1993): 14 ff., suggests that the image may depict Charlemagne and that he is carrying a crown of thorns in his hand. But even if this were so, the intent would be similar: to promote Alfonso's imperial status. See Maximo Gómez Rascón, *Catedral de León, las vidrieras: El simbolismo de la luz* (León: Edilesa, 2000), 130.

83 **He also patronized the stained glass workshop:** Ángela Franco Mata, "Alfonso X el Sabio y las Catedrales de Burgos y León," *Norba: Revista de arte* 7 (1987): 71–81.

83 **Here Alfonso carries both the orb and the scepter:** Fernández Arenas, *Las vidrieras de la Catedral de León*, 73–74. This is the first window of the "upper series."

83 **Huntsmen had shadowed the travelling courts:** S. D. Church, "Some Aspects of the Royal Itinerary in the Twelfth Century," *Thirteenth-Century England* 11 (2007): 31–45.

84 **Above all, however, Alfonso envisioned:** Manuel Núñez Rodríguez, "El rey, la catedral, y la expresión de un programa," *Espacio, tiempo y forma,* serie VII, *Historia del arte* 5 (1992): 27–52.

84 **"a town that is well fortified":** *Estoria de Espanna,* fol. 338r (the Hispanic Seminary of Medieval Studies digital edition is accessible online at http://www.hispanicseminary.org).

84 **It has long been thought that the young prince:** Muhammad ibn 'Abd Allah ibn 'Umar al-Bayzar, *Libro de los animales que cazan (Kitāb al-Yawāriḥ),* ed. José Manuel Fradejas Rueda (Madrid: Casariego, 1987); José Manuel Fradejas Rueda, "*Libro de los animales que cazan,*" in *Diccionario filológico de literatura medieval española: Textos y transmisión,* ed. Carlos Alvar and José Manuel Lucía Megías. (Madrid: Castalia, 2002), 792–795.

86 **From the Black Forest to Sicily:** David Abulafia, *Frederick II: A Medieval Emperor* (Oxford: Oxford University Press, 1988), 267–270.

86 **"Brilliant in colouring . . . the work is accurate and minute":** Charles H. Haskins, "The 'De arte venandi cum avibus' of the Emperor Frederick II," *English Historical Review* 36, no. 143 (July 1921): 334–355.

86 **"The chase is most similar to war for these reasons":** Cited in Richard Almond, *Medieval Hunting* (Stroud, UK: The History Press, 2003), 16–17.

86 **"remove the eggs of hawks, sparrowhawks, or falcons":** Antonio Ballesteros, *Las cortes de 1252* (Madrid: Real Academia de la Historia, 1911), 24, 27.

87 **an episode traceable to July 1254:** Antonio Ballesteros-Beretta, *Alfonso X el Sabio* (Barcelona: Salvat, 1963), 97.

87 **"The king of Castile came to Alicante":** Damian Smith and Helena Buffery, eds., *The Book of Deeds of James I of Aragon: A Translation of the Medieval Catalan Llibre dels fets* (Burlington, VT: Ashgate, 2003), ch. 377, p. 281.

87 **It is perfectly plausible that one of Alfonso's brothers:** Anthony J. Cárdenas, "*Libro de las animalias que caçan:* Is It Alfonso X's?," *La corónica* 15 (1986–1987): 85–86; Anthony J. Cárdenas, "A Medieval Spanish Version of the *Book of Moamín:* Observations on Date and Sponsorship," *Manuscripta* 31 (1987): 166–180.

88 **In the National Museum of Archaeology:** Josemi Lorenzo Arribas, "Los Aliceres del Palacio de Curiel de los Ajos (Valladolid): Iconografía del caballero medieval," *Museo Arqueológico Nacional,*

pieza del mes (ciclo 2003–2004) (March 2004), http://www.man
.es/man/estudio/publicaciones/materiales-didacticos/publicacion
-01054.

88 **"contributes much to diminish serious thoughts":** Robert I.
Burns, SJ, ed., *Las siete partidas*, trans. Samuel Parsons Scott, 5 vols.
(Philadelphia: University of Pennsylvania Press, 2001), law 2.5.20,
2:296.

89 **"The joy which they should receive from the sport":** Burns, *Las
siete partidas*, law 2.5.20, 2:296.

89 **"that birds of the sky and fishes of the deep":** Almond, *Medieval
Hunting*, 90–114.

89 **a satanic servant has convinced:** CSM 67: Kathleen Kulp-Hill,
trans., *Songs of Holy Mary of Alfonso X, the Wise: A Translation of the
Cantigas de Santa María* (Tempe: Arizona Center for Medieval and
Renaissance Studies, 2000), 88–89; see Almond, *Medieval Hunting*,
88, on the idea of a "noble Quarry."

89 **As today, the animals were given pet names:** Simon Barton, *The
Aristocracy in Twelfth-Century León and Castile* (Cambridge:
Cambridge University Press, 1997), 64.

90 **"be compelled to kiss the posterior of that dog publicly":** Joyce
Salisbury, *The Beast Within: Animals in the Middle Ages*, 2nd ed.
(New York: Routledge, 2010), ch. 1.

90 **At the top of the hierarchy was the fierce gyrfalcon:** Almond,
Medieval Hunting, 20–21, 39–47, and 48–51.

90 **When Edward I of England sent four grey gyrfalcons:** Robin
Oggins, *The Kings and Their Hawks: Falconry in Medieval England*
(New Haven, CT: Yale University Press, 2004), ch. 2.

91 **Contact with the Arabic world:** Haskins, "The 'De arte venandi
cum avibus,'" 334–355; Salisbury, *Beast Within*, ch. 2; Oggins, *Kings
and Their Hawks*, chs. 1 and 2.

91 **This tradition surfaces in the fourteenth-century cycle:** Jerrilynn
Dodds, "Hunting in the Borderlands," *Medieval Encounters* 14
(2008): 267–302.

91 **the hawk was a royal bird:** [Juan Gil de Zamora], *Johannis Aegidii
Zamorensis, historia naturalis*, ed. Avelino Domínguez García and
Luís Ballester (Salamanca: Junta de Castilla y León, 1994),
182–183.

92 **clergymen, too, were often keen hunters:** Carmel Ferragud and
Ricardo M. Olmos de León, "La cetrería en los ejemplos, similes y
metáforas de San Vicente Ferrer," *Anuario de estudios medievales* 42,
no. 1 (2012): 273–300.

92 **Just as the hawk beats his wings:** [Gil de Zamora], *Johannis Aegidii
Zamorensis*, 217–227.

92 **an almost regal dietary regimen:** Fradejas Rueda, *Libro de los animales que cazan*, 18 (fol. 10r), 24 (fol. 17r), and 59–60, (fols. 55r–v).

93 **He recounts a heron-hunting incident:** CSM 142: Kulp-Hill, *Songs of Holy Mary*, 175.

93 **Mary's divine protection of the birds:** CSM 243: Kulp-Hill, *Songs of Holy Mary*, 294; CSM 44: Kulp-Hill, *Songs of Holy Mary*, 59, and (Stephen Parkinson, ed., *Alfonso X the Learned, Cantigas de Santa María: An Anthology*, MHRA Critical Texts 40 (Cambridge, UK: Modern Humanities Research Association, 2015); , 48–49.

93 **an incident that probably took place in 1265:** CSM 366: Kulp-Hill, *Songs of Holy Mary*, 445–446.

94 **By the age of nine, Edward:** Oggins, *Kings and Their Hawks*, ch. 6.

94 **"By succession in you the empires divided":** Salvador Martínez, *Alfonso X, the Learned: A Biography*, trans. Odile Cisneros (Leiden: Brill, 2010), 136–137.

95 **On a deeper level, there were close:** Ana Rodríguez López, "El reino de Castilla y el imperio germánico en la primera mitad del siglo XIII: Fernando III y Federico II," in *Historia social, pensamiento historiográfico y Edad Media: Homenaje al profesor Abilio Barbero de Aguilera*, ed. Maria Isabel Loring (Madrid: Ediciones del Orto, 1997), 613–630.

95 **Certainly, Alfonso did not yet have a strong foothold:** Roberto Sabatino López, "Entre el Medioevo y el Renacimiento: Alfonso X y Federico II," *Revista de Occidente* 43 (1984): 7–14.

95 **Alexander IV may even have orchestrated:** Carlos de Ayala, *Directrices fundamentales de la política peninsular de Alfonso X (relaciones castellano aragonesas de 1252 a 1263)* (Madrid: Antiqua et Mediaevalia, 1986), 170–176.

97 **Much more than a simple translation:** Ana Echevarría, "Eschatology or Biography? Alfonso X, Muhammad's Ladder and a Jewish Go-Between," in *Under the Influence: Questioning the Comparative in Medieval Castile*, ed. Cynthia Robinson and Leyla Rouhi (Leiden: Brill, 2005), 133–152.

97 **In fact, it means "little lightning flash":** Christiane Gruber, "Al-Burāq," in *Encyclopedia of Islam*, 3rd. ed. (Leiden: Brill, 2012), 40–46, at 41.

98 **"I saw that some sinners":** No manuscript of the Castilian text survives, only rendering from Castilian into Old French and into Latin, a version that Dante may have read. This is my own translation from the bilingual Latin-French edition of the Gisèle Besson and Michèle Brossard-Dandré, trans., *Liber scale Machometi (Le livre de l'échelle de Mahomet)* (Paris: Le Livre de Poche, 1991), ch. 85.

99 **Alfonso had gained a narrow majority:** Ballesteros-Beretta, *Le livre de l'echelle de Mahomet (Liber scale Machometi)*, 177–183; Martínez, *Alfonso X*, 148–149.

99 **A spectacularly garbled version of the episode:** Manuel González Jiménez, ed., *Crónica de Alfonso X. según el ms. II/2777 de la Biblioteca del Palacio real (Madrid)* (Murcia: Real Academia Alfonso X el Sabio, 1998) [hereafter CAX], ch. 2, p. 9. Queen Yolant was twelve years old when she was married; her first child, Berenguela, was born when she was sixteen—hardly a "failure."

99 **the account of a Norwegian chronicle:** Marlen Ferrer, "Emotions in Motion: Emotional Diversity in 13th Century Spanish and Norse Society" (PhD diss., University of Oslo, 2008), 41–43, 142–143.

100 **"He also ordered all the scriptures to be translated into Romance":** CAX, ch. 9, p. 26.

100 **Finally, the royal workshops began:** On the language and aspirations of the *Siete partidas*, see Jesús Rodríguez-Velasco, "Theorizing the Language of Law," *diacritics* 36, no. 3–4 (fall-winter 2006): 64–86.

100 **"If the *Partidas* had been written in Latin":** Joseph F. O'Callaghan, *The Learned King: The Reign of Alfonso X of Castile* (Philadelphia: University of Pennsylvania Press, 1993), 274.

101 **"The king makes a book":** Antonio G. Solalindes, ed., *General estoria. Primera parte* (Madrid: Molina, 1930), 1:477b.

102 **"While King Alfonso was in Seville":** CAX, ch. 9, p. 28. The "king of Egypt" may have been one of two Mamluk sultans, Kutuz al-Muzaffar (r. 1259–1260) or possibly Baibars I (r. 1260–1277).

102 **a menanerie of exotic birds, mammals, and fishes:** CSM 29: Kulp-Hill, *Songs of Holy Mary*, 40; John E. Keller, "The Depiction of Exotic Animals in Cantiga XXIX of the *Cantigas de Santa María*," in *Studies in Honor of Tatiana Fotich*, ed. Josep M. Sola Solé, Alessandro S. Crisafulli, and Siegfried A. Schultz (Washington DC: Catholic University of America Press, 1972), 247–253.

103 **Throughout the early 1260s:** Joseph O'Callaghan, *The Gibraltar Crusade: Castile and the Battle for the Strait* (Philadelphia: University of Pennsylvania Press, 2011), 22–23; Ayala, *Directrices*, 265–269; Amy G. Remensnyder, *La Conquistadora: The Virgin Mary at War and Peace in the Old and New Worlds* (Oxford: Oxford University Press, 2014), 54.

104 **A Christian garrison was then stationed:** O'Callaghan, *Gibraltar Crusade*, 29.

104 **The *Chronicle of Alfonso X* is ungenerous:** CAX, ch. 6, p. 17.

104 **But from a strategic point of view:** O'Callaghan, *Gibraltar Crusade*, 30–31.

104 **the Doñana wetlands:** Charter of July 12, 1267: see Manuel González Jiménez, ed., *Diplomatario andaluz de Alfonso X* (Seville: El Monte, Caja de Huelva y Sevilla, 1991), doc. 329, 358–359.

NOTES TO CHAPTER FIVE

105 **a small coterie of Christians:** Alwyn Harrison, "Andalusī Christianity: The Survival of Indigenous Christian Communities" (PhD diss., University of Exeter, 2009), 417–418.

106 **In Jerez, as in Murcia, municipal government:** Alejandro García Sanjuan, "Causas inmediatas y alcance de la revuelta mudéjar de 1264," *Mudéjares y moriscos: Cambios sociales y culturales* (Teruel: Centro de Estudios Mudéjares, 2004), 505–518, at 513–516.

106 **Many, following the advice of their spiritual leaders:** L. P. Harvey, *Islamic Spain, 1200 to 1500* (Chicago: University of Chicago Press, 1990), 51–54.

106 **But either the ruler of Granada had no such understanding:** Barbara Boloix, "La inestable frontera castellano-nazarí en el siglo XIII: Del vasallaje a la insurrección (1246–1266)," in *Encrucijada de culturas: Alfonso X y su tiempo: Homenaje a Francisco Márquez Villanueva*, ed. Emilio González Ferrín (Seville: Fundación Tres Culturas, 2014), 201–211.

106 **Early in the 1260s, Alfonso and Muhammad formulated:** Joseph O'Callaghan, *The Gibraltar Crusade: Castile and the Battle for the Strait* (Philadelphia: University of Pennsylvania Press, 2011), 25; Joseph F. O'Callaghan, *The Learned King: The Reign of Alfonso X of Castile* (Philadelphia: University of Pennsylvania Press, 1993), 178.

107 **Alfonso then wrote:** Antonio Ballesteros-Beretta, *Alfonso X el Sabio* (Barcelona: Salvat, 1963), 362–365; the translation is my modification of the text in H. Salvador Martínez, *Alfonso X, the Learned: A Biography*, trans. Odile Cisneros (Leiden: Brill, 2010), 165.

107 **clearly signaled his intentions:** O'Callaghan, *Learned King*, 179, 181.

107 **Islamic combatants seeking holy war against the infidel:** Ibn Abi Zar' states that 3,000 Marinid knights had come to engage in holy war, but Ibn Idhari, who is more careful, gives the number 300 (O'Callaghan, *Gibraltar Crusade*, 34–35).

108 **The Arabic chronicler Ibn Idhari:** See García Sanjuan, "Causas inmediatas," 512–513.

108 **It is possible that Alfonso deliberately provoked:** The suggestion that Alfonso deliberately provoked the Mudéjar Rebellion is made

by Antonio Malpica Cuello, "Historia medieval de Andalucía cristiana: Algunas reflexiones y una propuesta de trabajo," in *España, Al-Andalus, Sefarad: Síntesis y nuevas perspectivas*, ed. Felipe Maíllo Salgado (Salamanca: Universidad de Salamanca, 1988; rpt. 1990), 69–81, at 72.

109 **"talked secretly with the Moors":** Ballesteros-Beretta, *Alfonso X el Sabio*, 368 (my translation).

109 **"all the castles and towns where there were Moors":** Damian Smith and Helena Buffery, eds., *The Book of Deeds of James I of Aragon: A Translation of the Medieval Catalan* Llibre dels fets (Burlington, VT: Ashgate, 2003), ch. 378, pp. 283–284.

110 **"Because of the wrongs he has done me":** Smith and Buffery, *Book of Deeds*, chs. 380–382, pp. 285–287.

110 **"The Moors took all the soldiers left in the castle":** CSM 345: Kathleen Kulp-Hill, trans., *Songs of Holy Mary of Alfonso X, the Wise: A Translation of the Cantigas de Santa María* (Tempe: Arizona Center for Medieval and Renaissance Studies, 2000), 420–421.

111 **the earliest of the *Cantigas de Santa María*:** Joseph O'Callaghan, *Alfonso X and the Cantigas de Santa María: A Poetic Biography* (Leiden: Brill, 1998), 8–9.

111 **"The king or ruler of the realm should be a good companion":** John K. Walsh, ed., *El libro de los doze sabios: O tractado de la nobleza y lealtad [ca. 1237]: Estudio y edición*, Anejos del boletín de la Real Academia Española 29 (Madrid, 1975), 85–86.

111 **The mirror had shown him that a good monarch:** Walsh, *El libro de los doze sabios*, 86, 89.

112 **"a man might take comfort when oppressed":** Robert I. Burns, SJ, ed., *Las siete partidas*, trans. Samuel Parsons Scott, 5 vols. (Philadelphia: University of Pennsylvania Press, 2001), law 2.5.21, 2:297.

112 **Ancient Greek ideas on the subject:** For this idea, I am most grateful to Juan Escourido for sharing a draft chapter, titled "Política de la alegría: Represión y modernidad al tablero en la Iberia alfonsí," from his forthcoming doctoral dissertation, *Poniendo en juego la Iberia premoderna (1250–1650): Alfonso X, Libro de Buen Amor, poesía de cancionero y novelas lipogramática* (University of Pennsylvania).

112 **"God desired that people might have all manner of happiness":** Alfonso X el Sabio, *Libro de los juegos: Acedrex, dados e tablas; Ordenamiento de las tafurerías*, ed. Raúl Orellana Calderón (Madrid: Biblioteca Castro, 2009), 19 (my translation, slightly modifying the version in Sonja Musser, "Los libros de acedrex dados e tablas: Historical, Artistic and Metaphysical Dimensions of Alfonso X's" *Book of Games* [PhD diss., University of Arizona, 2007], 106).

112 **Such pastimes, of course, are often more:** Johan Huizinga, *Homo ludens: A Study of the Play-Element in Culture* (Boston: Beacon Press, 1950), 13–14.

113 **One song relates how "in the land of Germany":** CSM 42: Kulp-Hill, *Songs of Holy Mary*, 55–56.

114 **a priest who uses black arts:** CSM 125: Kulp-Hill, *Songs of Holy Mary*, 154–156.

115 **"Whenever anyone gives in to violent laughter":** Plato, *Republic*, trans. C. D. C. Reeve (Indianapolis: Hackett, 2004), 69.

115 **A new comic spirit had begun to emerge:** Michael Camille, *Image on the Edge: The Margins of Medieval Art* (Cambridge, MA: Harvard University Press, 1992), 116.

116 **On the other side of the channel:** Jacques Le Goff, *Saint Louis* (Paris: Gallimard, 1996), 483–488.

116 **Jaune I's *Books of Deeds*:** Josep Pujol, "Jaume I, *rex facetus*: Notes de filología humorística," *Estudis romanics* 25, no. 2 (2003): 215–236, at 221–233.

116 **The *Dialog of Solomon and Marcolf*:** Jan Ziolkowski, ed., *Solomon and Marcolf* (Cambridge, MA: Harvard University Press, 2008), 57.

116 **The joke rests on a pun:** Ziolkowski, *Solomon and Marcolf*, 98–99; Benjamin M. Liu, *Medieval Joke Poetry: The Cantigas d'escarnho e de mal dizer* (Cambridge, MA: Harvard University Press, 2004), 104–105.

116 **The dialog circulated for centuries:** See Nancy Mason Bradbury and Scott Bradbury, eds. "The Dialogue of Solomon and Marcolf: Introduction," University of Rochester, Middle English Text Series, http://d.lib.rochester.edu/teams/text/bradbury-solomon-and-marcolf-intro (accessed September 24, 2014).

117 **Even in late-Renaissance Italy, scatological humor:** Alberto Montaner Frutos, "Alfonso V como rex facetus a través del Panormita," e-Spania, 2007, http://e-spania.revues.org/document 1503.html (accessed September 15, 2014); Peter Burke, "Frontiers of the Comic in Early Modern Italy, c. 1350–1750," in *A Cultural History of Humour*, ed. Jan Bremmer and Herman Roodenburg (Cambridge, UK: Polity Press, 1997), 61–75.

117 **songs of mockery and slander:** Kenneth R. Scholberg, *Sátira e invective en la España medieval* (Madrid: Gredos, 1971), esp. 106–109.

117 **"take in his wood":** Cantiga d'escarnho e de mal dizer [hereafter CEM] 11 in Manuel Rodrigues Lapa, ed., *Cantigas d'escarnho e de mal dizer dos cancioneiros medievais galego-portugueses*, 3rd ed. (rpt.; Lisbon: João da Costa, 1995), 21–22. All translations from the CEM are my own.

117   **"And pardons are a most precious thing":** Slightly modified version of the translation in Frede Jensen, ed. and trans., *Medieval Galician-Portuguese Poetry* (New York: Garland, 1992), 297.

117   **"Concern and care should always be given to the movements of the psyche":** Ariel Bar-Sela, Hebbel E. Hoff, and Elias Faris, "Moses Maimonides' Two Treatises on the Regimen of Health," *Transactions of the American Philosophical Society* 54 (1964): 3–50, at 38.

118   **Humor served then, as it serves now:** See Pujol, "Jaume I," 215–221, on the way in which Alfonso's father-in-law deployed humor for such purposes.

118   **The king himself wrote other poems:** Scholberg, *Sátira*, 109–119.

118   **Nobody—not Pedro García nor Pedro d'Espanha:** CEM 2: Lapa, *Cantigas d'escarnho*, 21–22.

118   **Ay, ay: Don Mendo has brought a horse:** CEM 6: Lapa, *Cantigas d'escarnho*, 23.

118   **The knight / When he spurs on:** CEM 21: Lapa, *Cantigas d'escarnho*, 33.

119   **He railed against the noblemen:** CEM 24: Lapa, *Cantigas d'escarnho*, 35. It is possible that the *cantiga* refers to the later rebellion of 1272, as is evidently the case for CEM 26, but the Vega de Granada (the plains of Granada) was also an important theater of war in 1265.

121   **The joke reveals real anxiety:** CEM 25: Lapa, *Cantigas d'escarnho*, 35; Liu, *Medieval Joke Poetry*, 100–102.

121   **The key garrison town of Jerez . . . by October 9, 1264:** O'Callaghan, *Learned King*, 187–188, initially rejected this date and argued that Jerez was not recaptured until October 4 to 9, 1266, drawing attention to the evidence of the *Libro del repartimiento de Jerez*, which stipulates that the Moors had capitulated on October 4, 1266. "I am convinced . . . that the Mudéjar revolt in lower Andalusia was much more alarming than has been recognized" (188). However, he now accepts Manuel González Jiménez's defense of the traditional date. See Manuel González Jiménez, *Documentación e itinerario de Alfonso X el Sabio* (Sevilla: Universidad de Sevilla, 2012), 50; Manuel González Jiménez, ed., *Crónica de Alfonso X. según el ms. II/2777 de la Biblioteca del Palacio real (Madrid)* (Murcia: Real Academia Alfonso X el Sabio, 1998) [hereafter CAX], ch. 14, p. 39n42); see also O'Callaghan, *Gibraltar Crusade*, 38.

121   **The schism between Muhammad I and the Banu Ashqilula:** Harvey, *Islamic Spain*, 31–37.

122   **Some time between late August and early September:** O'Callaghan, *Learned King*, 189, states that the meeting at Alcalá de Benzaide is

likely to have taken place much later, in June 1267. González Jiménez, *Documentación e itinerario*, 48, does not provide a clear date for this treaty, stating that it had been signed "months before" December 1265. O'Callaghan, *Gibraltar Crusade*, 44, now accepts that a truce was concluded in 1265 but cites González Jiménez's argument that there were two agreements, one in 1265 when they concluded a truce and the other in 1267 when they concluded a more permanent settlement.

122 **One historian has claimed that Alfonso:** Martínez, *Alfonso X*, 172–174.

122 **Charles was a distant relative of Alfonso:** Martínez, *Alfonso X*, 174–178.

123 **The wedding, it was agreed:** Ballesteros-Beretta, *Alfonso X el Sabio*, 407–416; Manuel González Jiménez, "El infante Don Fernando de la Cerda. Biografía e itinerario," in *Estudios alfonsíes* (Granada: Editorial Universidad de Granada, 2009), 301–314, at 303–304.

123 **Financial resentment widened a breach:** Simon R. Doubleday, *The Lara Family: Crown and Nobility in Medieval Spain* (Cambridge, MA: Harvard University Press, 2001), ch. 4.

124 **"all of them were silent":** CAX, ch. 19, p. 57.

124 **the dramatic reappearance of his exiled brother:** CAX, ch. 8, pp. 24–25.

124 **"In the battles and struggles":** CAX, ch. 8, p. 24.

125 **A source close to him suggests:** For the following account, see Aengus Ward, ed., *Sumario analístico de la historia gothica: Edition and study* (London: Department of Hispanic Studies, Queen Mary, University of London, 2007), 109–111.

125 **A tense and unstable situation:** Martínez, *Alfonso X*, 179–184.

125 **The Castilian prince then took command:** Ballesteros-Beretta, *Alfonso X el Sabio*, 415–416.

126 **"While the king of Granada was in his tent":** CAX, ch. 16, p. 45. Manuel González Jiménez suggests that this account of Lara alienation may be premature (CAX, ch. 16, p. 45n53), and indeed the chronology of this section of this chronicle is notoriously inaccurate, but the magnates' rebellion did not come out of a blue sky.

NOTES TO CHAPTER SIX

127 **Alfonso "was very happy to see us":** Damian Smith and Helena Buffery, eds., *The Book of Deeds of James I of Aragon: A Translation of the Medieval Catalan Llibre dels fets* (Burlington, VT: Ashgate, 2003), ch. 494, pp. 344–345.

127 **The public display of affection:** Smith and Buffery, *Book of Deeds*, chs. 476–477, pp. 334–335.

128 **The two rulers were not merely:** Smith and Buffery, *Book of Deeds*, chs. 380–381, pp. 285–286.

128 **Love and friendship between men:** Antonella Liuzzo Scorpo, *Friendship in Medieval Iberia: Historical, Legal and Literary Perspectives* (Farnham, UK: Ashgate, 2014), 9–40.

128 **One chronicler of the reign of Henry II:** C. Stephen Jaeger, *Ennobling Love: In Search of a Lost Sensibility* (Philadelphia: University of Pennsylvania Press, 1999), 1.

128 **a vital component of high-level political bonding:** Jesús Rodríguez-Velasco, "Leyes de la amistad" (unpublished paper, Universidad Autónoma de la Ciudad de Mexico, March 2014); Jesús Rodríguez-Velasco, "Perplexities: Narrative and Law in Medieval Cultures" (unpublished paper, Péter Pázmany Katolikus Egyetem, Budapest, April 2015).

128 **Prince Edward of England, the future Edward I:** Manuel González Jiménez, ed., *Crónica de Alfonso X. según el ms. II/2777 de la Biblioteca del Palacio real (Madrid)* (Murcia: Real Academia Alfonso X el Sabio, 1998) [hereafter CAX], ch. 18, pp. 49–50.

129 **Passing under the archway:** Francisco Javier Hernández, "Two Weddings and a Funeral: Alfonso X's Monuments in Burgos," *Hispanic Research Journal* 13, no. 5 (October 2012): 412–417.

129 **These have variously been seen as four sons:** Hernández, "Two Weddings and a Funeral," 418.

129 **"would sow discord and anger amongst them":** Smith and Buffery, *Book of Deeds*, ch. 495, p. 345.

130 **"Another day," he says, he found:** Smith and Buffery, *Book of Deeds*, ch. 496, p. 346.

131 **As usual, the chronicler is unreliable:** CAX, ch. 18, p. 52n69.

132 **"God loves these people more than the knights":** Smith and Buffery, *Book of Deeds*, ch. 498, pp. 347–348.

132 **"and some four or five knights went with us":** Smith and Buffery, *Book of Deeds*, ch. 499, p. 38.

132 **Alfonso's health steadily deteriorated:** Maricel Presilla, "The Image of Death and Political Ideology in the *Cantigas*," in *Studies on the Cantigas de Santa Maria: Art, Music, and Poetry*, ed. Israel J. Katz et al. (Madison: HSMS, 1987), 403–457.

132 **One diagnosis is cancer:** Richard Kinkade, "Alfonso X, Cantiga 235, and the Events of 1269–1278," *Speculum* 67, no. 2 (1992): 284–323, at 285–290.

133 **Ideas such as this:** Albrecht Classen, "Introduction: Friendship—the Quest for a Human Ideal and Value from Antiquity to the Early

Modern Time," in *Friendship in the Middle Ages and Early Modern Age: Explorations of a Fundamental Ethical Discourse*, ed. Albrecht Classen and Marilyn Standidge (Berlin: De Gruyter, 2010), 1–183, at 5–8.

133 **"As Aristotle said, no man":** Robert I. Burns, SJ, ed., *Las siete partidas*, trans. Samuel Parsons Scott, 5 vols. (Philadelphia: University of Pennsylvania Press, 2001), law 4.27.2, 4:1003.

134 **"arises solely from beneficence":** Burns, *Las siete partidas*, law 4.27.4, 4:1005.

134 **"nothing was so pleasant as to have, for a friend":** Burns, *Las siete partidas*, law 4.27.3, 4:1004; Liuzzo Scorpo, *Friendship in Medieval Iberia*, 68–80.

134 **The son returns home, lesson learned:** Kenneth S. Scholberg, "A Half-Friend and a Friend and a Half," *Bulletin of Hispanic Studies* 35 (1958): 187–198; Liuzzo Scorpo, *Friendship in Medieval Iberia*, 73.

134 **Transferred to the heavens:** Antonella Liuzzo Scorpo, "Spiritual Friendship in the Works of Alfonso X of Castile: Images of Interaction Between the Sacred and the Spiritual Worlds of Thirteenth-Century Iberia," in Classen and Standidge, *Friendship*, 445–475.

135 **"In friendship . . . there is no rank higher than another":** Burns, *Las siete partidas*, law 4.27.5, 4:1005.

135 **In his *Confessions*:** Stephen Jaeger, "Friendship of Mutual Perfecting in Augustine's *Confessions* and the Failure of Classical *Amicitia*," in Classen and Standidge, *Friendship*, 185–200.

135 **"having been condemned to death":** Burns, *Las siete partidas*, law 4.27.6, 4:1006; Liuzzo Scorpo, *Friendship in Medieval Iberia*, 78.

136 **reinvigorated in the twelfth century:** Julian Haseldine, "Monastic Friendship in Theory and Action in the Twelfth Century," in Classen and Standidge, *Friendship*, 349–393, at 349.

136 **"There was no pretense between us":** Aelred of Rievaulx, *Spiritual Friendship*, trans. Mary Eugenia Laker, SSND (Kalamazoo, MI: Cistercian Publications, 1977), 129.

136 **The letters of one of his most famous contemporaries:** On friendship between women, see Liuzzo Scorpo, *Friendship in Medieval Iberia*, 184–186.

136 **Thirteenth-century people:** Classen, "Introduction," 57–60.

137 **Assertions of friendship were doubtless:** On political friendships, see Liuzzo Scorpo, *Friendship in Medieval Iberia*, 111–139.

137 **Some letters in which churchmen express extravagant warmth:** Haseldine, "Monastic Friendship," 356–380.

137 **Lords became "friends" of their vassals:** Gerd Althoff, "Friendship and Political Order," in *Friendship in Medieval Europe*, ed. Julian Haseldine (Stroud, UK: Sutton, 1999), 91–105.

137 **At the Castilian court:** Jesús Rodríguez-Velasco, "Theorizing the Language of Law," *diacritics* 36, no. 3–4 (fall-winter 2006): 64–86, esp. 78.

137 **"should be good friends of the king":** Burns, *Las siete partidas*, law 2.9.5, 2:314.

137 **In the section of the *Partidas* that deals specifically with friendship:** Carlos Heusch, "Les fondements juridiques de l'amitié à travers les Partidas d'Alphonse X et le droit médiéval," *Cahiers de linguistique hispanique médiévale* 18–19 (1993): 5–48.

137 **One kind of friendship exists . . . "which in former times":** Burns, *Las siete partidas*, law 4.27.4, 4:1005.

138 **According to customary law:** Heusch, "Les fondements juridiques," 26–33; Liuzzo Scorpo, *Friendship in Medieval Iberia*, 24, 28–30.

138 **The Wise King recounts the simultaneously practical and emotional benefits:** Burns, *Las siete partidas*, law 4.27.5, 4:1005.

138 **The emotional texture of individual friendships:** Jaeger, *Ennobling Love*, 4.

138 **Andalusi attitudes would also have been formative:** Jonathan Decter, "A Hebrew 'Sodomite' Tale from Thirteenth-Century Toledo: Jacob Ben El'azar's Story of Sapir, Shapir, and Birsha," *JMIS* 3, no. 2 (2011): 187–202, at 199.

138 **This text, which ultimately has Sanskrit and Persian origins:** David Wacks, *Framing Iberia: Maqamat and Frametale Narratives in Medieval Spain* (Leiden: Brill, 2007), 89.

139 **"mirror for princes":** Christine Van Ruymbeke, "Murder in the Forest: Celebrating Rewritings and Misreadings of the Kalila-Dimna Tale of the Lion and the Hare," *Studia iranica* 41 (2012): 203–254, at 204–205.

139 **One such tale relates the capture of the Brightly Colored Dove:** John E. Keller and Robert White Linker, ed., *El libro de Calila e Digna* (Madrid: Consejo Superior de Investigaciones Científicas, 1967), 165–170 (my translation, modified from the original).

140 **"in the house of a man of religion":** My rendering is based on Keller and Linker, *Calila e Digna*, 177–186.

142 **As prince and then as king:** On the inheritance of friendship and enmity, see Liuzzo Scorpo, *Friendship in Medieval Iberia*, 126–128.

142 **"begged him as a friend, and ordered him as a vassal":** CAX, ch. 20, p. 64.

143 **In founding a new military order:** Amy G. Remensnyder, *La Conquistadora: The Virgin Mary at War and Peace in the Old and New Worlds* (Oxford: Oxford University Press, 2014), 52–53.

143 **news of a terrifying incursion:** CAX, ch. 22, pp. 70–76.

144 **Alfonso's reaction, if we can judge from the royal chronicle:** Francisco J. Hernández, "La reina Violante de Aragón, Jofré de

Loaysa y la *Crónica de Alfonso* X. Un gran fragmento cronístico del siglo XIII reutilizado en el XIV," *JMIS* 7, no. 1 (2015): 87–111, indicating that we can refer to this section as the *Estoria del alboroço* [History of the uprising].

145 **The program was cohesive:** Julio Escalona, "Los nobles contra su rey. Argumentos y motivaciones de la insubordinación nobiliaria de 1272–1273," *Cahiers de linguistique hispanique médiévale* 25 (2002): 131–162, at 154–156.

145 **When the rebels returned:** CAX, ch. 25, p. 89.

146 **"the queen kept them for two days":** CAX, ch. 27, p. 92.

146 **They appear to be transcriptions of letters:** Isabel Alfonso, "*Desheredamiento* y *desafuero*, o la pretendida justificación de una revuelta nobiliaria," *Cahiers de linguistique hispanique médiévale* 25 (2002): 99–129.

146 **"raising you and marrying you off":** CAX, ch. 28, p. 95.

147 **Alfonso's messengers rehearse the long trajectory:** CAX, ch. 30, pp. 99–102.

147 **"that we shall be friends for always to you and your sons":** CAX, ch. 43, pp. 123–127, at 125.

148 **Adopting a more militant tone:** CAX, ch. 49, pp. 138–140, at 139.

149 **"came to him as a friend, not as an emissary of the others":** CAX, ch. 51, pp. 142–143, at 143.

NOTES TO CHAPTER SEVEN

151 **"I saw the letter that you sent me":** Manuel González Jiménez, ed., *Crónica de Alfonso X. según el ms. II/2777 de la Biblioteca del Palacio real (Madrid)* (Murcia: Real Academia Alfonso X el Sabio, 1998) [hereafter CAX], ch. 52, pp. 144–151. See also Paula K. Rodgers, "Alfonso X Writes to His Son: Reflections on the *Crónica de Alfonso* X (Together with a Commentary on and Critical Text of the Unique Alfonsine Letter That It Preserves)," *Exemplaria hispánica* 1 (1991–1992): 58–79.

152 **Fernando had begun to take on important roles:** Manuel González Jiménez, "El infante Don Fernando de la Cerda. Biografía e itinerario," in *Estudios alfonsíes* (Granada: Editorial Universidad de Granada, 2009), 305–309.

153 **Achieving the difficult balance:** Rachel E. Moss, *Fatherhood and Its Representations in Middle English Texts* (Cambridge, UK: D. S. Brewer, 2013), 72.

153 **delegated responsibilities to his wife and son:** For Yolant's diplomatic role throughout this "uprising," Francisco J. Hernández, "La reina Violante de Aragón, Jofré de Loaysa y la *Crónica de*

Alfonso X. Un gran fragmento cronístico del siglo XIII reutilizado en el XIV," JMIS 7, no. 1 (2015): 87–111.

154   **"She resolved it better than the king had ordered":** CAX, ch. 53, p. 152.

154   **"He thanked the queen as much as he possibly could":** CAX, ch. 55, pp. 158–159.

155   **The popular imagination:** Barbara A. Hanawalt, "Medievalists and the Study of Childhood," *Speculum* 77, no. 2 (2002): 440–460.

155   **Even some scholarly experts on the medieval family:** Cf. Ruth Mazo Karras, *From Boys to Men: Formations of Masculinity in Late Medieval Europe* (Philadelphia: University of Pennsylvania Press, 2003), 165–166.

156   **"All animals which have young naturally exert themselves":** Robert I. Burns, SJ, ed., *Las siete partidas*, trans. Samuel Parsons Scott, 5 vols. (Philadelphia: University of Pennsylvania Press, 2001), laws 2.7.1–2, 2:300.

156   **generally believed that men contained greater heat than women:** Philip Grace, "Aspects of Fatherhood in Thirteenth-Century Encyclopedias," *Journal of Family History* 31, no. 3 (2006): 211–236, 224–225.

156   **childbirth was usually a moment restricted to women:** Nicholas Orme, *Medieval Children* (New Haven: Yale University Press, 2001), 13.

156   **two scenes of childbirth:** Gonzalo Menéndez Pidal, *La España del siglo XIII leída en imágenes* (Madrid: Real Academia de la Historia, 1986), 78.

156   **"Where they are not bad tempered":** Burns, *Las siete partidas*, law 2.7.3, 2:301.

157   **sleeveless robe of an unknown little child:** Menéndez Pidal, *La España del siglo XIII*, 62.

157   **heartbreaking tale of the mother:** CSM 139: Kathleen Kulp-Hill, trans., *Songs of Holy Mary of Alfonso X, the Wise: A Translation of the Cantigas de Santa María* (Tempe: Arizona Center for Medieval and Renaissance Studies, 2000), 172.

157   **But across Europe, miracle tales:** R. C. Finucane, *The Rescue of the Innocents: Endangered Children in Medieval Miracles* (New York: Saint Martin's Press, 1997), 99, suggests that in the texts studied, roughly a third of parents making vows to saints, seeking protection for their children, are fathers.

158   **"The girl went to drink from the irrigation ditch":** CSM 133: Kulp-Hill, *Songs of Holy Mary*, 165.

158   **a couple on their way to the Marian shrine at Salas:** CSM 171: Kulp-Hill, *Songs of Holy Mary*, 206.

158 **a knight who lived in the city of Segovia:** CSM 282: Kulp-Hill, *Songs of Holy Mary*, 341.

158 **"I shall tell a miracle which happened in Tudia":** On Alfonso's authorship of this *cantiga*, see Manuel Pedro Ferreira, "Alfonso X, compositor," *Alcanate: Revista de estudios alfonsíes* 5 (2006–2007): 117–137, esp. 127–129.

158 **the nearly fatal illness of . . . Fernando:** CSM 221: Kulp-Hill, *Songs of Holy Mary*, 264–265.

159 **"Is there anything more precious than a son":** Cited in Philip David Grace, "Providers and Educators: The Theory and Practice of Fatherhood in Late Medieval Basel, 1475–1529" (PhD diss., University of Minnesota, 2010), 107.

160 **metal toy soldiers:** Orme, *Medieval Children*, 173–174.

160 **the tradition of works written by fathers:** Orme, *Medieval Children*, 243.

160 **It is likely that Fernando's tutor was Jofré de Loaysa:** González Jiménez, "El infante Don Fernando de la Cerda," 302–303.

160 **Fathers typically greet their sons more laconically:** Moss, *Fatherhood*, 74–98.

161 **"to love and fear their father and mother":** Burns, *Las siete partidas*, law 2.7.9, 2:305.

161 **"not like slaves, but like sons":** Grace, "Aspects of Fatherhood," 227–228.

161 **horrific aberrations:** Burns, *Las siete partidas*, laws 4.18.2 and 7.8.12, 4:965 and 5:1348–1349; cf. Marilyn Stone, *Marriage and Friendship in Medieval Spain: Social Relations According to the Fourth Partida of Alfonso X* (New York: Peter Lang, 1990), 102.

162 **In one widely told medieval story:** Hanawalt, "Medievalists and the Study of Childhood," at 456.

162 **a daughter, and not a son:** Antonio Resende de Oliveira, "Beatriz Afonso, 1244–1300," in *As primeiras rainhas: Mafalda de Mouriana, Dulce de Barcelona e Aragão, Urraca de Castela, Mecia Lopes de Haro, Beatriz Afonso*, by María Alegria Fernandes Marques et al. (Lisbon: Círculo de Leitores, 2012), 387–463. On father-daughter relationships more generally, see Moss, *Fatherhood*, 112–113, 188.

163 **Here she is wearing a transparent dress:** Fols. 54r and 58r: see Sonja Musser, "Los libros de acedrex dados e tablas: Historical, Artistic and Metaphysical Dimensions of Alfonso X's *Book of Games*" (PhD diss., University of Arizona, 2007), 745–746; on her youth, see Resende de Oliveira, "Beatriz Afonso," 401–407.

163 **"blessed with an elegant body":** Leontina Ventura, *D. Afonso III* (Lisbon: Temas e Debates, 2009), 318–323.

163 **"so that they may read the Hours properly":** Burns, *Las siete partidas*, law 2.7.11, 2:306–307.

163   **Charlemagne . . . taught his girls:** Samuel Epes Turner, trans., "Einhard: The Life of Charlemagne," Fordham University, Medieval Sourcebook, http://www.fordham.edu/halsall/basis/einhard.asp (accessed September 3, 2014).

164   **a pretty girl called Musa:** CSM 79: Kulp-Hill, *Songs of Holy Mary*, 104; Stephen Parkinson, ed., *Alfonso X the Learned, Cantigas de Santa María: An Anthology*, MHRA Critical Texts 40 (Cambridge, UK: Modern Humanities Research Association, 2015), 68–69. See also Menéndez Pidal, *La España del siglo XIII*, 239.

164   **"Legitimate" children are sacred:** Burns, *Las siete partidas*, law 4.13, 4:948; cf. Stone, *Marriage and Friendship*, 90–91.

164   **The children of stable relationships:** Moss, *Fatherhood*, 167–183.

164   **Canon law ruled that a child born out of wedlock:** Ruth Mazo Karras, "Sexuality in the Middle Ages," in *The Medieval World*, ed. Peter Linehan and Janet L. Nelson (New York: Routledge, 2001), 279–293.

164   **in royal circles many natural children were well favored:** Orme, *Medieval Children*, 57.

165   **the most acute problem:** Resende de Oliveira, "Beatriz Afonso," 395–397.

166   **Dutifully fulfilling her obligations:** Ventura, *Afonso III*, 141–142, 246–247, 268–269.

166   **The "good" fathers of medieval romance:** Moss, *Fatherhood*, 127–147.

166   **thrived at the Portuguese royal court:** Ventura, *Afonso III*, 203, 247.

166   **she also intervened in political affairs:** Resende de Oliveira, "Beatriz Afonso," 424–426.

167   **She seems certain to have been involved:** Antonio Ballesteros-Beretta, *Alfonso X el Sabio* (Barcelona: Salvat, 1963), 420–421, 427–428.

167   **When, twelve years later, her husband died:** Pablo Martín Prieto, "Las Guzmán alfonsinas. Una dinastía femenina en la Castilla de los siglos XIII y XIV," *Mirabilia* 17, no. 2 (2013): 259–262.

167   **the famous *Alfonsine Tables*:** Laura Fernández Fernández, "El ms. 8322 de la Bibliothèque de l'Arsenal y su relación con las tablas alfonsíes. Hipótesis de trabajo," *Alcanate: Revista de estudios alfonsíes* 7 (2010–2011): esp. 253–258. The tables had initially been compiled and expanded, on Alfonso's initiative, by two Jewish scholars, Isaac ben Sid and Yehuda ben Mosé.

168   **"he should by no means go, because it was not fitting":** Damian Smith and Helena Buffery, eds., *The Book of Deeds of James I of*

Aragon: A Translation of the Medieval Catalan Llibre dels fets (Burlington, VT: Ashgate, 2003), ch. 552, p. 374.

168   **She then remained there with the rabbi:** Yitzhak F. Baer, "From the Age of the Reconquest to the Fourteenth Century," in A *History of the Jews in Christian Spain* (Philadelphia: Jewish Publication Society of America, 1978), 119–120.

168   **"he fell so gravely ill that they thought he would surely die":** CSM 235: Kulp-Hill, *Songs of Holy Mary,* 281–283.

169   **unspeakable news:** CAX, ch. 77, p. 240.

169   **Some medieval writers felt disdain:** Finucane, *Rescue of the Innocents,* 151–157.

170   **Even his battle-hardened father-in-law:** Smith and Buffery, *Book of Deeds,* ch. 545, p. 371.

170   **Lope Díaz and the young Prince Sancho headed quickly:** CAX, ch. 65, pp. 185–188.

170   **The body of the dead infante Fernando:** CAX, ch. 64; Francisco Javier Hernández, "Two Weddings and a Funeral: Alfonso X's Monuments in Burgos," *Hispanic Research Journal* 13, no. 5 (October 2012): 421.

170   **a set of rich fabrics:** J. Yarza Luaces, ed., *Vestiduras ricas: El monasterio de las Huelgas y su época, 1170–1340* (Madrid: Patrimonio Nacional, 2005), 148, 154–155, 157, 159, 162–165.

171   **The emir had now completed the preparations for his assault:** Ibn abi Zar, *Rawd al-Qirtas,* trans. Ambrosio Huici Miranda, 2nd ed. (Valencia: J. Nacher, 1964), 2:596–597.

171   **"like a flood, or a cloud of locusts":** Ibn abi Zar, *Rawd al-Qirtas,* 2:596–597.

171   **the grim setting for a *cantiga*:** CSM 323: Kulp-Hill, *Songs of Holy Mary,* 391–392.

172   **The Moroccans then received news:** Ibn abi Zar, *Rawd al-Qirtas,* 2:596–597.

172   **Among them was the head of Nuño González de Lara:** Ibn abi Zar, *Rawd al-Qirtas,* 2:601; CAX, ch. 62, pp. 178–180.

172   **"lamented the death of Don Nuño":** CAX, ch. 62, p. 179. A similar fate soon befell Queen Yolant's brother Sancho, the archbishop of Toledo: in a separate engagement, he was captured and decapitated, and the hand on which he wore his ring was cut off. However, the practice of decapitation was in no way distinctive to Islam: see Maribel Fierro, "Decapitation of Christians and Muslims in the Medieval Iberian Peninsula: Narratives, Images, Contemporary Perceptions," *Comparative Literature Studies* 45, no. 2 (2008): 137–164.

NOTES TO CHAPTER EIGHT

175 **Broken in spirit and body:** CSM 235: Kathleen Kulp-Hill, trans., *Songs of Holy Mary of Alfonso X, the Wise: A Translation of the Cantigas de Santa María* (Tempe: Arizona Center for Medieval and Renaissance Studies, 2000), 281–283; Manuel González Jiménez, ed., *Crónica de Alfonso X. según el ms. II/2777 de la Biblioteca del Palacio real (Madrid)* (Murcia: Real Academia Alfonso X el Sabio, 1998) [hereafter CAX], ch. 66, p. 188n278; "Anales Toledanos III," ed. Antonio Floriano, *Cuadernos de historia de España* 43–44 (1967): 154–187.

176 **The *Chronicle of Alfonso X* tells us blithely:** CAX, ch. 67, p. 189.

176 **"When he entered Castile, all the people of the lands":** CSM 235: Kulp-Hill, *Songs of Holy Mary*, 282.

177 **By the time the Cortes met in April:** CAX, ch. 68, p. 193.

177 **"our illness increased and worsened":** Damian Smith and Helena Buffery, eds., *The Book of Deeds of James I of Aragon: A Translation of the Medieval Catalan Llibre dels fets* (Burlington, VT: Ashgate, 2003), ch. 560, p. 378.

177 **In the brilliant creative vision:** Francisco Prado Vilar, "Sombras en el palacio de las horas: Arte, magia, ciencia y la búsqueda de la felicidad," in *Alfonso X el Sabio. Sala San Esteban, Murcia, 27 octubre 2009–31 enero 2010* [exhibition catalog] (Murcia: A. G. Novograf, 2009), 448–455.

178 **One recent biographer has speculated:** H. Salvador Martínez, *Alfonso X, the Learned: A Biography,* trans. Odile Cisneros (Leiden: Brill, 2010), 239, 279.

178 **"fine galleon / that will take me quickly away":** Juan Paredes, ed., *El cancionero profano de Alfonso X el Sabio. Verba (anuario Galego de filoloxía), anexo* 66 (Santiago de Compostela: Serviço de Publicacións e Intercambio Científico, 2010); Joseph O'Callaghan, *Alfonso X and the Cantigas de Santa María: A Poetic Biography* (Leiden: Brill, 1998), 200–201.

179 **Another poem associated with Alfonso:** The attribution is made by John Keller, taking the text from James Fitzmaurice-Kelly, *The Oxford Book of Spanish Verse* (Oxford: Clarendon Press, 1942), 8; see O'Callaghan, *Alfonso X and the Cantigas de Santa María,* 227.

179 **he recalls his illness in Vitoria:** CSM 209: Kulp-Hill, *Songs of Holy Mary*, 251 (Stephen Parkinson, ed., *Alfonso X the Learned, Cantigas de Santa María: An Anthology*, MHRA Critical Texts 40 [Cambridge, UK: Modern Humanities Research Association, 2015], 120–121); CSM 279: Kulp-Hill, *Songs of Holy Mary*, 338 (Parkinson, *Cantigas de Santa María*, 122–123).

180 **"Like David . . . he composed many beautiful songs":** Fidel Fita, "Biografías de San Fernando y de Alfonso el Sabio por Gil de Zamora," *Boletín de la Real Academia de la Historia* 5 (1885): 321.

180 **Henry, duke of Lancaster:** E. J. Arnould, Le livre de seyntz medicines: *The Unpublished Devotional Treatise of Henry of Lancaster* (Oxford: Anglo-Norman Text Society, 1940), 190.

180 **music . . . is essential to restoring the personal harmonies:** Christopher Callahan, "Music in Medieval Medical Practice: Speculations and Certainties," *College Music Symposium* 40 (2000): 151–164.

181 **a delightful comic tale:** CSM 64: Kulp-Hill, *Songs of Holy Mary*, 81–82; Parkinson, *Cantigas de Santa María*, 58–63.

181 **Once there was a maiden:** CSM 188: Kulp-Hill, *Songs of Holy Mary*, 225.

182 **In Alfonso's tale, there are echoes of Saint Paul's notion:** Ryan Giles, *Inscribed Tower*, unpublished manuscript.

182 **a minstrel in Lombardy:** CSM 293: Kulp-Hill, *Songs of Holy Mary*, 355.

182 **In a culture that blurred the division:** Caroline Walker Bynum, *Christian Materiality: An Essay on Religion in Late Medieval Europe* (New York: Zone Books, 2011), 105–112.

183 **a good woman who lived by the banks of the Guadiana River:** CSM 347: Kulp-Hill, *Songs of Holy Mary*, 422–423.

184 **Once there was a man from Aragon:** CSM 173: Kulp-Hill, *Songs of Holy Mary*, 208.

184 **"When half a drachma's weight of it is taken in a drink":** Ingrid Bahler and Katherine Gyékényesi Gatto, eds. and trans., *The Lapidary of King Alfonso X the Learned* (New Orleans, LA: University Press of the South, 2000), 141.

184 **a young shepherdess from Córdoba:** CSM 321: Kulp-Hill, *Songs of Holy Mary*, 389–390.

185 **acerbic wit of Alfonso's satirical songs:** Benjamin M. Liu, *Medieval Joke Poetry: The Cantigas d'escarnho e de mal dizer* (Cambridge, MA: Harvard University Press, 2004), 118–130.

185 **In the *Book of Stones*, gold:** Bahler and Gyékényesi Gatto, *Lapidary*, 67–69.

186 **The culture of royalty in Castile:** Joseph O'Callaghan, "The *Cantigas de Santa Maria* as an Historical Source: Two Examples (nos. 321 and 386)," in *Studies on the Cantigas de Santa Maria: Art, Music, and Poetry*, ed. Israel J. Katz et al. (Madison: HSMS, 1987), 387–402.

186 **In his *Book of Holy Medicines* (*Livre de seyntz medicines*):** Cited in Naoë Kukita Yoshikawa, "Holy Medicine and Disease of the

Soul: Henry of Lancaster and *Le livre de seyntz medicines*," *Medical History* 53, no. 3 (2009): 397–414.

186   **King Duarte of Portugal:** Iona McCleery, "Both 'Illness and Temptation of the Enemy': Melancholy, the Medieval Patient, and the Writings of King Duarte of Portugal (r. 1433–1438)," *JMIS* 1, no. 2 (2009): 163–178, at 165–172.

187   **The cutting-edge hospital wards:** John Henderson, *The Renaissance Hospital: Healing the Body and Healing the Soul* (New Haven, CT: Yale University Press, 2006), chs. 4–5.

187   **Her capacity for spectacular, sometimes magnanimous medical intervention:** CSM 81: Kulp-Hill, *Songs of Holy Mary*, 105.

187   **heals a man who cuts out his own tongue:** CSM 174: Kulp-Hill, *Songs of Holy Mary*, 209.

188   **a man who . . . has his foot amputated:** CSM 37: Kulp-Hill, *Songs of Holy Mary*, 50.

188   **incident in the town of Lugo:** CSM 77: Kulp-Hill, *Songs of Holy Mary*, 101.

188   **Alfonso, lying on his four-poster sickbed:** This description of the CSM 209 draws on John E. Keller and Richard P. Kinkade, "Iconography and Literature: Alfonso Himself in Cantiga 209," *Hispania* 66, no. 3 (1983): 348–352; Prado Vilar, "Sombras," 449–450; and Francisco Corti, "Narrativa visual de la enfermedad en las *Cantigas de Santa María*," *Cuadernos de historia de España* 75 (1998–1999): 85–115, at 87–93.

190   **The early church fathers had seen such amulets:** Don Skemer, *Binding Words: Textual Amulets in the Middle Ages* (University Park: Pennsylvania State University Press, 2006), 58–68.

191   **the codicil to his last will and testament:** Manuel González Jiménez, ed., *Diplomatario andaluz de Alfonso X* (Seville: El Monte, Caja de Huelva y Sevilla, 1991), doc. 521, 557–564, at 559.

191   **Might the books associated with Louis IX of France:** Bynum, *Christian Materiality*, 136.

192   **"I am sweet herb in all greenness":** Hildegard of Bingen, *Selected Writings*, trans. Mark Atherton (London: Penguin, 2001), 142.

192   **blessing for radishes:** Bynum, *Christian Materiality*, 147–148.

192   **the mineral was perceived to be alive:** Bynum, *Christian Materiality*, 109.

193   **inherited from al-Andalus a belief in the supernatural:** Julio Navarro Palazón and Pedro Jiménez Castillo, "Religiosidad y creencias en la Murcia musulmana: Testimonios arqueológicos de una cultura oriental," in *Huellas: Catedral de Murcia; Exposición 2002, 23 de enero–22 de julio*, ed. Julio Navarro Palazón (Murcia: Caja de Ahorros de Murcia, 2002), 58–87, at 63–65.

194   **the bezoar stone:** J. K. Rowling, *Harry Potter and the Sorcerer's Stone* (New York: Scholastic, 1998), 137.

194   **These ideas underpinned the *Book of Stones*:** On the dating of the revised edition, see Anthony Cárdenas-Rotunno, "El *Lapidario* alfonsí: La fecha problemática del códice escurialense h.I.15," in *Actas del XIII Congreso de la Asociación Internacional de Hispanistas, Madrid 6–11 de julio de 1998*, ed. Florencio Sevilla Arroyo and Carlos Alvar Ezquerra. 4 vols. (Madrid: Castalia / Fundación Duques de Soria, 2000), 1:81–87.

195   **It was swept into being:** Nancy Siraisi, *Medieval and Early Renaissance Medicine: An Introduction to Knowledge and Practice* (Chicago: University of Chicago Press, 1990), esp. 11–13 and, on Iberian Muslim, Jewish, and Salernitan influences on Montpellier, 58–59. On the *Book of Stones*, see Marcelino V. Amasuno, "El contenido médico en el *Lapidario* alfonsí," *Alcanate: Revista de estudios alfonsíes* 5 (2006–2007): 139–161; see also J. Horace Nunemaker, "In Pursuit of the Sources of the Alfonsine Lapidaries," *Speculum* 14, no. 4 (1939): 483–489.

196   **There was no medical school:** Siraisi, *Medieval and Early Renaissance Medicine*, 13, 57–58.

196   **chairs of medicine at Salamanca:** Marcelino Amasuno, *La escuela de medicina del studio salmantino (siglos XIII–XV)* (Salamanca: Universidad de Salamanca, 1990), 52–53.

197   **"The powders of this stone":** Bahler and Gyékényesi Gatto, *Lapidary*, 166.

197   **the stone called *tutya*:** Bahler and Gyékényesi Gatto, *Lapidary*, 185–186. Grace Mitchell speculates on the value of these stones for Alfonso in "Cures from the Lapidario," in *Estudios alfonsinos y otros escritos en homenaje a John Esten Keller y a Anibal A. Biglieri*, ed. N. Toscano Liria (New York: National Hispanic Foundation for the Humanities, National Endowment for the Humanities, 1991), 156–164.

198   **"In the mountain they called Culequin":** Bahler and Gyékényesi Gatto, *Lapidary*, 203.

198   **"stone that attracts gold":** Bahler and Gyékényesi Gatto, *Lapidary*, 33.

198   **Black coral:** Bahler and Gyékényesi Gatto, *Lapidary*, 53–54.

198   **Several varieties of jasper (yzf):** Bahler and Gyékényesi Gatto, *Lapidary*, 36–38.

198   **The divine presence of Mary, we are reminded:** CSM 376: Kulp-Hill, *Songs of Holy Mary*, 457–458; CSM 29: Kulp-Hill, *Songs of Holy Mary*, 40.

199 **These ideas might, in isolation:** Siraisi, *Medieval and Early Renaissance Medicine*, 149–152; Prado Vilar, "Sombras," 451.

199 **antidotes for black magic and witchcraft:** J. Horace Nunemaker, "An Additional Chapter on Magic in Mediaeval Spanish Literature," *Speculum* 7, no. 4 (1932): 556–564, at 562.

199 **alchemy entails the skill:** Bahler and Gyékényesi Gatto, *Lapidary*, 68.

200 **But as his health declined:** Francisco Márquez Villanueva, "La magia erotica del *Lapidario* alfonsí," *Anuario de letras* (Mexico) 35 (1997): 349–369, esp. 361. Francisco Prado Vilar argues that in Alfonso's cultural production during these years, the goal is always "the elimination of pain, protection against evil, the achievement of love, and the obtaining of knowledge" ("Sombras," 453).

200 **"They swore on their crosses that if Alfonso did not accept":** Ibn abi Zar, *Rawd al-Qirtas*, trans. Ambrosio Huici Miranda, 2nd ed. (Valencia: J. Nacher, 1964), 2:608–617.

201 **"King Alfonso of Castile treated his wife, King Pedro's sister, wrongfully":** Lynn H. Nelson, trans., *The Chronicle of San Juan de la Peña: A Fourteenth-Century Official History of the Crown of Aragon* (University of Pennsylvania Press: Philadelphia, 1991), 70.

201 **"her brother the king of Aragon came for her at night":** Jofré de Loaysa, *Crónica de los reyes de Castilla Fernando III, Alfonso X, Sancho IV y Fernando IV*, ed. Antonio García Martínez (Murcia: Patronato de Cultura de la Excma. Diputación de Murcia, 1961), ch. 219.24, 96.

201 **Pere III's actions:** Pere III was able to negotiate a very favorable set of agreements with Castile, the Treaty of Campillo-Ágreda (March 27, 1281), regarding the territorial borders between the two realms (CAX, ch. 75, p. 213n316).

201 **By August, a naval siege was in place:** CAX, chs. 69–70, pp. 195–198.

202 **"the only people who remained in Ceuta":** Ibn abi Zar, *Rawd al-Qirtas*, 2:623.

202 **As the besieging Christian armies abandoned their encampments:** Ibn abi Zar, *Rawd al-Qirtas*, 2:626–629.

Notes to Chapter Nine

203 **"Whenever somebody wrongs you, ask yourself at once":** Marcus Aurelius, *Meditations, with Selected Correspondence*, trans. Robin Hard (New York: Oxford University Press, 2011), 62, 109 (Books 7.26, 11.18).

204   **This vision of anger as a self-destructive vice:** Richard Barton, "Gendering Anger: *Ira, Furor,* and Discourses of Power and Masculinity in the Eleventh and Twelfth Centuries," in *In the Garden of Evil: The Vices and Culture in the Middle Ages,* ed. Richard Newhauser (Toronto: Pontifical Institute of Medieval Studies, 2005), 371–392, at 371–378.

204   **state bedroom at Westminster Palace:** Paul Hyams, "What Did Henry III of England Think in Bed and in French About Kingship and Anger?," in *Anger's Past: The Social Uses of an Emotion in the Middle Ages,* ed. Barbara Rosenwein (Ithaca, NY: Cornell University Press, 1998), 92–124.

204   **Among them, in the company of Avarice and Vanity:** See Maximo Gómez Rascón, *Catedral de León, las vidrieras: El simbolismo de la luz* (León: Edilesa, 2000), 134–143, on representations of vice and virtue in the windows.

204   **"discovered some things about the infante Fadrique":** Manuel González Jiménez, ed., *Crónica de Alfonso X. según el ms. II/2777 de la Biblioteca del Palacio real (Madrid)* (Murcia: Real Academia Alfonso X el Sabio, 1998) [hereafter CAX], ch. 68, p. 194.

204   **A separate source, another contemporary chronicle:** Manuel González Jiménez, "Unos anales del reinado de Alfonso X," *Boletín de la Real Academia de la Historia* 192 (1995): 461–491, at 477.

205   **Some have seen these events:** François Foronda, *El espanto y el miedo. Golpismo, emociones políticas y constitucionalismo en la Edad Media* (Madrid: Dykinson, 2013), 79.

205   **"The son of God wished that he take vengeance":** CSM 235: Kathleen Kulp-Hill, trans., *Songs of Holy Mary of Alfonso X, the Wise: A Translation of the Cantigas de Santa María* (Tempe: Arizona Center for Medieval and Renaissance Studies, 2000), 282.

205   **Their visual silence speaks to their horror:** Richard Kinkade and John E. Keller, "An Orphaned Miniature of Cantiga 235 from the Florentine Codex," *Cantigueiros* 10 (1998): 27–50.

207   **Some historians speculate that Alfonso's deteriorating health:** Joseph F. O'Callaghan, *The Learned King: The Reign of Alfonso X of Castile* (Philadelphia: University of Pennsylvania Press, 1993), 245.

207   **"demented and leprous":** Manuel González Jiménez, *Diplomatario andaluz de Alfonso X* (Seville: El Monte, Caja de Huelva y Sevilla, 1991), doc. 503bis, 532–535 (November 9, 1282, *recte* November 8) (my translation).

207   **Sancho is cast . . . as the heroic figure:** CAX, ch. 74, pp. 207–209.

208   **a capricious act of revenge:** CAX, ch. 74, pp. 209–210; cf. Melissa Katz, "The Final Testament of Violante de Aragón (c. 1236–1300/01): Agency and (Dis)empowerment of a Dowager Queen," in *Queenship in the Mediterranean*, ed. Elena Woodacre (New York: Palgrave Macmillan, 2013), 51–71.

208   **moment of crisis for the Jews:** Yitzhak F. Baer, "From the Age of the Reconquest to the Fourteenth Century," in *A History of the Jews in Christian Spain* (Philadelphia: Jewish Publication Society of America, 1978), 126–130; Alexandra Cuffel, "Ibn Sahula's Meshal ha-Qadmoni as Restorative Polemic," *JMIS* 3, no. 2 (2011): 173–174.

208   **In the autumn of 1280, secret negotiations:** CAX, ch. 74, pp. 210–211.

209   **"more with fear than with affection":** CAX, ch. 75, p. 216.

209   **"for fear of incurring his disfavor":** CSM 386: Kulp-Hill, *Songs of Holy Mary*, 471.

209   **"All should fear his wrath and be afraid of erring and angering him":** John K. Walsh, ed., *El libro de los doze sabios: O tractado de la nobleza y lealtad [ca. 1237]: Estudio y edición*, Anejos del boletín de la Real Academia Española 29 (Madrid, 1975), 84–85

210   **"King Alfonso became enraged at this reply":** CAX, ch. 75, p. 219.

210   **"If the lord or prince does not temper his anger with moderation":** Walsh, *El libro de los doze sabios*, 82.

211   **a narrative deeply sympathetic to his cause:** CAX, ch. 76, 220–230.

211   **a sentence condemning Alfonso:** CAX, ch. 76, p. 223n337.

211   **deliberately damaged with a wet cloth:** Rosa María Rodríguez Porto, "Inscribed/Effaced: The *Estoria de Espanna* after 1275," *Hispanic Research Journal* 13, no. 5 (October 2012): 387–406.

212   **For his part, Edward I of England:** There had been extensive correspondence between the two kingdoms in the preceding few years. Thomas Rymer, *Foedera, conventiones, literae, et cujuscunque generis acta publica inter reges angliae et alios quosvis imperatores, reges, pontifices, principes vel comunitates*, 3rd ed., 10 vols. (The Hague: Joannes Neaulme, 1739–1745), I, 2:157–158, 177, 184–186, and "Omissa," 81, 86. A letter from Alfonso X to Edward I, dated April 1, 1279, had addressed the English king as his beloved brother-in-law (Antonio Ballesteros-Beretta, *Alfonso X el Sabio* [Barcelona: Salvat, 1963], 921).

212   **Angrily, he swore that he did not wish:** Ibn abi Zar, *Rawd al-Qirtas*, trans. Ambrosio Huici Miranda, 2nd ed. (Valencia: J. Nacher, 1964), 2:629–630.

212   A newly agreed pact between the rulers: Ibn abi Zar, *Rawd al-Qirtas*, 2:630–631.

213   "O victorious king . . . the Christians have violated their oath of fidelity": Ibn abi Zar, *Rawd al-Qirtas*, 2:635.

213   Instead of righteous anger, they behaved: Barton, "Gendering Anger," 371–392.

213   "You see, my friends, to what situation": CAX, ch. 98, p. 251. This is MS 563 in the *Biblioteca Menéndez y Pelayo*, an early fourteenth-century manuscript and one of the oldest manuscripts of the chronicle. See Paula Kelley Rodgers, "Prolegomena to a Critical Edition of the *Crónica de Alfonso X*" (PhD diss., University of California, Davis, 1984), 210.

214   The emir arrived in Algeciras: CAX, ch. 98, pp. 251–252.

214   In his testament: González Jiménez, ed., *Diplomatario andaluz*, doc. 518, 548–554, at 552. On the correct dating of this document—1282 and not 1283—see Francisco Javier Hernández, "Alfonso X in Andalucía," in *Historia instituciones documentos* 22 (1995): 293–306, at 296–297.

214   "This was an expedition such as": Ibn abi Zar, *Rawd al-Qirtas*, 2:636–637.

215   The chronicle tells us that Ferrán Muñoz: CAX, ch. 77, p. 232.

215   If Ferrán Muñoz were still alive: CAX, ch. 99, pp. 257–262.

215   A papal bull: Rymer, *Foedera*, I, 2:222.

215   "the people whom anger seizes": Lucius Annaeus Seneca, *Anger, Mercy, Revenge*, trans. Robert A. Kaster and Martha C. Mussbaum (Chicago: University of Chicago Press, 2010), 14.

216   He saw him quite rightly as a fountain of practical, real-life wisdom: On the reception of Seneca, see Karl Alfred Blüher, *Séneca en España: Investigaciones sobre la recepción de Séneca en España desde el siglo XIII hasta el siglo XVII* (Madrid: Gredos, 1983).

216   "On account of the great desire": Robert I. Burns, SJ, ed., *Las siete partidas*, trans. Samuel Parsons Scott, 5 vols. (Philadelphia: University of Pennsylvania Press, 2001), law 2.5.9, 2:290. The *Partidas* are more emphatic in dissociating themselves from anger than, say, the Norwegian *Konungs skuggsjá* [The king's mirror], written ca. 1250. See Marlen Ferrer, "Emotions in Motion: Emotional Diversity in 13th Century Spanish and Norse Society" (PhD diss., University of Oslo, 2008), 144–160.

216   "rage obstructs the heart of man": Burns, *Las siete partidas*, law 2.5.11, 2:291.

217   "when he conducted himself so harshly": Burns, *Las siete partidas*, laws 2.1.3 and 7.33.7, 2:271 and 5:1574; Foronda, *El espanto y el miedo*, 78.

217 **a gambler . . . seizes a crossbow:** CSM 154: Kulp-Hill, *Songs of Holy Mary*, 188 (my adaptation). On Alfonso's awareness of the need for emotional restraint in relation to games and gambling, see also Juan Escourido, "Política de la alegría: Represión y modernidad al tablero en la Iberia alfonsí," in *Poniendo en juego la Iberia premoderna (1250–1650): Alfonso X, Libro de Buen Amor, poesía de cancionero y novelas lipogramática* (PhD diss., University of Pennsylvania, forthcoming).

218 **words were an instrument of war:** Matthew Paris adopted a similar strategy in his portrait of Henry III (Hyams, "What Did Henry III of England Think in Bed," 120–121).

218 **a masterpiece of pro-Sancho propaganda:** CAX, "El porqué de una nueva edición de la crónica de Alfonso X," introduction, xxxviii–xliii.

219 **last will and testament:** González Jiménez, *Diplomatario andaluz*, doc. 518, 548–554.

221 **legal sentence condemning Sancho's rebellion:** González Jiménez, *Diplomatario andaluz*, doc. 503bis, 534–535.

222 **All royal charters were ceremonially read aloud:** Liam Moore, "By Hand and by Voice: Performance of Royal Charters in Eleventh- and Twelfth-Century León," *JMIS* 5, no. 1 (2013): 18–32.

222 **codicil to his testament:** González Jiménez, *Diplomatario andaluz*, doc. 521, at 560–561.

223 **the king was struck with grief:** Kim Bergqvist, "Tears of Weakness, Tears of Love: Kings as Sons and Fathers in Medieval Spanish Prose," in *Tears, Sighs, and Laughter: Medieval Studies*, ed. Per Förnegård, Erika Kihlman, and Mia Åkestam (Stockholm: Royal Swedish Academy of Letters, History, and Antiquities, forthcoming 2016), suggests that the chronicle's account reveals the existence of an "emotional community" in which the expression of private emotions at the expenses of fulfilling political demands is not considered appropriate.

223 **"I am not crying for the infante Sancho":** CAX, ch. 87, pp. 240–241.

224 **appears to have written to the pope:** Rymer, *Foedera*, I, 2:230.

224 **The letter survives in a "certificate of authenticity":** This certificate was issued on October 10, 1284. Hernández, "Alfonso X in Andalucía," 298–300.

NOTES TO EPILOGUE

225 **The new king would rule for eleven years:** Mercedes Gaibrois de Ballesteros, *Historia del reinado de Sancho IV de Castilla* (Madrid: Voluntad, 1922–1928), 1:6–11.

226 **she devoted her patronage:** Melissa Katz, "The Final Testament of Violante de Aragón (c. 1236–1300/01): Agency and (Dis)empowerment of a Dowager Queen," in *Queenship in the Mediterranean*, ed. Elena Woodacre (New York: Palgrave Macmillan, 2013), 55–59; Melissa Katz, "The Non-gendered Appeal of *Vierge Ouvrante* Sculpture: Audience, Patronage, and Purpose in Medieval Iberia," in *Reassessing the Roles of Women as "Makers" of Medieval Art and Architecture*, ed. Therese Martin (Leiden: Brill, 2012), 1:37–91.

226 **In contrast, the king had been generous:** Manuel González Jiménez, ed., *Diplomatario andaluz de Alfonso X* (Seville: El Monte, Caja de Huelva y Sevilla, 1991), doc. 521, 557–564, at 561.

226 **She lived until 1303:** Pablo Martín Prieto, "Las Guzmán alfonsinas. Una dinastía femenina en la Castilla de los siglos XIII y XIV," *Mirabilia* 17, no. 2 (2013): 261–264.

226 **"the first place that God wished us to gain":** González Jiménez, *Diplomatario andaluz*, doc. 521, 557–564, at 558.

227 **In medieval society, the division of a body:** Caroline Walker Bynum, *Christian Materiality: An Essay on Religion in Late Medieval Europe* (New York: Zone Books, 2011), 177–216.

227 **his conception of an ideal, unified state:** Joseph F. O'Callaghan, *The Learned King: The Reign of Alfonso X of Castile* (Philadelphia: University of Pennsylvania Press, 1993), 273.

228 **transmitter of Arabic astronomical studies:** M. T. Gousset, "Le *Liber de locis stellarum fixarum* d'Al-Sûfi, ms. 1036 de la Bibliothèque de l'Arsenal à Paris: Une reattribution," *Arte medievale* 2 (1984): 93–106.

228 **Italian scholars also helped to diffuse:** Ángel Gómez Moreno, "Del duecento al quattrocento: Italia en España, España en Italia," *Insula* 757–758 (January–February 2010): 7–11, at 8.

229 **intimate relations:** Jerry Brotton, *The Renaissance Bazaar: From the Silk Road to Michelangelo* (Oxford: Oxford University Press, 2002), esp. 48–54.

230 **the codex landed in the hands of the Medici family:** Laura Fernández, "*Cantigas de Santa María*: Fortuna de sus manuscritos," *Alcanate: Revista de estudios alfonsíes* 6 (2008–2009): 323–348, at 341–344.

230 **Alfonso's personal fame:** Manuel Alvar Ezquerra, "Alfonso X contemplado por Don Juan Manuel," en *La literatura en la época de Sancho IV: Actas del congreso internacional 'La literatura en la época de Sancho IV'* (Alcalá de Henares, 21–24 de febrero de 1994) (Alcalá: Universidad de Alcalá, 1996), 91–106, at 92–93, cited in Nicasio Salvador Miguel, "La labor literaria de Alfonso X y el contexto

europeo," *Alcanate: Revista de estudios alfonsíes* 4 (2004–2005): 79–99, at 96–97.

230 **an Italian setting:** CSM 73, 132, 219, 307: Kathleen Kulp-Hill, trans., *Songs of Holy Mary of Alfonso X, the Wise: A Translation of the Cantigas de Santa María* (Tempe: Arizona Center for Medieval and Renaissance Studies, 2000), 95, 163–164, 263, 372; cf. Walter Mettmann, "A Collection of Miracles from Italy as a Possible Source of the CSM," *Cantigueiros* 1, no. 2 (1988): 75–82; Jesús Montoya Martínez, "Italia y los italianos en las *Cantigas de Santa María*," in *Composición, estructura y contenido del cancionero marial de Alfonso X* (Murcia: Real Academia de Alfonso X el Sabio, 1999), 211–231.

230 **incident . . . in the Cathedral of Foggia:** CSM 136, 294: Kulp-Hill, *Songs of Holy Mary*, 169, 356; Mettmann, "Collection of Miracles from Italy," 78–81; Montoya, "Italia y los italianos," 227.

231 **Ironically, the *Cantigas de Santa María*—so intimately linked:** Stephen Parkinson, ed., *Alfonso X the Learned, Cantigas de Santa María: An Anthology*, MHRA Critical Texts 40 (Cambridge, UK: Modern Humanities Research Association, 2015), 3.

231 ***Alfonsine Tables* were similarly admired:** Laura Fernández Fernández, "El ms. 8322 de la Bibliothèque de l'Arsenal y su relación con las tablas alfonsíes. Hipótesis de trabajo," *Alcanate: Revista de estudios alfonsíes* 7 (2010–2011): esp. 253–258.

231 **the science of astrology:** Nancy Siraisi, *Medieval and Early Renaissance Medicine: An Introduction to Knowledge and Practice* (Chicago: University of Chicago Press, 1990), 152, 189.

232 **A century ago, a Spanish priest:** María Rosa Menocal, "An Andalusianist's Last Sigh," *La corónica* 24, no. 2 (1996): 179–189.

232 **"Averroes, who wrote the weighty glosses":** Dante Alighieri, *Inferno*, trans. Robert and Jean Hollander (New York: Doubleday, 2000), 75.

232 **"He shall not feed on lands or lucre":** Dante, *Inferno*, canto I, lines 101 ff.

233 **"greatest gift to posterity":** Robert I. Burns, SJ, "Jews and Moors in the *Siete partidas* of Alfonso X the Learned: A Background Perspective," in *Medieval Spain: Culture, Conflict and Coexistence. Studies in Honour of Angus MacKay*, ed. Roger Collins and Anthony Goodman (New York: Palgrave Macmillan, 2002), 46; for the Louisiana connection, see Agustín Parise, "Translators' Preface to the Laws of *Las siete partidas* Which Are Still in Force in the State of Louisiana," *Journal of Civil Law Studies* 7, no. 1 (2014): 311–353.

233 **Building on the legacy of the twelfth-century Renaissance:** Darrin McMahon, *Happiness: A History* (New York: Atlantic Monthly Press, 2006), 140–164.

234 **"There is no pleasure in this world":** John E. Keller and Robert White Linker, ed., *El libro de Calila e Digna* (Madrid: Consejo Superior de Investigaciones Científicas, 1967), 185.

235 **"While he contemplated the heavens":** "Dumque coelum considerat, observatque astra, terram amisit." Juan de Mariana, *Historia de rebus hispaniae* (Toledo, 1592), 649, cited in Evelyn S. Procter, "Materials for the Reign of Alfonso X of Castile, 1252–84," *Transactions of the Royal Historical Society, Fourth Series* 14 (1931): 39–63, at 39.

235 **"I will illustrate my meaning by the jest":** "Theaetetus," in *The Dialogues of Plato*, trans. B. Jowett, 5 vols. (Oxford: Clarendon Press, 1871), 4:341.

Index

Abbasids, 56, 102, 139

Abu Ya'qub, son of Abu Yusuf, 202, 212

Abu Ya'qub al-Mansur, Almohad caliph, 42

Abu Ya'qub Yusuf, Almohad caliph, 42

Abu Yusuf, Marinid emir of Morocco, 104, 121, 143, 151, 170–172, 200, 207, 213–214

Abu Zayan, son of Abu Yusuf, 169

Adelard of Bath, 91

Aelred of Rievaulx, 136

Afonso III, king of Portugal, 95, 165–166

Albertus Magnus, 194

Alcalá de Benzaide, Treaty of (1265), 122, 147, 149

alchemy, 199

Alcobaça, Portugal, 226

Alexander IV, Pope, 77, 79, 95, 165

Alexios IV Angelos, 3

Alfonsine Tables, xx, 54, 167, 231

Alfonso de la Cerda, grandson of Alfonso X, 208, 218, 221
 See also de la Cerda, infantes

Alfonso de Molina, 130, 131

Alfonso IX, king of León, 2

Alfonso Raimúndez, 90

Alfonso VIII, king of Castile, 8, 14, 22, 73, 151

Alfonso X, attitudes and beliefs
 Andalusi culture, admiration for, xxvi, xxviii–xxix, 6, 40, 43–44, 52
 anger and restraint of anger, 207–210, 216–217, 219 (*See also* anger)
 faith and religion, xxiii, xxiv, 10, 34, 118, 135, 181, 186–187, 190–193, 199, 204
 fatherhood, 155–162, 234
 friendship, 138, 234 (*See also* friendship; Lara, Nuño Gonzalez de)
 happiness, 199, 233–235 (*See also* humor)
 hunting, 84, 85 (fig.), 86–87, 103 (*See also* hunting)
 leadership, 50, 56–57
 learning and wisdom, 54–56 (*See also* Book of the Twelve Wise Men)
 monarchy, 54, 227–228
 writing and music, as therapeutic exercise, 180
 See also Alfonso X, cultural projects; Alfonso X, family relationships; chess; sexuality
Alfonso X, cultural projects
 architecture, interest in, 101 (*See also* Burgos cathedral; Giralda, La; León cathedral; Seville)

Alfonso X, cultural projects
(*continued*)
  astrology and astronomy, xx–xxi,
    xxviii, 57, 62, 75–76 (*See also*
    Book of Crosses; Book of the
    Eighth Sphere; Book of the Fixed
    Stars; Books of Astrological
    Knowledge; Perfect Book of the
    Judgment of the Stars)
  Castilian Spanish in education
    and government, 52, 100
  histories (*See History of Spain;*
    Universal History)
  law codes (*See Fuero Real; Siete*
    Partidas)
  musical projects of, xxi, 180 (*See*
    also Cantigas de Santa María;
    Cantigas d'escarnho e de mal
    dizer)
  universities, schools, and students,
    73–75
  writing and music, as therapeutic
    exercise, 180
Alfonso X, diplomacy
  Abu Yusuf, alliance with, 207,
    212–215
  England, treaties with, 61–62
  French, secret negotiations with,
    208
  Holy Roman Emperor, aspiration
    to office of, 54, 77, 94–95, 99,
    103, 167–169
  Jaume I, relationship with, 31–33,
    127–128
  Muhammad I, relationship with,
    106–108
  Muhammed II, knighting of, 154
  political astuteness of, 235–236
  rebellion of noblemen, 142–149
Alfonso X, family relationships
  Beatrix of Swabia (mother),
    illness and recovery, 9–10
  Beatriz, queen of Portugal
    (daughter), 35, 162–167

Berenguela (daughter), 60
Berenguela (sister), 10
Enrique, conflict relationship
    with, 70–72, 124–125
Fernando de la Cerda (eldest son),
    72, 151–155, 169–170
Fernando III (father), relationship
    with, 25, 51
Jeanne de Dammartin
    (stepmother), relationship with,
    48
Mayor Guillén de Guzmán,
    relationship with, 34–35,
    49–50, 163, 166, 234
Yolant (wife), relationship with,
    xviii, 30, 44, 48–49, 154,
    200–201
See also Fadrique; Felipe; Jaime;
    Juan; Leonor (daughter);
    Leonor ("Eleanor of Castile");
    Manuel; Pedro; Sancho IV;
    individual entries for the above
Alfonso X, life events
  birth, 6
  death and burial, 225, 227–228
  health and illness, 132, 168–169,
    172–173, 175, 177–179,
    200
  last will and testament, 191, 212,
    219–221
  See also Alfonso X, family
    relationships
Alfonso X, military activities
  al-Andalus, desire to conquer,
    xxvi
  alférez of Castilian army, 34
  Algeciras, siege of, 201–202
  Cádiz, annexation of, 103
  Cartagena, capture of, 44
  Jerez, 59, 104, 111, 121
  Marinid attack on Castile,
    169–172
  Mudéjar Rebellion, 109–111, 122,
    227

Murcia, occupation of, 30–31, 33, 35, 46, 62, 84, 106, 196
Muslims, attack on Spain by, 169–172
Niebla, 59, 104
as participant in Fernando III's military campaigns, 11–12
Portugal, incursion into, 44–45
Salé, expedition at, 104
Tejada, capture of, 59
See also Marinids; Puerto de Santa María
Alfonso X, portraits and depictions
Book of Games (?), 12, 40
Cantigas de Santa María, during illness, 172–173
Cantigas de Santa María, heron-hunting with falcons, 85 (fig.)
cartulary of Tojos Outos, 49
cloister of Burgos cathedral (?), 129
Estoria de Espanna, 211
stained glass of León cathedral, 83
US House of Representatives, xx
Alfonso XI, king of Castile-León, 86
Algarve, 14, 165, 167
Algeciras, 107, 148, 170, 171, 201, 202, 208, 212, 214
Alhambra palace, Granada, 91
Alí Abbas, 7
Alighieri, Dante, 96–98, 136, 232
Almería, xxiv, 16
Almohads, 18–23, 41–42, 57–58
Almoravids, xxv, 19, 41, 57
Alphonso, Prince (son of Edward I and Leonor), 115, 160
amulets, 189–192
Andalusi culture, xxiv–xxix
amuletic images in, 193
Christian assimilation of, xxv–xxvi, 23–24, 38, 91, 96–98, 138, 193, 228–229
economic foundations of, 16–17, 43–44

intellectual sophistication of, 4–7, 20–21, 56–58, 62, 74, 180
sexuality in, 38, 40, 138
See also Jews; Seville
Andalusia, xxiv, 11, 19, 30, 47, 103, 105, 107, 109, 211
anger, 203–204, 209, 213, 215–219
See also Alfonso X, attitudes and beliefs: anger and restraint of anger
Aragon, xviii, 14, 23, 27
See also Jaume I; Pere III
Aristotle, 73, 133, 137, 218, 232
Arnaldo de Vilanova, 189
Augustine of Hippo, Saint, 135, 187
Averroes (Ibn Rushd), 21, 232
Avicenna (Ibn Sina), 7, 196
al-Azraq, 87

Bacon, Roger, 190
Badajoz, 207, 214, 222–223
Baghdad, 18, 56, 57, 102, 139
Banu Ashqilula, 108, 121, 126
Barcelona, xxiv, 14, 16, 72, 99, 110, 168
barragana (concubine), 35, 49
Bartholomew the Englishman, 36, 161
Bayad and Riyad, Tale of, 51 (fig.)
Beatrix of Swabia ("Beatriz"), mother of Alfonso X, 3–4, 5 (fig.), 9–10, 101, 103
Beatriz, queen of Portugal (daughter of Alfonso X), 35, 40, 50, 124, 125, 162–167, 207, 212, 223, 226
Beaucaire, France, 168–169, 229
Berbers, xxiv, 19, 41, 57
See also Almohads; Almoravids; Marinids
Berenguela, daughter of Alfonso X, 60
Berenguela, queen of Castile and León, 2–3, 11, 15, 26–27
Berenguela, sister of Alfonso X, 10

Blanca, 226. *See* Branca
Blanche, wife of Fernando de la
　　Cerda, xix, 123, 127–128, 152,
　　170, 200
Boccaccio, Giovanni, 37–38
Bologna, 15, 64, 73, 101, 228
Bonaventura of Siena, 232
Boniface VIII, Pope, 189–190
Book of Crosses (Libro de las cruzes),
　　75–77
Book of Deeds (Llibre dels fets) by
　　Jaume I, 31, 87, 109, 116, 127,
　　129
Book of Games, 2, 12, 13 (fig.), 27,
　　40, 112, 163
*Book of Hunting Animals (Kitab
　　al-Jawarih)*, 84–85, 87,
　　92–93
*Book of Mohammed's Ladder (Libro de
　　la escala de Mahoma)*, 96–98,
　　232
Book of Stones (Lapidario), 33, 62,
　　177–179, 184, 185, 194–195,
　　195 (fig.), 196–197, 199, 234
Book of the Eighth Sphere, 68
*Book of the Fixed Stars (Liber de locis
　　stellarum fixarum)* by al-Sufi,
　　63–64, 65 (fig.), 228
Book of the Twelve Wise Men, xvii,
　　11, 35, 55, 72–73, 111, 209,
　　210, 236
*Books of Astrological Knowledge
　　(Libros de saber de astrología)*,
　　179–180
Branca, daughter of Beatriz, 167,
　　226
Burckhardt, Jacob, xix
Burgos, 3, 14, 69, 71, 72, 101, 127
Burgos cathedral, 5, 69, 128–129,
　　236

Cádiz, 103, 105, 107
Calatrava, military order of, 151,
　　211, 221
Calila and Digna, xxviii, 96,
　　139–142, 141 (fig.)
Cameros family, 176
Canon of Medicine (Ibn Sina),
　　196
*Cantares de los miraglos e de loor de
　　Sancta María*, 191
Canterbury Tales (Chaucer),
　　185
*Cantigas de Santa María (Songs of
　　Holy Mary)*, xxi–xxii, xxiii
　　(fig.), 111, 231
　　Alfonso X heron-hunting with
　　　falcons, 85 (fig.)
　　Alfonso X's ill health, 168–169,
　　　172–173
　　anti-Semitic stereotypes in,
　　　64
　　authorship of, 180–181
　　childhood, 156–159, 159 (fig.),
　　　171, 183
　　friendship, 134
　　healing, health, and illness,
　　　172–173, 181–189, 191, 234
　　humor in, 113–114, 114 (fig.)
　　hunting, 89
　　Italian settings in, 230
　　Mudéjar rebellion, 110
　　rape, 75
　　sexuality and chastity, 36–38, 39
　　　(fig.), 181, 230
　　vengeance and violence, 75, 205,
　　　206 (fig.), 217
　　*See also Códice de Florencia; Códice
　　　de los músicos; Códice rico (Rich
　　　Codex)*
Cantigas d'escarnho e de mal dizer,
　　117–118, 123, 185, 231
Cartagena, 35, 44, 109
Castile, kingdom of, 14–15
　　economic crisis in, 123, 126
　　internal conflict in, 142–149,
　　　210–211, 214–215
　　Renaissance in, 228–232

vernacular language, use of in education and government, xix, 63, 100
    See also Alfonso VIII; Alfonso X; Alfonso XI; Berenguela; Enrique I; Fernando III; Sancho IV; Yolant
Castro, Alvar Pérez de, 11
Castro, Esteban Fernández de, 124, 152
Cato the Wise, 88
Ceuta, 41, 43, 107, 202
Chansonnier Manesse, 103
Charlemagne, 102, 163
Charles of Anjou, 122, 125
Chaucer, Geoffrey, 160, 185, 190
chess, 12, 13 (fig.), 14, 24–26, 27, 163
childhood and infancy, 9–10, 35–36, 48, 49, 55, 67, 99, 111, 156–157, 183–184
    See also Cantigas de Santa María (Songs of Holy Mary
Chronicle of Alfonso X, 71, 99–100, 102, 104, 122, 124, 126, 128, 131, 143, 144, 146, 153, 176, 202, 213, 218, 220, 223
Chronicon mundi (Chronicle of the world), 55
Cicero, 134, 228, 232
Clement IV, Pope, 123, 126
clothing and shoes, 17–18, 157, 170–171, 181
Códice de Florencia (Florentine Codex), 159 (fig.), 205, 206 (fig.), 229
Códice de los músicos (Musicians' Codex), xxii, xxiii (fig.)
Códice rico (Rich Codex), xxi, 39 (fig.)
Colocci, Angelo, 231
Conrad of Hohenstaufen, 15
Conradin, duke of Swabia, 103, 125
Constanza, sister of Yolant, 71
convivencia, xxv

Copernicus, xx, 231
Córdoba, xvii, 12, 17, 23, 56, 57, 105, 214–215
Cortes, 59–60, 86, 95, 106, 128, 145, 155, 177, 209
courtesans, 40, 117, 120
    See also Eanes, Dominga; Pérez, María (La Balteira)
Crusades and crusading movements, xix, 15–16, 18, 22, 64, 68, 86, 103, 107, 116, 117, 122, 123, 143, 168, 212
Cuenca, 9
Cuenca, bishop of, 106, 108

Dammartin, Jeanne de, 10, 47, 70–71
Dante. See Alighieri, Dante
De arte venandi cum avibus (Frederick II), 86, 90–91
de la Cerda, infantes, 176, 225
    See also Alfonso de la Cerda; Fernando de la Cerda
De preconiis hispaniae (Gil de Zamora), 217
De proprietabus rerum (Bartholomew), 161
Dee, John, 68
Denia, emir of, 16
Dialog of Solomon and Marcolf, 116
Dinís, grandson of Alfonso X, 124, 167, 207
Disciplina clericalis (Pedro Alfonso), 134
Dominic, Saint, and, 232
Dominicans, 90, 217
    See also Thomas Aquinas, Saint; Vincent de Beauvais
Doñana wetlands, 104
Duarte, king of Portugal, 186–187

Eanes, Dominga, 120
Écija, 107, 170, 172
Edward I, king of England, xviii, 61, 69–70, 90, 94, 128, 215

Edward II, king of England, 115
Egidio de Tebaldis, 168
Eleanor of Aquitaine, 8
Eleanor of Castile. *See* Leonor
    ("Eleanor of Castile")
Eleanor of England, 7–8, 14
elephant and giraffe, 102
emotions. *See* anger; fatherhood;
    friendship; melancholy/
    depression; sexuality
Enrique, brother of Alfonso X, 9, 48,
    70–72, 124–125
Enrique, Maestro, 101
Enrique I, king of Castile, 2
Erasmus, 159
*Estoria de Espanna. See History of
    Spain*

*Fables of the Distant Past (Meshal
    ha-Qadmoni)* by Ibn Sahula,
    66
Fadrique, brother of Alfonso X, 72,
    78, 79, 87, 100, 124, 176, 204
falconry, 84–86, 90–94
    See also Alfonso, attitudes,
        hunting; hunting
fatherhood
    See also Alfonso X, attitudes,
        fatherhood
Felipe, brother of Alfonso X, 87, 100,
    124, 142
Fernández, Martín, 83
Fernando de la Cerda, son of Alfonso
    X
    betrothal and marriage to
        Blanche, xix, 123, 127–129
    birth, 72
    childhood and education, 160
    death and burial, 169, 179–171
    depiction of, 49
    diplomatic and political role,
        152–154
    letter of advice from father,
        151–152

    responsibility on Andalusi
        frontier, 143
Fernando I, king of Castile, 17
Fernando III, king of Castile and
    León
    alliance with Almohads, 20, 23
    Córdoba, capture of, xvii, 11–12,
        23
    courtly tastes of, 25
    death, 50
    diplomacy of, 44, 78
    health and illness, 30
    Jaén, occupation of, 46
    León, inheritance of, 11
    marriage to Beatrix of Swabia,
        3–4, 5 (fig.)
    military prowess of, xvii, 1–2,
        11–12
    Portuguese incursion, disapproval
        of, 45
    sculpture of, 101
    Seville, occupation of, 46–47
Ficino, Marsilio, 232
Florence, Italy, xxii, 24, 67, 96, 187,
    196, 231
Francis, Saint, and Franciscans, 92,
    115, 217, 229
Frederick II, Holy Roman Emperor,
    xix, 3, 44, 77–78, 85–86, 90–91
friendship, 128, 133–142
    See also Alfonso X, attitudes and
        beliefs: friendship
Fuero real, 100, 145

Galicia, xxi, 11, 14, 49, 145, 147,
    181, 188, 226
Galilei, Galileo, 231
Games, Diego de, 61
García, Ovieto, 32
Gascony, 43, 61, 208
General estoria. See Universal History
Genoa, 16, 20, 43, 58, 95, 100, 101,
    229
Gerard of Cremona, 228

Gerardus Falconarius, 91
Gerbert, "Scientist Pope," xxvi
Gervase of Tilbury, 61
Ghibellines (pro-imperial party), 44,
    77, 232
Gibraltar, 19
Gil de Zamora, Juan, 10, 45, 52,
    91–92, 163, 180, 217–218
Giles of Rome, 6
Giralda, La (Seville), xxvi (fig.),
    xxvii, 43, 52
Glanvill, 164
gold, medicinal properties of, 185,
    198
Granada, city of, 91, 148
Granada, kingdom of, 23, 35,
    106–108, 119, 122–123, 145,
    147–149, 154, 171–172,
    207–208, 221
    See also Muhammad I;
    Muhammad II
Gregory X, Pope, 142, 168, 169, 230
Guadix, 121, 147, 152
Guelphs (pro-papal party), 44, 85,
    96, 122, 125
Guillelmus Falconarius, 91
Guillem, Bernat, 110

al-Hakam I, 57
Hákon Hákonarsson, king of Norway,
    99
Hákonar saga Hákonarsonar, 99
Haro, Lope Díaz de, 71, 124, 131,
    152, 170
Haro family, 48, 71, 72, 130–131,
    152, 176
    See also Haro, Lope Díaz de
Hayy ibn Yaqzan (Ibn Tufayl), 21
healing objects, 191–194
    See also stones
Henry, duke of Lancaster, 180, 186
Henry I, king of England, 165
Henry II, king of England, 8, 83
Henry III, king of England, xviii, 61

Henry VI, Holy Roman Emperor,
    77–78
Hildegard of Bingen, 136, 192, 194
Historical Mirror (Espejo ystorial) by
    Louis IX, 191
History of Spain (Estoria de Espanna),
    11, 26, 46, 47, 56, 111, 211
Hohenstaufen dynasty, 3, 15, 78, 125
    See also Conrad of Hohenstaufen;
    Frederick II; Manfred of
    Hohenstaufen
Holy Grail, 17
humor, 112–121
    See also Alfonso X, attitudes and
    beliefs: happiness
hunting, 84–90, 104
    See also Alfonso X, attitudes and
    beliefs: hunting; Book of
    Hunting Animals; De arte
    venandi cum avibus
Hunting window (Cacerías), León,
    81–83

Ibn al-Ahmar. See Muhammed I,
    king of Granada
Ibn al-Wafid, 56
Ibn Arabi, 33
Ibn Ezra, Abraham, 63
Ibn Hud, 11, 23, 31
Ibn Idhari, 108
Ibn Mahfut, 104
Ibn Mansur, Muhammad, 195
Ibn Quzman, 38
Ibn Rushd (Averroes), 21, 232
Ibn Sahib al-Sala, 42
Ibn Sahula, 66, 208
Ibn Said, Ibrahim, 56
Ibn Sina (Avicenna), 7, 196, 232
Ibn Tufayl, 21
Ibn Tumart, 18–20
Ibn Waqar, Abraham, 97, 189
Ibn Zadoq, Isaac, 208
Ibn Zuhr (Avenzoar), 194
al-Idrisi, 16

Innocent III, Pope, 22
Innocent IV, Pope, 44, 48, 78
Irene Angelina, 3
Isabella (Isabel la Católica), 24
Isabelle of France, 192
Isidore of Seville, 47
Italy, xviii, xix, xxii, xxviii, 20, 44,
    77–79, 101, 124–125, 142–143,
    168, 181, 183, 195–196
    See also Bologna; Florence; Genoa;
    Ghibellines; Guelphs; Naples;
    Pisa; Renaissance, in Spain and
    Italy; Renaissance, of the
    twelfth century; Sicily; Siena;
    Venice

Jacobo de las Leyes, 101
Jaén, 22, 46, 106, 107, 171, 208,
    211
Jaime, son of Alfonso X, 159, 207,
    215, 223
jamsa ("hand of Fatima"), 193
Jaume I, king of Aragon
    conquest of Mallorca and
    Valencia, xviii
    death, 177
    marriage to Yolanda of Hungary,
    30
    Mudéjar Rebellion and conquest
    of Murcia, 109–110, 122, 146
    reaction to death of Fernando de
    la Cerda, 170
    relationship with Alfonso X,
    30–33, 45, 48, 70, 77, 87,
    131–132, 168
    relationship with Castilian
    dissidents, 48, 70–72,
    127–131
    See also Book of Deeds
Jefferson, Thomas, 233
Jerez, 59, 71, 104, 105, 106, 107,
    110–111, 121, 123
Jews
    anti-Semitic stereotypes, 64

cultural and intellectual
    importance of, 6, 57, 62–64, 66,
    97
    in Seville, 58
Jiménez de Rada, Rodrigo, 22, 26–27,
    55, 60, 64
Joan, Master, 132
Jofré of Loaysa, 160, 201
John, king of England, 83, 145
John of Gaddesden, 190
John of Salisbury, 54, 73, 89
Juan, son of Alfonso X, 129, 159,
    207, 210–211, 222, 225
Juan, son of Fernando III and Jeanne
    Dammartin, 10
Juana, daughter of Alfonso de
    Molina, 131

Knights Hospitaler, 221
Knights Templar, 221
Kristín, princess of Norway, 99–100
Kutubiyya, 20

Lara, Gonzalo Núñez de, 2, 3
Lara, Juan Núñez de, 126, 143–144,
    148
Lara, Nuño González de
    Alfonso X's opinion of, 152
    death of, 172
    deterioration of friendship with
    Alfonso X, 124, 130–131
    friendship with Alfonso X, 7, 27,
    45, 48, 71, 104, 110
    rebellion against Alfonso X,
    142–148, 152
    reconciliation with Alfonso X,
    154–155
Lara, Nuño González de, son of Nuño
    González de Lara, 126
Lara family, 7, 71, 110, 142, 144, 176
    See also Lara, Gonzalo Núñez de;
    Lara, Juan Núñez de; Lara,
    Nuño González de
Latini, Brunetto, 96, 136–137, 230

León, cathedral of, 81–84, 101, 103, 204, 236
León, kingdom of, xvii, xxv, 2–3, 11, 14, 15, 17, 27–28, 34, 40, 45, 145, 152, 169, 211, 221
    See also Alfonso IX; Berenguela; Fernando III; Teresa of Portugal
Leonor, daughter of Alfonso X, 175
Leonor ("Eleanor of Castile"), half-sister of Alfonso X, xviii, 59, 61, 69–70
Lerma, 142, 144
Liber lapidum (Hildegard), 194
Libro de los animales que cazan (Kitab al-Jawarih), 86
Livre de seyntz medicines (Henry of Lancaster), 180
Livre dou tresor (Latini), 136
Louis IX, king of France (saint), xix, 116, 122, 123, 127, 143, 191–192
Louisiana Territory, Partidas and, 233
Lucas, bishop of Tuy, 55
Luis, son of Fernando III and Jeanne Dammartin, 10

Maghreb, xxv, 18, 20, 21, 41, 74, 103, 106, 212
Maimonides, Moses, 20, 117
Makejoy, Matilda, 115
Málaga, 16, 121, 147, 148, 152
al-Mamun, king of Toledo, 6, 56, 75
Manfred, king of Sicily, 79, 95, 122
Manfred of Hohenstaufen, 125
manners, 7–9, 17, 55
al-Mansur, 139
Manuel, brother of Alfonso X, 93–94, 99, 124, 207, 211
Manuel I Comnenus, 94
Marcus Aurelius, 203–204, 215
Marguerite of Provence, xix
margul, 33–34
Mariana, Juan de, 235
marina, 184

Marinids, 104, 121, 143, 169–172, 200, 202, 212
    See also Abu Ya'qub; Abu Yusuf
Marrakech, xxv, 16, 19, 20, 21, 41, 42, 213
Martin IV, Pope, 215
Martínez de Fe, Pedro, 201–202
Matilde, countess of Boulogne, 165
Maunsell, John, 61
Mayor Guillén de Guzmán, 34–35, 49–50, 163, 166, 234
Medici family, 230
melancholy/depression, 172, 175, 178–179, 185–186, 194, 196, 197, 198, 234
Mineralia (Albertus Magnus), 194
Mirandola, Pico della, 233
mirrors for princes, xvii, 139, 155, 161, 217
Montpellier, France, 9, 168, 175, 196, 199
Morandi, Benedetto, 233
Mozarabs, 4, 64
Mudéjar Rebellion, 108–111, 121–122
mudéjares, 105–106
Muhammad I, king of Granada (Ibn al-Ahmar), 23, 46, 60, 106–109, 121–122, 126, 148
Muhammad II, king of Granada, 148, 172, 200, 213, 221
mujaheddin, 107, 121
Mula, 84
Muñoz, Ferrán, 215
Murcia, 11, 30–31, 33, 106, 109, 122, 193, 223
Muret, battle of, 14
al-Mu'tamid ibn Abbad, king of Seville, 40

Naples, 16, 229
Nasrids, 121–122, 126

Navarre, kingdom of, 14, 59, 61
 See also Sancho VI; Thibault I;
  Thibault II
Las Navas de Tolosa, battle of, 22,
 64
necromancy, 199
Niebla, 104, 107, 226
nobility and aristocracy, 7, 15–16, 17,
 46, 47, 48, 55, 58, 60, 61, 70,
 71, 81, 88, 89, 92, 118–120,
 123, 126, 128, 137, 138, 151,
 176, 207, 212, 215, 223, 227,
 235
 See also Alfonso X, diplomacy,
  rebellion of noblemen; entries
  for Castro, Haro, and Lara
  families; Sancho IV, king of
  Castile and León, rebellion
  against Alfonso X

Otto IV of Brunswick, Holy Roman
 Emperor, 3

Palacios, Miguel Asín, 232
Paris, Matthew, 61, 69
Pedro, son of Alfonso X, 129, 159,
 207, 210, 215
Pedro Alfonso, 134
Pere III (Pedro), king of Aragon,
 177, 201, 225
Pérez, María (La Balteira), 117
Pérez, Teresa, 17
Perfect Book of the Judgment of the
 Stars (Libro conplido en los
 iudizios de las estrellas), 62,
 66–69, 231
Perpignan, 168, 175, 187
Petrarca, Francesco (Petrarch), 180
Phares, Simon de, 68
Philip, duke of Swabia, 3
Philippe III, king of France, 176, 177,
 208
Picatrix, 68
Pietro de Reggio, 168, 231

Pisa, 9, 16, 20, 43, 94, 95, 96, 98,
 229, 230
Plato, 115, 232, 235
Policraticus (John of Salisbury), 73
Ponce, Fernán Pérez, 214
Poridat de las poridades, 73
Portugal, 14, 165
Portugal, kingdom of, 14, 165
 See also Afonso III; Beatriz;
  Sancho I Capelo; Sancho II
Ptolemy, 63, 68
Puerto de Santa María, El, 103, 107

al-Rashid, Harun, 102
Rawd al-Qirtas, 169, 172, 200, 201,
 212, 214
al-Razi, 7
Renaissance
 in Spain and Italy, xviii–xxiv, 6,
  21, 52, 54, 56, 62, 63, 96, 117,
  136, 179, 180, 187, 196, 199,
  228–232, 236
 of the twelfth century, xxii, xxiv,
  4, 6, 15–18, 20, 21, 43–44, 54,
  58, 136, 228
Richard, earl of Cornwall, 98–99,
 143
al-Riquti, Muhammad, 33
Rodríguez, Juan, 117
Rudolf of Habsburg, 168
Ruiz de Girón, Gonzalo, 207
Ruiz de los Cameros, Simón, 204,
 206 (fig.)

Salamanca, 28, 73, 75, 196, 223
Salé, 104, 202
Salerno, Italy, 196
Sánchez, Diego, 158
Sancho (archbishop of Toledo),
 brother of Yolant, 148
Sancho I Capelo, king of Portugal,
 165
Sancho II, king of Portugal, 44, 45,
 176

Sancho IV, king of Castile and León
  Alfonso X, disparagement and
    disinheritance of, 207, 220–221
  Alfonso X's forgiveness of,
    221–222
  birth, 100
  claim to throne of Castile, 170,
    176–177
  illness of, 223–224
  as king of Castile, 225
  knighting of, 129
  rebellion against Alfonso X,
    210–211, 214–215, 221–222
  sculpture of, 129
  Simón Ruiz, execution of, 204
Sancho VI, king of Navarre, 55, 59
Santa María la Blanca, Toledo, 60
Santiago, military order of, 211
Santiago de Compostela, 14, 36, 152,
  193, 209
Secretum secretorum, 73
Seneca, 215–216, 229, 232
Seville
  Alfonso X's admiration for, xxvi,
    40, 43–44
  Aljarafe of, 40–41, 47
  as Almohad capital, xxiv, 16, 19,
    42–46
  Almohad minaret (La Giralda),
    xxvii (fig.)
  capture by Castile, 46–47, 50
  expulsion of Muslim inhabitants,
    47, 58
  post-conquest decline of, 58–59
  resistance to Sancho IV's
    authority, 225
sexuality, 35–40
al-Shaqundi, Abu 'l Walid Isma'il ibn
  Mohammad, 40–41
Sicily, xix, 43, 77–78, 86, 91, 95,
  122, 125, 228
Siena, 230, 232
Siete partidas (Seven Divisions)
  on education for girls, 163
  on fatherhood, 155, 160–161
  on friendship, 133–134, 137–138
  influence of, xx, 232–233
  on "legitimate" children, 164
  on marriage, 49
  on pleasure, 111–112
  on ruler's treatment of subjects,
    216–217
  vernacular, use of in, 100
  on womanizing and excessive
    drinking, 35
Simón, son of Fernando III and
  Jeanne Dammartin, 10
Socrates, 115, 235
Solomon, King, 55, 112, 116, 156,
  193
Sendebar, 72
stones, medicinal properties of,
  33–34, 184, 185, 193–198, 195
  (fig.)
  See also alchemy; amulets; Book of
    Stones(Lapidario); gold; healing
    objects
students, behavior of, 74–75
al-Sufi (Azophi Arabus), 63–64,
  228
Sybil, queen of Scotland, 165

table manners, 8
Tagliacozzo, battle of, 125
taifa period, xxviii, 56–57, 75
Tarifa, 107, 148, 169, 171, 200
Teresa of Portugal, queen of León,
  11
Thibault I, king of Navarre, 59
Thibault II, king of Navarre, 59
Thomas Aquinas, Saint, 190, 233
Tlemcen, 213
Todros ben Judah Abulafia, 63, 168
Toledo
  birthplace of Alfonso X, 6
  Castilian recapture of, xxv, 4
  Cortes at, 59–61
  death and exile of Sancho II, 45

Toledo (*continued*)
   as hub of learning, xxviii, 4, 6, 33,
     52, 56, 59, 66, 75–76, 97,
     167–178, 228
   Jewish community and, 4
   religious diversity in, 4, 6–7, 62,
     64, 66, 97, 196
   Sancho's behavior in, 221
   See also al-Mamun; Jiménez de
     Rada, Rodrigo
Toledo cathedral, 59–60
trade and commerce, 16–18, 41, 228

Ubayd Allah, 'Abu Marwan
   (Oueydalla), 75–76
Uclés, military order of, 151, 207,
   221
Umayyads, 57
Universal History (*General estoria*),
   100, 101
Urban IV, Pope, 123

Valencia, 16, 23, 27, 31, 72, 87, 177,
   189
Valladolid, 44, 47, 48, 71, 200, 211,
   213, 222
vengeance and violence, 75, 205,
   206 (fig.), 217
Venice, 16, 229, 231
Villa Real (Ciudad Real), 169
Villamayor, Garcia Fernández de, 7

Vincent de Beauvais, 7, 36, 161, 191
Violante, queen of Castile and León.
   See Yolant
Virgil, 232

Walter of Henley, 160
wet nurses, 6–7, 156–157

Xàtiva, 31–32, 177, 225

Yehuda ben Mosé, 62, 66, 68, 75
Yehuda Mosca, 175, 197
Yolanda of Hungary, queen of
   Aragon, 30, 32, 47
Yolant ("Violante"), queen of Castile
   and León
   betrothal and marriage to Alfonso
     X, xviii, 30, 44, 47–49, 166, 234
   depictions of, 49, 83
   diplomatic and political skills of,
     xix, 30, 109–110, 146, 148,
     153–154
   later relationship with Alfonso X,
     168, 200–201, 208, 226
   motherhood, 49, 60, 72, 99, 100
   patronage of Clarissan convent,
     226

Zamora, 155, 211, 224
al-Zarkali (Azarquiel), 56–57, 62,
   167, 228

ABOUT THE AUTHOR

Simon R. Doubleday is a professor of history at Hofstra University, editor in chief of the *Journal of Medieval Iberian Studies*, and president of the American Academy of Research Historians of Medieval Spain. He lives in New York City and Santiago de Compostela, Spain.